Fortran 90
for Scientists and Engineers

Brian D Hahn

Department of Applied Mathematics
University of Cape Town

ELSEVIER

Elsevier Ltd.
Linacre House, Jordan Hill, Oxford OX2 8DP
200 Wheeler Road, Burlington, MA 01803

Transferred to digital printing 2004

British Library Cataloguing in Publication Data
Hahn, Brian D.
Fortran 90 for Scientists and Engineers
I. Title
005.13

ISBN 0 340 60034 9

3 4 5 6 7 8 9 10

Contents

Preface

The Fortran 90 standard represents the first significant change in Fortran in over 20 years, and brings it into line with most modern structured programming languages. This book is one of a handful on Fortran 90, and one of even fewer in which every program (unless otherwise clearly stated) has been tested on a working compiler: the FTN90 compiler for PCs.

If you are a newcomer to Fortran, you should read the book in the conventional way, from the beginning.

However, if you are a Fortran 77 user you may like to dip immediately into later chapters to see some of the new features of the language. Probably the two most important advances are the new array facilities (Chapters 9 and 15) and the impressively enlarged collection of intrinsic procedures (Appendix C), including the so-called elemental functions which operate on all or selected elements of array arguments. You may now define your own types, or structures (Chapter 12) and even construct linked lists with them using pointers (Chapter 13). Modules (Chapter 8) may be independently compiled, and may contain type definitions and variable declarations, as well as procedures. The use of interface blocks (Chapter 8) makes it possible to overload specific procedure names with generic names, and also to overload operators. Conditional loops are possible now with DO WHILE (Chapter 6), and there is a new CASE statement (Chapter 6). However, you should probably first have a look at Sections 2.2–2.5 (program layout, variable declarations, etc.) and Section 3.5 (kind) to see some important changes in the basics of Fortran.

In keeping with the spirit of the earlier edition, this book is a problem-solving exposition of Fortran 90, and not a technical reference manual. You will therefore not necessarily find all the references to a particular topic in one place in the text (e.g. arrays are covered in Chapters 9 and 15) as this would interfere with the informal style of the book. There are, however, appendices with summaries of all the statements and the intrinsic procedures, and a comprehensive index.

I should like to thank the following in particular: David Mackin of Edward Arnold for his helpful editorial suggestions, and for arranging the loan of an FTN90 compiler; Peter Anderton of The Numerical Algorithms Group for the loan of the compiler; the University of Cape Town for leave in order to write this book, and for financial support for the project; my long-suffering colleagues for leaving me alone while I was writing; and my wife, Cleone, who patiently reminds me when programs won't work, that computers are like that, aren't they?

Brian D. Hahn
Department of Applied Mathematics
University of Cape Town
Rondebosch
South Africa
June 1993

Preface to Problem Solving with FOR-TRAN 77

So many books on FORTRAN have been written that the appearance of yet another one seems to require some justification. There are three particular areas where this book can claim to make a distinctive contribution.

Firstly, the approach taken is a problem-solving one, developed over many years of teaching programming to first-year university students with no computing experience. The computer is presented as a tool (probably the most exciting one of the 20th century) for solving interesting, real world problems, and examples from many areas, particularly science and engineering, are discussed. The technicalities of each new FORTRAN construction are therefore generally presented only after motivation by the posing of a suitable problem. Since the objective of this book is to enable you to solve problems using a computer, the first 12 chapters are in a sense a preparation for the final three. In these later chapters you will be introduced to some modern computer applications such as simulation, modelling and numerical methods. There are also a large number of exercises, involving a variety of applications. Most of these have solutions provided. Those that do not have solutions may be suitable for use as class projects in a teaching situation.

Secondly, structured problems are developed throughout. The beginner is shielded from the devastating effect of the GOTO statement until well into the text. When it is introduced, the use of GOTO is encouraged in one well-defined situation only: this feature appears to be unique in all the vast literature on FORTRAN.

Thirdly, emphasis is laid throughout the book on what has come to be called programming style, and guidelines for writing clear, readable programs are presented.

This book has developed out of notes originally written as a supplement to lectures for students taking courses in applied mathematics at the University of Cape Town, with no prior experience of computing. It can therefore be used as a "teach yourself" guide by anyone who wants to learn FORTRAN 77 (officially known as FORTRAN ANSI X3-9 1978), the current international standard, which is the version used here.

Although this is primarily a text for beginners, the more experienced programmer should be able to find plenty of interest, particularly in the applications. He may even learn something! The appendices contain summaries of all the FORTRAN 77 intrinsic functions and statements (including those which are not recommended for stylistic reasons), with examples of their general usage.

No specialized mathematical background is needed to follow most of the examples. There are occasional forays into first-year university mathematics, but these are self-contained and may be glossed over without loss of continuity (you may even find them instructive!).

Thanks are due to John Newmarch of the University of Cape Town Information Technology Services for his critical reading of the original manuscript on which this book is based, and for his invaluable suggestions regarding programming style. Thanks are also due to the generations of students who have patiently endured my efforts to improve my methods of teaching computing. I also wish to thank my colleague, Ruth Smart, who collaborated with me on an earlier version of this book, for her helpful advice and painstaking reading of the manuscript. Finally, I should like to acknowledge a deep debt of gratitude to my wife, Cleone, for her continual support and encouragement during the preparation of this book.

It is hoped this book will give some insight into the ways that computers may be used to solve real problems, and that after working through it you will be better able to find out more about this fascinating subject for yourself.

1986

1

Getting Going

1.1 Introduction

In the period since I first became an undergraduate student, some 25 years ago, I have been fortunate enough to witness the remarkable revolution in computer technology which future historians will surely regard as one of the outstanding features of the twentieth century. The first computer I programmed occupied a large room. Only one person could use it at a time, by pressing an impressive array of switches, and programs had to be punched on cards. Its "fast" memory could store about 240 numbers. Its slow memory could hold a few thousand numbers, and was located on a rotating drum which you could hear ticking as it spun.

As technology advanced, and computers became more powerful, they also became much smaller. From occupying a whole room, they now only require part of a desk, a lap, or even a palm. They have banded together to form networks, and during an average working day, it is not uncommon to send electronic mail messages around the world, and to connect directly to a computer on the other side of the world.

You may not have used a computer before (except possibly to play games) but you are probably familiar with using a calculator. The simplest sort can only do arithmetic and display an answer. Smarter ones have memory locations—where intermediate results may be stored—and function keys such as sin, log, etc. The most sophisticated calculators allow you to store the sequence of operations (instructions) needed to calculate the solution of the problem. This sequence of instructions is called a *program*. To carry out the entire set of calculations you only need to load the program into the calculator, press the run key, supply the necessary data, and sit back while the calculator churns out the answer. A computer, whether it is a small personal one like the IBM PC, or a large impersonal mainframe, is in principle only an advanced programmable calculator, capable of storing and executing sets of instructions, called programs, in order to solve specific problems.

You may have used a computer before, but only to run software packages that have been written by someone else. Spreadsheets, databases and word processors fall into this category. If you have taken the trouble to start reading this book, you probably have an interest in science or engineering, and are curious enough about programming to want to write your *own* programs to solve your particular problems, instead of relying on someone else's more general package.

1.2   Fortran

The particular set of rules for coding the instructions to a computer is called a *programming language*. There are many such languages, for example Fortran, BASIC, Pascal and C++. Fortran, which stands for FORmula TRANslation, was the first "high level" programming language. It made it possible to use symbolic names to represent mathematical quantities, and to write mathematical formulae in a reasonably comprehensible form, such as X = B/(2*A). The idea of Fortran was proposed in late 1953 by John Backus, in New York, and the first Fortran program was run in April 1957.

The use of Fortran spread so rapidly that it soon became necessary to standardize it, so that a program written in the standard would be guaranteed to run at any installation which claimed to support the standard. In 1966 the first ever standard for a programming language was published. This version became known as Fortran 66 (more correctly FORTRAN 66, but the practice of capitalizing acronyms is becoming unfashionable). A new standard, Fortran 77, was published in 1978. In spite of competition from newer languages such as Pascal and C, Fortran continued to flourish, so much so that the latest standard, Fortran 90, came out in August 1991. This is the version used in this book. Connoisseurs of Fortran will be interested in the history of the language sketched by Michael Metcalf and John Reid in *Fortran 90 Explained*, Oxford University Press (Oxford, 1990).

If you are already experienced in Fortran, you might like to consult the Preface, which indicates where the new features may be found. You will also need to know that some old features have been declared *obsolescent*. These (which may include some of your old favourites) have been made redundant by the new standard, and are *recommended* for deletion in the next standard, i.e. the recommendation is not binding. Appendix B contains a summary of all Fortran 90 statements, and indicates which are obsolete and/or not recommended.

1.3   Running Fortran Programs

If you are new to Fortran, you should run the sample programs in this section as soon as possible, without trying to understand in detail how they work. Explanations will follow in due course. You will need to find out, from a manual or from someone else, how to enter and run Fortran programs on your computer system.

Greetings   This program will greet you if you give it your name:

```
! My first Fortran 90 program!
! Greetings!

CHARACTER NAME*20

PRINT*, 'What is your name?'
READ*, NAME
PRINT*, 'Hi there, ', NAME
END
```

You should get the following output (your response is in italics):

```
  What is your name?
```
Garfield
```
  Hi there, Garfield
```

AIDS cases   The following program computes the number of accumulated AIDS cases $A(t)$ in the United States in year t according to the formula

$$A(t) = 174.6(t - 1981.2)^3.$$

```
PROGRAM AIDS
 ! Calculates number of accumulated AIDS cases in USA
   INTEGER T                    ! year
   REAL    A                    ! number of cases

   READ*, T
   A = 174.6 * (T - 1981.2) ** 3
   PRINT*, 'Accumulated AIDS cases in US by year', T, ':', A
 END PROGRAM AIDS
```

If you supply the value 2000 for the year you should get the output

```
   Accumulated AIDS cases in US by year 2000 :    1.1601688E+06
```

The answer is given in *scientific notation*. E+06 means multiply the preceding number by 10^6, so the number of cases is about 1.16 million. Using trial and error run the program repeatedly to find out when there will be about 10 million accumulated cases.

Try typing a mistake in the value of t (2,000 for example) to see how Fortran responds.

Compound interest   Suppose you have $1000 saved in the bank, which compounds interest at the rate of 9% per year. What will your bank balance be after one year? You must obviously be able to do the problem in principle yourself, if you want to program the computer to do it. The logical breakdown, or *structure plan*, of the problem is as follows:

(1) Get the data (initial balance and interest rate) into the computer
(2) Calculate the interest (9% of $1000, i.e. $90)
(3) Add the interest to the balance ($90 + $1000, i.e. $1090)
(4) Print (display) the new balance.

This is how the program looks:

```
PROGRAM MONEY
 ! Calculates balance after interest compounded
   REAL BALANCE, INTEREST, RATE

   BALANCE = 1000
   RATE = 0.09
   INTEREST = RATE * BALANCE
   BALANCE = BALANCE + INTEREST
   PRINT*, 'New balance:', BALANCE
END PROGRAM MONEY
```

Run the program and note that no input (from the keyboard) is required now (why not?). The output should be 1.0900000E+03 (1090).

Summary

- A computer program is a set of coded instructions for solving a particular problem.
- The Fortran statement READ* is for getting data into the computer.
- The Fortran statement PRINT* is for printing (displaying) results.

Exercises

1.1 Write a program to compute and print the sum, difference, product and quotient of two numbers A and B (supplied from the keyboard). The symbols for subtraction and division are - and / respectively. Use the program to discover how Fortran reacts to an attempted division by zero.

1.2 The energy stored on a condenser is $CV^2/2$, where C is the capacitance and V is the potential difference. Write a program to compute the energy for some sample values of C and V.

Solutions to most exercises are in Appendix E.

2

Elementary Fortran: I

In this chapter and the next one we will look in detail at how to write Fortran programs to solve simple problems. There are two essential requirements for successfully mastering this art:

- The exact rules for coding instructions must be learnt;
- A logical plan for solving the problem must be developed.

These two chapters are devoted mainly to the first requirement: learning some basic coding rules. Once you have mastered these, we can go on to more substantial problems.

All Fortran 90 statements introduced in this and subsequent chapters (and some which are not) are summarized in Appendix B.

2.1   Compound Interest Again

In Chapter 1 you ran the program MONEY to compute compound interest:

```
PROGRAM MONEY
 ! Calculates balance after interest compounded
   REAL BALANCE, INTEREST, RATE

   BALANCE = 1000
   RATE = 0.09
   INTEREST = RATE * BALANCE
   BALANCE = BALANCE + INTEREST
   PRINT*, 'New balance:', BALANCE

END PROGRAM MONEY
```

We will now discuss in detail how the program works. When you run a Fortran 90 program two separate processes take place. Firstly the program is *compiled*. This means that each statement is translated into some sort of *machine code* that the computer can understand. Secondly, the compiled program is *executed*. In this step each translated instruction is carried out. The software package that carries out both these processes is generally called a *compiler*.

During compilation, space in the computer's *random access memory* (RAM) is allocated for any numbers (data) which will be generated by the program. This part of the memory may be thought of as a bank of boxes, or *memory locations*, each of which can hold only one number at a time. These memory locations are referred to by symbolic names in the program. So the statement

```
BALANCE = 1000
```

allocates the number 1000 to the memory location named BALANCE. Since the contents of BALANCE may change during the program it is called a *variable*.

The translated (compiled) form of our program looks roughly as follows:

(1)   Put the number 1000 into memory location BALANCE
(2)   Put the number 0.09 into memory location RATE
(3)   Multiply the contents of RATE by the contents of BALANCE and put the answer in INTEREST
(4)   Add the contents of BALANCE to the contents of INTEREST and put the answer in BALANCE
(5)   Print (display) a message followed by the contents of BALANCE
(6)   Stop.

During execution, these translated statements are carried out in order from the top down. After execution, the memory locations used will have the following values:

```
BALANCE  : 1090
INTEREST : 90
RATE     : 0.09
```

Note that the original contents of BALANCE is lost.

The PROGRAM statement in the first line introduces the program. It is optional, and may be followed by an optional name. The second line, starting with an exclamation mark, is a comment for the benefit of the reader, and has no effect on the compilation. Variables in a program can be of different *type*; the REAL statement declares their type in this example. The first three non-blank lines of this program are *non-executable*, i.e. no action is carried out by them (they have no counterpart in the translated form of the program above).

Try the following exercises:

(1)   Run the program.
(2)   Change the first *executable* statement to read

```
BALANCE = 2000
```

and make sure that you understand what happens when you run the program again.
(3)   Leave out the line

```
BALANCE = BALANCE + INTEREST
```

and re-run. Can you explain what happens?
(4)   Try to rewrite the program so that the original contents of BALANCE is *not* lost.

A number of questions have probably occurred to you by now, such as

- What names may be used for memory locations?
- How can numbers be represented?
- What happens if a statement won't fit on one line?
- How can we organize the output more neatly?

These questions, and hopefully many more, will be answered in the following sections.

2.2 Program Layout

The general structure of a simple Fortran program is as follows (items in square brackets are optional):

[PROGRAM *program name*]
  [*declaration statements*]
  [*executable statements*]
END [PROGRAM [*program name*]]

As you can see, the only compulsory statement in a Fortran program is END. This statement informs the compiler that there are no further Fortran statements to compile.

The notation

END [PROGRAM [*program name*]]

means that the program name may be omitted from the END statement, but that if there is a program name, the keyword PROGRAM may *not* be omitted.

Statements   Statements form the basis of any Fortran program, and may contain from 0 to 132 characters (a statement may be blank; blank statements are encouraged to make a program more readable by separating logical sections). Earlier versions of Fortran insisted that certain parts of a statement start in certain columns; Fortran 90 has no such restriction.

All statements, except the *assignment* statement (e.g. BALANCE = 1000), start with a *keyword*. Some keywords encountered so far are END, PRINT, PROGRAM, and REAL.

Generally, there will be one statement per line. However, multiple statements may appear on a line if they are separated by semi-colons. For the sake of clarity, this is recommended only with very short assignments, such as

A = 1; B = 1; C = 1

Long statements may continue over several lines as discussed below.

Significance of blanks   Blanks are generally not significant, i.e. you can use them to improve readability by indenting statements (adding blanks on the left) or padding within statements. However, there are places where blanks are *not* allowed. To be specific it is necessary to define a technical term: the token.

A *token* in Fortran 90 is a basic significant sequence of characters, e.g. labels, keywords, names, constants, operators and separators (these items are all discussed later). Blanks may not appear within a token. So INTE GER, BAL ANCE and < = are not allowed (<= is an operator), while A * B is allowed and is the same as A*B.

A name, constant or label must, however, be separated from an adjacent keyword, name, constant or label by at least one blank. So REALX and 30CONTINUE are not allowed (30 is the label in the second case).

Comments   Any characters following an exclamation mark (!) (except in a character string) are commentary, and are ignored by the compiler. An entire line may be a comment. A blank line is also interpreted as comment. Comments should be used liberally to improve readability.

Continuation lines   If a statement is too long to fit on a line, it will be continued on the next line if the last non-blank character in it is an ampersand (&):

A = 174.6 *   &
    (T - 1981.2) ** 3

Continuation is normally to the first character in the next non-comment line. However, if the first non-blank character of the continuation line is &, continuation is to the first character after the &. In this way a token may be split over two lines, although this is not recommended, since it makes the code less easy to read.

An & at the end of a comment line will not continue the comment, since the & is construed as part of the comment.

2.3 Data Types

The concept of a *data type* is fundamental in Fortran 90. A data type consists of a set of data values (e.g. the whole numbers), a means of denoting those values (e.g. −2, 0, 999), and a set of operations (e.g. arithmetic) that are allowed on them.

The Fortran 90 standard requires five *intrinsic* (i.e. built-in) *data types*, which are divided into two classes. The *numeric* types are integer, real and complex. The *non-numeric* types are character and logical.

Associated with each data type are various *kinds*. This is a basically the number of bits available for storage, so that, for example, there might be two kinds of integer: short and long. There is a full discussion of kind in Chapter 3.

In addition to the intrinsic data types, you may define your own *derived data types*, each with their own set of values and operations. This is discussed in Chapter 12.

Integer and real intrinsic types are discussed below. Character and complex intrinsic types are discussed in Chapter 3; the remaining intrinsic type, logical, is dealt with in Chapter 5.

2.4 Literal Constants

Literal constants (often simply called constants) are the tokens used to denote the values of a particular type, i.e. the actual characters that may be used. Before we consider constants in detail we need to look briefly at how information is represented in a computer.

Bits 'n bytes The basic unit of information in a computer is a *bit*: something which has only two possible states, usually described as on and off. The *binary digits* 0 and 1 can therefore be used to represent these two states mathematically (hence the term *digital* computer). The word "bit" in a contraction of "**binary digit**".

Numbers in a computer's memory must therefore be represented in *binary code*, where each bit in a sequence stands for a successively higher power of 2. The decimal numbers 0 to 15, for example, are coded in binary as follows:

Decimal	Binary	Hexadecimal	Decimal	Binary	Hexadecimal
0	0000	0	8	1000	8
1	0001	1	9	1001	9
2	0010	2	10	1010	A
3	0011	3	11	1011	B
4	0100	4	12	1100	C
5	0101	5	13	1101	D
6	0110	6	14	1110	E
7	0111	7	15	1111	F

A *byte* is the amount of computer memory required for one character, and is eight bits long. Since each bit in a byte can be in two possible states, this gives 2^8, i.e. 256, different combinations.

Hexadecimal code (see table) is often used because it is more economical than binary. Each hexadecimal digit stands for a power of 16. E.g.

$$2A = 2 \times 16^1 + 10 \times 16^0 = 32 + 10 = 42$$

One byte can be represented by two hex digits.

Microcomputer memory size (and disk capacity) is measured in bytes, so 64K for example means slightly more than 64 000 bytes (since 1K actually means 1024). Microcomputers are sometimes referred to as 8-, 16- or 32-bit machines. This describes the length of the units of information handled by their microprocessors (chips). The longer these units, the faster the computer.

Integer literal constants   *Integer literal constants* are used to denote the values of the integer intrinsic type. The simplest and most obvious representation is an unsigned or signed integer (whole number), e.g.

```
1000   0   +753   -999999   2501
```

In the case of a positive integer constant, the sign is optional.

The *range* of the integers is not specified in the standard, but on a 16-bit computer, for example, could be from -32768 to $+32767$ (i.e. -2^{n-1} to $+2^{n-1} - 1$).

The range may be specified on a particular computer by using a *kind parameter*. This is discussed in Chapter 3.

Positive whole numbers may also be represented in binary, octal (base 8) or hexadecimal form, e.g.

```
binary:          B'1011'
octal:           O'0767'
hexadecimal:     Z'12EF'
```

Lower case may be used. Quotation marks (") may be used instead of apostrophes (') as *delimiters*. These forms are restricted to use with the DATA statement, and in internal and external files as digit strings, without the leading letters and the delimiters.

Real literal constants   These are used to denote values of real intrinsic type, and take two forms.

The first form is the obvious one and is called *positional form* or *fixed point* and consists of a string of digits with a decimal point. It may be signed or unsigned. Examples:

```
0.09   37.   37.0   .0   -.6829135
```

There may be no digits to the left of the decimal point, or no digits to the right of the decimal point, but a decimal point by itself is not allowed.

The second form is called *exponential form* or *floating point*. It basically consists of either an integer (signed or unsigned) or a fixed point real (signed or unsigned) followed in both cases by the letter E followed by an integer (signed or unsigned). The number following the E is the *exponent* and indicates the power of 10 by which the number preceding the E must be multiplied. E.g.

2.0E2	(= 200.0)
2E2	(= 200.0)
4.12E+2	(= 412.0)
−7.321E−4	(= −0.0007321)

Real constants are stored in exponential form in memory, no matter how they are actually written. If a real has a fractional part it may therefore be represented approximately (this is sometimes referred to as *finite machine precision*). Even if there is no fractional part the real is stored differently from an integer of the same value. E.g. 43 is an integer, while 43.0 is a real. They will be represented differently in memory.

The range and precision of real constants are not specified by the standard. Typically, reals will range between 10^{-38} and 10^{+38}, with a precision of about seven decimal digits. The range and precision may be specified with a kind parameter.

2.5 Names and Variables

We have already seen that memory locations can be given symbolic *names*, such as BALANCE and RATE. In Fortran 90, names can be given to other things apart from memory locations, such as the program itself. A name must consist of between 1 and 31 *alphanumeric* characters, and must start with a letter. The alphanumeric characters are the 26 letters, the 10 digits, *and the underscore* (_). (Fortran 77 users will note that names may now be longer than six characters.)

Except in the case of character strings, Fortran 90 is *case insensitive*, i.e. the names MYNAME and MyName represent the same thing. Perhaps it should be noted that Fortran programmers have a long tradition of writing programs in uppercase only. This goes back to the days (which I remember well!) when card punch machines had to be used—these can represent only uppercase letters. A mixture of upper- and lowercase is, however, much easier to read (it contains more information than pure uppercase). So it might be better to use NoOfStudents than NOOFSTUDENTS. It is also generally better to use meaningful names (which are not *too* long however), such as NoOfStudents, instead of simply N.

There are no *reserved words* in Fortran; you may therefore use the name END for a memory location, although this is certainly not recommended!

The following table shows some valid and invalid names.

Valid names	Invalid names (why?)
X	X+Y
R2D2	SHADOW FAX
Pay_Day	2A
ENDOFTHEMONTH	OBI-WAN
TIME	NAME$

A *variable* is a memory location whose value may be changed during execution of a program. A variable's name is constructed according to the above rules. A variable has a type which determines the type of constant it may hold. It is given a type in a *type declaration*, e.g.

```
INTEGER X
REAL INTEREST
CHARACTER LETTER
REAL :: A = 1
```

Note that a variable may be *initialized* in its declaration. In this case a double colon (::) must be used. The value of a variable initialized in this way may be changed later in the program. Although more complicated expressions are allowed when initializing, it is recommended for stylistic reasons that initialization be restricted to simple assignments as shown above.

Although the variables X, INTEREST and LETTER have been *declared* in the program fragment above, they are as yet *undefined*, as they have no value. You should avoid referencing an undefined variable. A variable may be defined in a number of ways, e.g. by initializing it (A above) or assigning a value to it, as in other examples we have seen.

A variable may also be given an initial value in a DATA statement, after being declared, e.g.

```
REAL A, B
INTEGER I, J
DATA A, B / 1, 2 / I, J / 0, -1 /
```

A name in a program must be unique. For example, if a program is named MONEY, an attempt to declare a variable of the same name will cause an error.

The variables described here are *scalar* because they can hold only a single value.

Implicit type rule   Earlier versions of Fortran had what was called an *implicit type rule*. Variables starting with the letters I to N inclusive were automatically specified with integer type, while variables starting with any other letter were automatically specified real. **This (unhelpful) rule still applies in Fortran 90 by default**, to ensure compatibility of code written under earlier versions.

The implicit type rule can lead to serious programming errors. A real value might unwittingly be assigned to a variable which is integer by default; the fractional part is then truncated (chopped off). For example, the statement

```
Interest_rate = 0.12
```

in a program where Interest_rate is not declared explicitly will assign the value 0 to the variable.

To guard against such errors it is **strongly recommended** that the statement

```
IMPLICIT NONE
```

be used at the start of all programs. This statement switches off the implicit type rule; consequently *all* variables used in the program *must* be declared. This incidentally promotes good programming style; having to declare a variable means that you have been forced to think about what it represents.

2.6   Vertical Motion under Gravity

If a stone is thrown vertically upward with an initial speed u, its vertical displacement s after a time t has elapsed is given by the formula $s = ut - \frac{1}{2}gt^2$, where g is the acceleration due to gravity. Air resistance has been ignored. We would like to compute the value of s, given u and t. Note that we are not concerned here with how to derive the formula, but how to compute its value. The logical preparation of this program is as follows:

1. Get values of g, u and t into the computer
2. Compute the value of s according to the formula
3. Print the value of s
4. Stop.

This plan may seem trivial to you, and a waste of time writing down. Yet you would be surprised how many beginners, preferring to rush straight to the computer, try to program step 2 before step 1. It is well worth developing the mental discipline of planning your program first—if pen and paper turns you off why not use your word processor? You can ever enter the plan as comment lines in the program.

The program is as follows:

```
PROGRAM Vertical
! Vertical motion under gravity

IMPLICIT NONE

REAL, PARAMETER :: G = 9.8   ! acceleration due to gravity
REAL S                       ! displacement (metres)
REAL T                       ! time
REAL U                       ! initial speed (metres/sec)

PRINT*, ' Time        Displacement'
PRINT*
U = 60
T = 6
S = U * T - G / 2 * T ** 2
PRINT*, T, S

END PROGRAM Vertical
```

The strange way of declaring G makes it a *named constant*, since its value should definitely not change in the program. Named constants are discussed further below.

Table 2.1   Numeric intrinsic operators

Operator	Precedence	Meaning	Example
**	1	Exponentiation	2 ** 4 (= 2^4)
*	2	Multiplication	2 * A
/	2	Division	B / DELTA
+	3	Addition or unary plus	A + 6.9
-	3	Subtraction or unary minus	X - Y

2.7   Programming Style

Programs that are written any old how, while they may do what is required, can be difficult to follow when read a few months later, in order to correct or update them (and programs that are worth writing will need to be maintained in this way). It is therefore extremely important to develop the art of writing programs which are well laid out, with all the logic clearly described. This is known as *programming style*, and should be manifest in most of the programs in this book (occasional lapses are in order to save space ...). Guidelines for good style are laid out in the Epilogue.

The program in the previous section has been written with this in mind:

- There is a comment at the beginning describing what the program does.
- All the variables have been declared *and described* on separate lines, in alphabetical order. You may like to include initialization with the declaration and description, e.g.

      REAL :: T = 6   ! time

- Blanks have been used on either side of the equal signs and the operators (e.g. **), and after commas.
- Blank lines have been used to separate distinct parts of the program.

You may like to develop your own style; the point is that you **must** pay attention to readability.

2.8   Numeric Expressions

The program Vertical in Section 2.6 makes use of the following code:

      U * T - G / 2 * T ** 2

This is an example of a *numeric expression*—a formula combining constants, variables (and functions like square root) using *numeric intrinsic operators*. It specifies a rule for computing a value. Since it only computes a single value it is a *scalar* numeric expression. There are five numeric intrinsic operators, shown in Table 2.1. Typing blanks on either side of operators will make expressions more readable.

These operators are called intrinsic because they are built-in. We will see later how to define new operators, and how to *overload* an intrinsic operator, i.e. give it a different meaning.

An operator with two operands, as in A + B, is called a *binary* or *dyadic* operator. When an operator appears with only one operand, as in −Z, it is called *unary* or *monadic*.

The order in which operations in an expression are carried out is determined by the *precedence* of the operators, according to the table above, except that parentheses ( ) always have the highest precedence. Since multiplication has a higher precedence than addition, this means, for example, that 1 + 2 * 3 is evaluated as 7, while (1 + 2) * 3 is evaluated as 9. Note also that −3 ** 2 evaluates to −9, not 9.

When operators with the same precedence occur in the same expression, they are with one exception always evaluated from left to right, so 1 / 2 * A is evaluated as (1 / 2) * A and not 1 / (2 * A).

The **exception** to the precedence rules is that in an expression of the form

A ** B ** C

the **right-hand** operation B ** C is evaluated **first**.

Integer division This causes so much heartache amongst unsuspecting beginners that it deserves a section of its own. When an integer quantity (constant, variable or expression) is divided by another integer quantity the result is also of integer type, so it is **truncated towards zero**, i.e. the fractional part is lost. E.g.

10 / 3	evaluates to 3
19 / 4	evaluates to 4
4 / 5	evaluates to 0 (which could cause an unwanted division by zero!)
− 8 / 3	evaluates to −2
3 * 10 / 3	evaluates to 10
10 / 3 * 3	evaluates to 9

Mixed-mode expressions Fortran 90 allows operands in an expression to be of different type. The general rule is that the weaker or simpler type is converted, or *coerced*, into the stronger type. Since integer type is the simplest, this means that operations involving real and integer operands will be done in real arithmetic. This applies to each operation separately, not necessarily to the expression as a whole. So, for example,

10 / 3.0	evaluates to 3.33333
4. / 5	evaluates to 0.8
2 ** (− 2)	evaluates to 0 (?)

However, note that

3 / 2 / 3.0

evaluates to 0.333333 because 3 / 2 is evaluated first, giving integer 1.

2.9   Numeric Assignment

The purpose of the numeric assignment is to compute the value of a numeric expression and assign it to a variable. Its general form is

$$variable = expr$$

The equal sign does *not* have the same meaning as the equal sign in mathematics, and should be read as "becomes". So the assignment

```
X = A + B
```

should be read as "(the contents of) X becomes (the contents of) A plus (the contents of) B".

In this way the assignment

```
N = N + 1
```

is meaningful, and means "increase the value of N by 1", whereas the mathematical *equation*

$$n = n + 1$$

is not generally meaningful.

If *expr* is not of the same type as *var*, it is converted to that type before assignment. This means that there might be loss of precision. For example, assuming N is integer, and X and Y are real:

```
N = 10. / 3     (value of N is 3)
X = 10 / 3      (value of X is 3.0)
Y = 10 / 3.     (value of Y is 3.33333)
```

The danger of performing integer divisions inadvertently cannot be stressed too much. For example, you might want to average two marks which happen to be integers M1 and M2. The most natural statement to write is

```
FINAL = (M1 + M2) / 2
```

but this loses the decimal part of the average. It is always safest to write constants as reals if real arithmetic is what you want:

```
FINAL = (M1 + M2) / 2.0
```

Examples   The formulae

$$F = GME/r^2,$$
$$c = \sqrt{a^2 + b^2}/(2a),$$
$$A = P(1 + r/100)^n$$

may be translated into the following Fortran assignments:

```
F = G * M * E / R ** 2
C = (A ** 2 + B ** 2) ** 0.5 / (2 * A)
A = P * (1 + R / 100) ** N
```

The second can also be written with the SQRT *intrinsic function* as

```
C = SQRT( A ** 2 + B ** 2 ) / (2 * A)
```

but never as

```
C = (A ** 2 + B ** 2) ** (1/2) / (2 * A)
```

(1/2 in the exponent evaluates to zero because of integer division).

2.10   Simple Input and Output

In this section we will look at the READ* and PRINT* statements more closely. The process of getting information into and out of the computer is an aspect of what is called *data transfer*. The simplest form of data transfer in Fortran 90 is with READ* and PRINT* and is called *list-directed*. More advanced forms of data transfer are discussed in Chapter 10.

Input   So far in this chapter variables have been given values by using numeric assignment statements, as in the program MONEY:

```
BALANCE = 1000
RATE = 0.09
```

This is an inflexible way of supplying data, since to run the program for different balances or interest rates you would have to find and change these statements. There may be many such assignments in a more complicated program, and it is a waste of time to recompile them every time you want to change the data. The READ* statement, however, which we saw in Chapter 1, allows you to supply the data *while the program is running*. Replace these two assignment statements with the single statement

```
READ*, BALANCE, RATE
```

When you run the program, the compiler will wait for you to type the values of the two variables at the keyboard, if you are using a PC (an IBM compatible personal computer). They may be on the same line, separated by blanks, a comma, or a slash, or on different lines. You can correct a number with the **backspace** key while entering it. If you are using some other system, you may need some advice on how to supply data for READ*.

The general form of the READ* statement is

```
READ*, list
```

where *list* is a list of variables separated by commas.

Note the following general rules:
- A single line of input or output is called a *record* (e.g. in the case of a PC, from the keyboard or on the screen).
- Each READ statement requires a *new* input record. E.g. the statement

```
READ*, A, B, C
```

will be satisfied with one record containing three values:

```
3   4   5
```

whereas the statements

```
READ*, A
READ*, B
READ*, C
```

require three input records, each with one value in it:

```
3
4
5
```

- When the compiler encounters a new READ, unread data on the current record is discarded, and the compiler looks for a new record to supply the data.
- Data for a READ may run over onto subsequent records. Basically the compiler searches all input records for data until the I/O (Input/Output) list has been satisfied.
- If there are not enough data to satisfy a READ the program will crash with an error message.

Example   The statements

```
READ*, A
READ*, B, C
READ*, D
```

with the input records

```
1   2   3
4
7   8
9   10
```

have the same effect as the assignments

```
A = 1
B = 4
C = 7
D = 9
```

Reading data from text files   It often happens that you need to test a program by reading a lot of data. Suppose you were writing a program to find the average of, say, 10 numbers. It becomes a great nuisance to have to type in the 10 numbers each time you run the program (since programs seldom work correctly the first time). The following trick is very useful.

The idea is to put the data in a separate (external) file which is stored on your computer system, e.g. on its hard disk if you are using a PC. The program then reads the data from the file each time it is run, instead of from the PC keyboard. As an example, use your word processor to store the following line in the ASCII (text) file called DATA:

```
3   4   5
```

Now use this program to read these three numbers from the file and display them on the screen:

```
OPEN( 1, FILE = 'DATA' )
READ(1, *) A, B, C
PRINT*, A, B, C
END
```

The OPEN statement connects the *unit number* (1) to the *external* file DATA. The form of the READ statement shown here then directs the compiler to look in the file connected to unit 1 for its data (the unit number may typically be from 1 to 99).

Output The PRINT* statement is very useful for output of small amounts of data, usually while you are developing a program, since you don't need to be concerned with the exact details of the form of the output.

The general form is

```
PRINT*, list
```

where *list* may be a list of constants, variables, expressions, and *character strings*, separated by commas. A character string is a sequence of characters delimited by quotes (") or apostrophes ('). E.g.

```
PRINT*, "The square root of", 2, 'is', SQRT( 2.0 )
```

Here are some general rules:

- Each PRINT* statement generates a new output record.
- The way reals are printed depends on your particular system. The FTN90 compiler on a 386, for example, displays reals between -99.999 and $+99.999$ in fixed point form, and all others in exponential form. If you want to be fussy, you have to use *format specifications* (Chapter 10). E.g. the following statements will print the number 123.4567 in fixed point form over 8 columns correct to two decimal places:

```
      X = 123.4567
      PRINT 10, X
  10  FORMAT( F8.2 )
```

- If a character string in PRINT* is too long to fit on one line it will be displayed without a break if & also appears in the continuation line:

```
   PRINT*, 'Now is the time for all go&
           &od men to come to the aid of the party'
```

Sending output to the printer   This may be done as follows (on a PC):

```
OPEN( 2, FILE = 'prn' )
WRITE(2, *) 'This is on the printer'
PRINT*, 'This is on the screen'
```

Note that WRITE must be used in conjunction with a unit number. This is a more general statement than PRINT.

Summary

- Successful problem solving with a computer requires knowledge of the coding rules and a sound logical plan.
- The compiler translates the program statements into machine code.
- Fortran statements may be up to 132 characters long and may start anywhere on the line.
- All statements, except assignments, start with a keyword.
- A Fortran token is a sequence of characters forming a label, keyword, name, constant, operator or separator.
- Blanks should be used to improve readability, except inside keywords and names.
- Comments may be typed after the exclamation! They should be used liberally to describe variables and to explain how a program works.
- A statement with & as its last non-blank character will be continued onto the next line.
- There are five intrinsic data types: integer, real, complex, logical and character.
- Values of each data type are represented by literal constants.
- Integer constants may also be represented in binary, octal and hexadecimal.
- Real constants are represented in fixed point or floating point (exponential) form.
- Alphanumeric characters are the letters, digits and the underscore.
- Names may contain up to 31 alphanumeric characters, starting with a letter.
- A variable is the symbolic name of a memory location.
- The IMPLICIT NONE statement should be used to avoid variables being given a type implicitly.
- A numeric variable should be declared integer or real in a type declaration statement.
- Numeric expressions may be formed from constants and variables with the five numeric intrinsic operators, which operate according to strict rules of precedence.
- Decimal parts are truncated when integers are divided, or when integers are assigned to reals.
- Numeric assignment computes the value of a numeric expression and assigns it to a real or integer variable.
- Groups of variables may be given initial values in a DATA statement.
- PRINT* is used to print (display) output.
- READ* is used to input data from the keyboard while a program is running.
- Data may also be read from an external file (e.g. a disk file).

Exercises

2.1 Evaluate the following numeric expressions, given that A = 2, B = 3, C = 5 (reals); and I = 2, J = 3 (integers). Answers are given in parentheses.

A * B + C	(11.0)
A * (B + C)	(16.0)
B / C * A	(1.2)
B / (C * A)	(0.3)
A / I / J	(0.333333)
I / J / A	(0.0)
A * B ** I / A ** J * 2	(4.5)
C + (B / A) ** 3 / B * 2.	(7.25)
A ** B ** I	(512.0)
- B ** A ** C	(−45.0)
J / (I / J)	(division by zero)

2.2 Decide which of the following constants are not written in standard Fortran, and state why not:

(a) 9,87   (b) .0   (c) 25.82   (d) -356231
(e) 3.57*E2 (f) 3.57E2.1 (g) 3.57E+2 (h) 3,57E-2

2.3 State, giving reasons, which of the following are not Fortran variable names:

(a) A2   (b) A.2   (c) 2A   (d) 'A'ONE
(e) AONE   (f) _X_1   (g) MiXedUp (h) Pay Day
(i) U.S.S.R. (j) Pay_Day (k) min*2   (l) PRINT

2.4 Find the values of the following expressions by writing short programs to evaluate them (answers in parentheses):

(a) $\sqrt{2}$ (1.41421)
(b) the sum of 5 and 3 divided by their product (0.53333)
(c) the cube root of the product of 2.3 and 4.5 (2.17928)
(d) the square of 2π (39.4784—take $\pi = 3.1415927$)
(e) $2\pi^2$ (19.7392)
(f) $1000(1 + 0.15/12)^{60}$ (2107.18—the balance when $1000 is deposited for 5 years at 15% p.a. compounded monthly)

2.5 Translate the following expressions into Fortran:

(a) $p + \frac{w}{u}$ (b) $p + \frac{w}{u+v}$ (c) $\frac{p + \frac{w}{u+v}}{p + \frac{w}{u-v}}$ (d) $x^{1/2}$
(e) y^{y+z} (f) x^{y^z} (g) $(x^y)^z$ (h) $x - x^3/3! + x^5/5!$

2.6 Suppose that the largest integer on your system is $2^{31} - 1$. Write a Fortran statement which will compute this number, bearing in mind that an attempt to compute 2^{31} will cause an overflow error.

2.7   Write a program to calculate x, where

$$x = \frac{-b + \sqrt{b^2 - 4ac}}{2a}$$

and $a = 2$, $b = -10$, $c = 12$ (use Read* to input the data). (Answer 3.0)

2.8   There are eight pints in a gallon, and 1.76 pints in a litre. The volume of a tank is given as 2 gallons and 4 pints. Write a program which reads this volume in gallons and pints and converts it to litres. (Answer: 11.36 litres)

2.9   Write a program to calculate petrol (gas) consumption. It should assign the distance travelled (in kilometres) and the amount of petrol used (in litres) and compute the consumption in km/litre as well as in the more usual form of litres per 100 km. Write some helpful headings, so that your output looks something(?) like this:

Distance	Litres used	Km/L	L/100Km
528	46.23	11.42	8.76

2.10   Write some lines of Fortran which will exchange the contents of two variables A and B, using only one additional variable T.

2.11   Try the previous problem *without* using any additional variables!

2.12   Try to spot the syntax errors (i.e. mistakes in coding rules) in this program before running it on the computer to check your answers with the error messages generated by your compiler:

```
PROGRAM Dread-ful
REAL: A, B, X
X:= 5
Y = 6,67
B = X \ Y
PRINT* 'The answer is", B
END.
```

2.13   A mortgage bond (loan) of amount L is obtained to buy a house. The interest rate r is 15% (0.15) p.a. The fixed monthly payment P which will pay off the bond exactly over N years is given by the formula

$$P = \frac{rL(1 + r/12)^{12N}}{12[(1 + r/12)^{12N} - 1]}.$$

(a)   Write a program to compute and print P if $N = 20$ years, and the bond is for $50\,000$. You should get $658.39.

(b)   It's interesting to see how the payment P changes with the period N over which you pay the loan. Run the program for different values of N (use READ*). See if you can find a value of N for which the payment is less than $625.

(c) Now go back to having N fixed at 20 years, and examine the effect of different interest rates. You should see that raising the interest rate by 1% (0.01) increases the monthly payment by about $37.

2.14 It's useful to be able to work out how the period of a bond repayment changes if you increase or decrease your monthly payment P. The formula for the number of years N to repay the loan is given by

$$N = \frac{\log(\frac{P}{P-rL/12})}{12\log(1 + r/12)}.$$

(a) Write a new program to compute this formula. Use the intrinsic function LOG for the logarithm. How long will it take to pay off the loan of $50\,000$ at $800 a month if the interest remains at 15%? (Answer: 10.2 years—nearly twice as fast as when paying $658 a month!)

(b) Use your program to find out by trial-and-error the smallest monthly payment that can be made to pay the loan off—ever. **Hint:** recall that it is not possible to find the logarithm of a negative number, so P must not be less than $rL/12$.

2.15 The steady-state current I flowing in a circuit that contains a resistance $R = 5$, capacitance $C = 10$, and inductance $L = 4$ in series is given by

$$I = \frac{E}{\sqrt{R^2 + (2\pi\omega L - \frac{1}{2\pi\omega C})^2}}$$

where $E = 2$ and $\omega = 2$ are the input voltage and angular frequency respectively. Compute the value of I. (Answer: 0.0396)

3

Elementary Fortran: II

So far we have seen how to read data into a Fortran program, how to do some arithmetic with them, and how to output answers. In this chapter we look at two powerful constructions which feature in most real programs: DO and IF. We also look at two more intrinsic types, character and complex, and discuss the concept of kind. The chapter ends with a brief introduction to intrinsic functions.

3.1   DO Loops

Run the following program:

```
INTEGER I
REAL R
```

```
DO I = 1, 10
   PRINT*, I
END DO

END
```

To get some random numbers instead, replace the PRINT statement with the following two statements:

```
CALL RANDOM_NUMBER( R )
PRINT*, R
```

Every time you run the new program you will get the same 10 "random" numbers, which is rather boring. To see how to get a different set each time you will have to wait until Chapter 14.

For a change, try the following:

```
DO I = 97, 122
   WRITE( *, 10, ADVANCE = 'NO' )ACHAR( I )
   10    FORMAT( A1 )
END DO
```

The form of the WRITE statement above introduces a new feature which old hands will welcome with rejoicing: non-advancing I/O.

To get the alphabet backwards, replace the DO with

```
DO I = 122, 97, -1
```

The DO loop (or its equivalent) is one of the most powerful statements in any programming language. One of its simplest forms is

```
DO I = J , K
   block
END DO
```

where I is an integer variable, J and K are integer expressions, and *block* stands for any number of statements. The block is executed repeatedly; the values of J and K determine how many repeats are made. On the first loop, I takes the value of J, and is then increased by 1 at the end of each loop (including the last). Looping stops once I has reached the value of K, and execution proceeds with the statement after END DO. I will have the value $K + 1$ after completion of the loop (normal exit).

You can probably guess how DO works in reverse.

Square rooting with Newton   The square root x of any positive number a may be found using only the arithmetic operations of addition, subtraction and division, with *Newton's method*. This is an iterative (repetitive) procedure that refines an initial guess; there are more general examples in Chapter 16.

The structure plan of the algorithm to find the square root, and the program with sample output for $a = 2$ is as follows:

1. Input *a*
2. Initialize *x* to 1
3. Repeat 6 times (say)

    Replace *x* by $(x + a/x)/2$

    Print *x*
4. Stop.

```
PROGRAM Newton
! Square rooting with Newton

IMPLICIT NONE
REAL    A            ! number to be square rooted
INTEGER I            ! iteration counter
REAL    X            ! approximate square root of A

WRITE( *, 10, ADVANCE = 'NO' ) 'Enter number to be square rooted: '
10  FORMAT( A )
READ*, A
PRINT*
X = 1                ! initial guess (why not?)

DO I = 1, 6
   X = (X + A / X) / 2
   PRINT*, X
ENDDO

PRINT*
PRINT*, 'Fortran 90''s value:', SQRT( A )

END
```

Output:

```
Enter number to be square rooted: 2

    1.5000000
    1.4166666
    1.4142157
    1.4142135
    1.4142135
    1.4142135

Fortran 90's value:    1.4142135
```

The value of X converges to a limit, which is $\sqrt{a}$. Note that it is identical to the value returned by Fortran 90's intrinsic SQRT function. Most computers and calculators use a similar method internally to compute square roots and other standard mathematical functions.

Note:

- the use of a "prompt" in a WRITE statement to elicit input from the user—old hands note again that non-advancing I/O allows the input on the same line as the prompt;
- that to print an apostrophe (') in a string the apostrophe must be repeated ('');
- that some pairs of keywords, such as ENDDO, do not have to be separated.

Money again   The next program computes compound interest on an initial balance over a number of years. Run it for a period of about 10 years and see if you can follow how it works. Save it for use in Exercise 3.14 at the end of the chapter.

```
PROGRAM Invest
! compound growth of an investment

IMPLICIT NONE
REAL      Bal          ! balance
INTEGER   Period       ! period of investment
REAL      Rate         ! interest rate
INTEGER   Year         ! year counter

PRINT*, 'Initial balance:'
READ*, Bal
PRINT*, 'Period of investment (years):'
READ*, Period
PRINT*, 'Interest rate (per annum, as a decimal fraction):'
READ*, Rate
PRINT*
PRINT*, 'Year    Balance'
PRINT*

DO Year = 1, Period
  Bal = Bal + Rate * Bal
  PRINT*, Year, Bal
END DO

END
```

If you feel up to it try to implement non-advancing I/O to get each input on the same line as its prompt.

The next program is a variation on the last one. Suppose we have to service four different savings accounts, with balances of $1000, $500, $750 amd $12050. We want to compute the new balance for each of them after 9% interest has been compounded. Try it out.

```
PROGRAM Accounts
! processes customers accounts

IMPLICIT NONE
INTEGER   Acct        ! counter
REAL      NewBal      ! new balance after interest
```

```
REAL        OldBal      ! original balance
REAL        Rate        ! interest rate

Rate = 0.09             ! 9% pa

DO Acct = 1, 4
  WRITE( *, '(A)', ADVANCE = 'NO' ) 'Old balance: '
  READ*, OldBal
  NewBal = OldBal + Rate * OldBal
  PRINT*, 'New balance: ', NewBal
END DO

END
```

Note the effects of indenting the statements inside the DO loop. It makes it easier for you to spot the block when you read the program.

Differential interest rates Most banks offer differential interest rates—more for the rich, less for the poor. Suppose in the above example that the rate is 9% for balances less than $5000, but 12% otherwise. We can easily amend the program to allow for this by deleting the statement Rate = 0.09 and inserting a new block of statements after the READ* as follows:

```
IF (OldBal < 5000) THEN
  Rate = 0.09
ELSE
  Rate = 0.12
ENDIF
```

Try this out with sensibly chosen data to verify that it works. For example, $4000 will grow to $4360, whereas $5000 will grow to $5600.

3.2 Deciding with IF-THEN-ELSE

We will discuss the IF-THEN-ELSE statement just introduced more fully in this section.

As an example, suppose that the final course mark of students attending a university course is calculated as follows. Two examination papers are written at the end of the course. The final mark is either the average of the two papers, or the average of the two papers and the class record mark (all weighted equally), whichever is the higher. The following program computes and prints each student's mark, with the comment PASS or FAIL (50% being the pass mark).

```
PROGRAM Final_Mark
! Final mark for course based on class record and exams

IMPLICIT NONE
REAL      CRM         ! Class record mark
```

```
REAL      ExmAvg      ! average of two exam papers
REAL      Final       ! final mark
REAL      P1          ! mark for first paper
REAL      P2          ! mark for second paper
INTEGER   Stu         ! student counter

OPEN( 1, FILE = 'MARKS' )
PRINT*, ' CRM          Exam Avg     Final Mark'
PRINT*

DO Stu = 1, 3
   READ( 1, * ) CRM, P1, P2
   ExmAvg = (P1 + P2) / 2.0
   IF (ExmAvg > CRM) THEN
     Final = ExmAvg
   ELSE
     Final = (P1 + P2 + CRM) / 3.0
   END IF
   IF (Final >= 50) THEN
      PRINT*, CRM, ExmAvg, Final, 'PASS'
   ELSE
      PRINT*, CRM, ExmAvg, Final, 'FAIL'
   END IF
END DO

END
```

As explained above, the data are stored in an external file (MARKS) to make reading more efficient. For example, for a sample class of three students, the data could be:

```
40  60  43
60  45  43
13  98  47
```

i.e. the first student has a class record of 40 with exam marks of 60 and 43. Her final mark should be 51.5 (class record not used), whereas the second student's mark should be 49.3 (class record used). Run the program as it stands.

The IF construct   In the above example we see a situation where the computer must make decisions: whether or not to include the class record, and whether to pass or fail the student. The programmer cannot anticipate which of these possibilities will occur when writing the program, so it must be designed to allow for all of them. We need a *conditional branch*, which is another of the most powerful facilities in any programming language. A common form of the IF construct, as it is called in Fortran 90, is

```
IF condition THEN
    block1
[ELSE
    blockE]
END IF
```

where *condition* is a *logical expression* having a "truth" value of either true or false, and *block1* and *blockE* are blocks of statements. If the condition is true, *block1* is executed (and not *blockE*), otherwise *blockE* is executed (and not *block1*). The ELSE part is optional and may be left out. Execution continues in the normal sequential way with the next statement after END IF.

The condition may be formed from numeric expressions with the *relational operators*, such as <, <=, == (equals) and /= (not equals), and from other logical expressions with the *logical operators*, such as .NOT., .AND. and .OR.. These are all discussed fully with the most general form of IF in Chapter 5.

The IF statement A shorter form of the IF construct is the IF *statement*:

```
IF (condition) statement
```

In this case only a single statement is executed if the condition is true. Nothing happens if it is false.

The word "construct" implies a construction with more than one statement (and hence more than one keyword).

3.3 Characters

A glaring shortcoming of the above program is that the students' *names* are neither read nor printed. To remedy this we make use of *character* variables. Make the following changes to Final_Mark:

Insert the statement

```
CHARACTER (Len = 15) Name      ! Name
```

into the declaration section. Change the statement that prints the heading:

```
PRINT*, 'Name              CRM        Exam Avg    Final Mark'
```

Change the READ statement:

```
READ( 1, * ) Name, CRM, P1, P2
```

Change the two statements that print the marks:

```
PRINT*, Name, CRM, ExmAvg, Final, 'PASS'
PRINT*, Name, CRM, ExmAvg, Final, 'FAIL'
```

Finally, change the data file MARKS by inserting some names (don't forget the apostrophes):

```
'Able, RJ'      40 60 43
'Nkosi, NX'     60 45 43
'October, FW'   13 98 47
```

If you run the amended program you should get output like this:

```
Name            CRM         Exam Avg    Final Mark

Able, RJ        40.0000000  51.5000000  51.5000000 PASS
Nkosi, NX       60.0000000  44.0000000  49.3333321 FAIL
October, FW     13.0000000  72.5000000  72.5000000 PASS
```

Character constants   So far we have dealt mainly with two of Fortran 90's intrinsic types: integer and real. We now come to the intrinsic type character.

The basic *character literal constant* is a string of characters enclosed in a pair of either apostrophes (') or quotes ("). Most characters supported by your computer are permitted, with the exception of the "control characters" (e.g. **escape**). The apostrophes and quotes serve as *delimiters* and are not part of the constant.

A blank in a character constant is significant, so that

```
"B Shakespeare"
```

is not the same as

```
"BShakespeare"
```

Fortran 90 is "case sensitive" only in the case of character constants, so

```
Charlie Brown
```

is not the same as

```
CHARLIE BROWN
```

There are two ways of representing the delimiter characters themselves in a character constant. Either sort of delimiter may be embedded in a string delimited by the other sort, as in

```
'Jesus said, "Follow me"'
```

Alternatively, the delimiter should be repeated, as in

```
'Pilate said, ''What is truth?'''
```

A character string may be empty, i.e. '' or "". The number of characters in a string is called its *length*. An empty string has a length of zero.

Character variables   The statement

```
CHARACTER LETTER
```

declares LETTER to be a character variable of length 1, i.e. it can hold a single character. Longer characters may be declared, as in the program `Final_Mark`:

```
CHARACTER (Len = 15) Name
```

This means that the character variable `Name` can hold a string of up 15 characters. An alternative form of the declaration is

```
CHARACTER Name*15
```

Character constants may be assigned to variables in the obvious way:

```
Name = 'J. Soap'
```

On an input record, the quote or apostrophe delimiters are not needed for a character constant if the constant does not contain a blank, comma or slash. Since the names in the example above contain commas and blanks, delimiters are needed in the input file.

3.4 Named Constants

In the program `Vertical` in Chapter 2, the declaration statement

```
REAL, PARAMETER :: G = 9.8
```

was used to declare `G` as a *named constant*, or *parameter*. The effect of this is that `G` may not be changed later in the program—any attempt to do so will generate an error message.

The `PARAMETER` *attribute* is one of many that may be specified in a type declaration statement. Further attributes will be introduced later.

Named constants may themselves be used when initializing. The expression thus formed is an *initialization expression* (initialization expressions are in fact special cases of *constant expressions*, which may appear in other contexts). E.g.

```
REAL, PARAMETER :: Pi = 3.141593
INTEGER, PARAMETER :: Two = 2
REAL, PARAMETER :: OneOver2Pi = 1 / (2 * Pi)
REAL, PARAMETER :: PiSquared = Pi ** Two
```

Since initialization expressions are evaluated at compile time, there are certain restrictions on their form. At this stage, the relevant ones are:

- they may only involve intrinsic operators;
- the exponentiation operator must have an integer power;
- intrinsic functions must have integer or character arguments and results.

The following is therefore *not* allowed, given the definition of `Pi` above:

```
REAL, PARAMETER :: OneOverRoot2Pi = 1 / SQRT(2 * Pi)
```

In general, a double colon *must* appear wherever an attribute is specified or an initialization expression is used; otherwise it is optional. If the `PARAMETER` attribute is specified, an initialization expression *must* appear.

If the named constant is of character type, its length may be declared with an asterisk. The actual length is then determined by the compiler, saving you the bother of counting all the characters. E.g.

```
CHARACTER (LEN = *), PARAMETER &
 :: Message = 'Press ENTER to continue'
```

3.5   Kind

The concept of *kind* is a new feature of Fortran 90 with which experienced Fortran programmers will need to get to grips.

Each of the five intrinsic types has a default kind—this is required by the standard. There may be a number of other kinds—these will be system-dependent and are not specified by the standard. Associated with each kind is a non-negative integer called the *kind type parameter*. The value of the kind parameter enables you to identify the various kinds available.

Integer kinds   For example, the FTN90 compiler supports three integer kinds on a PC. The default kind has a kind parameter value of 3, and represents integers in the range -2^{31} to $2^{31} - 1$.

There are a number of intrinsic functions which enable you to establish kind related properties, and, more importantly, to specify a kind which will suit your precision requirements.

Integer constants automatically have default kind (that is what the word default means). The function KIND(I) returns the value of the kind parameter of its argument (real or integer), so KIND(0) will return the default integer kind. The simple declaration

```
INTEGER I
```

specifies I with default integer kind.

The function HUGE(I) returns the largest value represented by its argument (real or integer). To find the *smallest* value, simply add 1 and print the result. The values of an integer kind *cycle* between their lower and upper bounds (under the FTN90 compiler). The following fragment will establish default integer kind and upper and lower bounds:

```
INTEGER I, BIG, SMALL

BIG = HUGE(I)
SMALL = BIG + 1
PRINT*, 'Default kind: ', KIND( I )
PRINT*, 'Largest:      ', BIG
PRINT*, 'Smallest:     ', SMALL
```

Note that the arguments of KIND and HUGE need not be defined.

Having established the default kind parameter value, you can experiment a bit to establish the other kinds available on your compiler. E.g. the statement

```
INTEGER ([KIND =] 2) I
```

specifies I with a kind parameter of 2—more precisely, a *kind type parameter* (contents of square brackets is optional).

The function SELECTED_INT_KIND(N) returns the kind parameter value for the kind that will be able to represent all integer values in the range -10^N to 10^N. This function can be used to establish what kinds are available:

```
INTEGER K, N
N = 0

DO
  N = N + 1
  K = SELECTED_INT_KIND( N )
  IF( K == -1 ) EXIT
  PRINT*, N, K
END DO

END
```

The numerical value of the kind parameters is system-dependent. That is, while the integer kinds available under FTN90 are 1, 2 and 3, under a different compiler their values may be 2, 4 and 8, although the kinds may have identical properties. This raises the question of portability—can we write a program which specifies a certain kind, and which will run on any compiler that supports the standard? The answer is that we can, using the SELECTED_INT_KIND function to name a constant which is in turn used in the type declaration statement:

```
INTEGER, PARAMETER :: K6 = SELECTED_INT_KIND( 6 )
INTEGER (K6) I
```

The right-hand side of the first statement is an example of a *constant expression*. This guarantees that kind K6 will be able to represent all integers in the range -999999 to 999999 (and possibly more).

Although literal constants have default kind, a different kind may be specified by following the constant with an underscore and an unsigned integer constant or named integer constant, e.g.

```
123_2    123456_K6
```

specifies 123 with kind 2 (which is system-dependent), while 123456 is specified with the kind K6 selected by the declaration above (which is portable). Clearly the portable form is safer to use, and is therefore recommended.

In the evaluation of expressions where operands have different kind parameter values, the result has the kind parameter of the operand with the greater precision.

Real kinds   The functions KIND and HUGE described above also take real arguments. With real type, an attempt to go beyond HUGE causes an overflow error.

The function SELECTED_REAL_KIND(P, R) returns the kind parameter of the real type with precision at P (number of significant decimals) and an exponent range of at least 10^{-R} to 10^{R} (if available). P and R must be integers.

The kind of a real constant may be specified in the same way as an integer constant.

The standard requires that in addition to a default real kind, there must be at least one real kind with a greater precision than the default (this corresponds to the now obsolete DOUBLE PRECISION type of earlier versions). If this more accurate representation has, for example, a kind parameter value of 2, the AIDS program of Chapter 1 may be amended by replacing the REAL statement with

```
REAL (KIND=2)  A     ! number of cases
```

and the numeric assignment with

```
A = 174.6 * (T - 1981.2_2) ** 3
```

Note that to get a significantly different answer the expression must be coerced into the stronger type. Run this to see how the answer differs.

Further functions relating to real kind are described in the appendices.

Character kinds   The default kind of character constant includes all characters supported by your computer system with the exception of the control characters. The standard requires that the default kind satisfies a certain *collating sequence*. This is to enable sorting of characters, which is discussed in Chapter 11.

Other character sets (e.g. Greek) may be supported by your system, and these would have different kind parameters. In the case of character constants, the kind parameter, if any, *precedes* the constant. So if the named constants ASCII and GREEK had the values of the default and Greek kind, constants of those kinds could be written as

```
ASCII_"abcde"
GREEK_"αβγδε"
```

We saw in the case of integers and reals above that the kind parameter may be specified with a type parameter. Since the length of a character variable may also be specified on declaration, character is the only type to have *two* type parameters: one for length, and one for kind. Examples:

```
CHARACTER (LEN = 10, KIND = GREEK) Greek_Word
CHARACTER (LEN = 10) English_Word            ! default kind
CHARACTER (KIND = GREEK) Greek_Letter        ! default length of 1
CHARACTER (10, GREEK ) Greek_Word
```

Note that the specifiers "LEN =" and "KIND =" are optional. However, if only one unnamed parameter is given, it is taken to be the length, not the kind.

The function KIND also takes a character argument. (You may be wondering how the same function can take arguments of so many different types. If so, you will have to wait for the discussion of overloading to see how this may be done.)

3.6 Complex Type

Complex numbers and complex arithmetic are supported by Fortran 90. E.g.

```
COMPLEX, PARAMETER :: i = (0, 1)     ! sqrt(-1)
COMPLEX X, Y
X = (1, 1)
Y = (1, -1)
PRINT*, CONJG(X), i * X * Y
```

Output:

```
(  1.0000000, -1.0000000) (  0.0000000E+00,  2.0000000)
```

When a complex constant is input with READ* it must be enclosed in parentheses. Many of the intrinsic functions can take complex arguments.

3.7 Introduction to Intrinsic Functions

So far you should be able to write a program which gets data into the computer, performs simple arithmetic operations on the data, and outputs the results of the computation in a comprehensible form. However, more interesting problems are likely to involve special mathematical functions like sines, cosines, logarithms, etc. Just as most calculators have keys for these functions, Fortran allows you to compute many functions directly. These functions are called *intrinsic* (or built-in) functions.

Projectile motion We want to write a program to compute the position (x and y co-ordinates) and the velocity (magnitude and direction) of a projectile, given t, the time since launch, u, the launch velocity, a, the initial angle of launch (in degrees), and g, the acceleration due to gravity.

The horizontal and vertical displacements are given by the formulae

$$x = ut \cos a, \quad y = ut \sin a - gt^2/2.$$

The velocity has magnitude V such that $V^2 = \sqrt{V_x^2 + V_y^2}$, where its horizontal and vertical components, V_x and V_y, are given by

$$V_x = u \cos a, \quad V_y = u \sin a - gt,$$

and V makes an angle θ with the ground such that $\tan \theta = V_x/V_y$. The program is:

```
PROGRAM Projectile
IMPLICIT NONE

REAL, PARAMETER :: g = 9.8         ! acceleration due to gravity
REAL, PARAMETER :: Pi = 3.1415927  ! a well-known constant

REAL A      ! launch angle in degrees
REAL T      ! time of flight
```

```
REAL Theta   ! direction at time T in degrees
REAL U       ! launch velocity
REAL V       ! resultant velocity
REAL Vx      ! horizontal velocity
REAL Vy      ! vertical velocity
REAL X       ! horizontal displacement
REAL Y       ! vertical displacement

READ*, A, T, U
A = A * Pi / 180        ! convert angle to radians
X = U * COS( A ) * T
Y = U * SIN( A ) * T - g * T * T / 2.
Vx = U * COS( A )
Vy = U * SIN( A ) - g * T
V = SQRT( Vx * Vx + Vy * Vy )
Theta = ATAN( Vy / Vx ) * 180 / Pi
PRINT*, 'x: ', X, 'y: ', Y
PRINT*, 'V: ', V, 'Theta: ', Theta
END
```

If you run this program with the data

```
45  6  60
```

you will see from the negative value of θ that the projectile is coming down.

The argument of a function may be any valid Fortran expression of appropriate type, including another function. So *V* could have been computed directly as follows:

```
V = SQRT( (U * COS( A )) ** 2 + (U * SIN( A ) - g * T) ** 2 )
```

(The argument of SQRT is always positive here (why?) so no problems can arise.)

Angles for the trigonometric functions must be expressed in radians, and are returned in radians where appropriate. To convert degrees to radians, multiply the angle in degrees by $\pi/180$, where π is the well-known transcendental number 3.1415926.... If you want to impress your friends, however, you can cunningly exploit the mathematical fact that the arc tangent (inverse tangent) of 1 is $\pi/4$, and use the ATAN function (try it).

Some useful intrinsic functions   Descriptions of all the intrinsic procedures supported by Fortran 90 appear in Appendix C. A list of some of the more common ones follows. X stands for a real expression unless otherwise stated. Optional arguments are indicated in square brackets.

ABS(X): absolute value of integer, real or complex X.
ACOS(X): arc cosine (inverse cosine) of X.
ASIN(X): arc sine of X.
ATAN(X): arc tangent of X in the range $-\pi/2$ to $\pi/2$.
ATAN2(Y, X): arc tangent of y/x in the range $-\pi$ to π.
COS(X): cosine of real or complex X.
COSH(X): hyperbolic cosine of X.

EXP(X): value of the exponential function e^x, where X may be real or complex.

INT(X [,KIND]): converts integer, real or complex X to integer type *truncating towards zero*, e.g. INT(3.9) returns 3, INT(-3.9) returns −3. If the optional argument KIND is present, it specifies the value of the kind parameter of the result. Otherwise the result has default integer kind.

LOG(X): natural logarithm of real or complex X. Note that an integer argument will cause an error.

LOG10(X): base 10 logarithm of X.

MAX(X1, X2[, X3, ...]): maximum of two or more integer or real arguments.

MIN(X1, X2[, X3, ...]): minimum of two or more integer or real arguments.

MOD(K, L): remainder when K is divided by L. Arguments must be both integer or both real.

NINT(X [,KIND]): *nearest* integer to X, e.g. NINT(3.9) returns 4, while NINT(-3.9) returns −4.

REAL(X [,KIND]): converts integer, real or complex X to real type, e.g. REAL(2)/4 returns 0.5, whereas REAL(2/4) returns 0.0.

SIN(X): sine of real or complex X.

SINH(X): hyperbolic sine of X.

SQRT(X): square root of real or complex X.

TAN(X): tangent of X.

TANH(X): hyperbolic tangent of X.

Intrinsic subroutines   Fortran 90 also has a number of intrinsic subroutines. Subroutines differ slightly from functions in that they are invoked with a CALL statement, and results are returned through arguments. They are also described in Appendix C. The example below shows how you can display the date and time. It also illustrates the use of character substrings and concatenation.

```
CHARACTER*10 DATE, TIME, PRETTY_TIME
CALL DATE_AND_TIME( DATE, TIME )
PRINT*, DATE
PRETTY_TIME = TIME(1:2) // ':' // TIME(3:4) // ':' // TIME(5:10)
PRINT*, PRETTY_TIME
END
```

Output:

```
19930201
15:47:23.0
```

Summary

- A DO loop is used to repeat a block (set) of statements.
- The IF-THEN-ELSE construct enables a program to decide between alternatives.
- The IF statement is a shorter form of the IF construct.
- Character constants are strings of characters enclosed in apostrophes (') or quotes (").
- Named constants (parameters) may not be changed in a program.

- Variables may be initialized in a type declaration.
- Each of the intrinsic data types has a default kind, and a system-dependent number of other kinds.
- The kind type parameter associated with a data type is an integer which evaluates to the kind of that data type.
- The value of kind type parameters is system-dependent.
- Characters may have two type parameters in their type declarations: one for length, and one for kind.
- Complex numbers and arithmetic are supported by the COMPLEX intrinsic type.
- Complex constants must be enclosed in parentheses for input with READ*.
- Intrinsic (built-in) functions may be used to compute a variety of mathematical, trigonometric and other functions directly.

Exercises

3.1   Translate the following into Fortran statements:

(a)   Add 1 to the value of I and store the result in I.

(b)   Cube I, add J to this, and store the result in I.

(c)   Set G equal to the larger of the two variables E and F.

(d)   If D is greater than zero, set X equal to minus B.

(e)   Divide the sum of A and B by the product of C and D, and store the result in X.

3.2   If C and F are Celsius and Fahrenheit temperatures respectively, the formula for conversion from Celsius to Fahrenheit is $F = 9C/5 + 32$.

(a)   Write a program which will ask you for the Celsius temperature and display the equivalent Fahrenheit one with some sort of comment, e.g.

```
The Fahrenheit temperature is: ...
```

Try it out on the following Celsius temperatures (answers in parentheses): 0 (32), 100 (212), −40 (−40!), 37 (normal human temperature: 98.6).

(b)   Change the program to use a DO loop to compute and write the Fahrenheit equivalent of Celsius temperatures ranging from 20° to 30° in steps of 1°.

3.3   Write a program that displays a list of integers from 10 to 20 inclusive, each with its square root next to it.

3.4   Write a program to find and display the sum of the successive integers 1, 2, ..., 100. (Answer: 5050)

3.5   Write a program to find and display the sum of the successive *even* integers 2, 4, ..., 200. (Answer: 10100)

3.6   Ten students in a class write a test. The marks are out of 10. All the marks are entered in an external file MARKS. Write a program which will read all ten marks from the file and find and display the average mark. Try it on the following marks (each on a separate line in the file):

5   8   0   10   3   8   5   7   9   4   (Answer: 5.9)

3.7 The pass mark for the test in the previous problem is 5 out of 10. Change your program so it uses an IF–THEN to find out how many students passed the test.

3.8 Write a program which generates some random numbers R with

```
CALL RANDOM_NUMBER( R )
```

and counts how many of them are greater than 0.5, and how many are less than 0.5. Try increasing the number of random numbers generated. What do you expect?

3.9 What are the values of X and A (both real) after the following program section has been executed?

```
A = 0
I = 1
X = 0
A = A + I
X = X + I / A
A = A + I
X = X + I / A
A = A + I
X = X + I / A
A = A + I
X = X + I / A
```

3.10 Rewrite the program in the previous exercise more economically by using a DO loop.

3.11 Work out by hand the output of the following program:

```
PROGRAM Mystery
REAL S, X
INTEGER N, K

N = 4
S = 0

DO K = 1, N
  X = K
  S = S + 1 / (X * X)        ! faster than X ** 2
END DO

   PRINT 10, Sqrt( 6 * S )
10 FORMAT( F10.6 )

   END
```

If you run this program for larger and larger values of N you will find that the output approaches a well-known limit.

3.12 The electricity accounts of residents in a very small town are calculated as follows:

- if 500 units or less are used the cost is 2 cents (100 cents = $1) per unit;
- if more than 500, but not more than 1000 units are used, the cost is $10 for the first 500 units, and then 5 cents for every unit in excess of 500;
- if more than 1000 units are used, the cost is $35 for the first 1000 units plus 10 cents for every unit in excess of 1000;
- in addition, a basic service fee of $5 is charged, no matter how much electricity is used.

Write a program which reads the names and consumptions of the following users from an external file and displays the name, consumption and total charge for each user:

```
Ahmed, A B          200
Baker, C D          500
Essop, S A          700
Jansen, G M         1000
Smith, Q G          1500
```

(Answers: $9, $15, $25, $40, $90)

3.13 Suppose you deposit $50 per month in a bank account every month for a year. Every month, after the deposit has been made, interest at the rate of 1% is added to the balance. E.g. after one month, the balance is $50.50, and after two months it is $101.51.

Write a program to compute and print the balance each month for a year. Arrange the output to look something like this:

```
MONTH           MONTH-END BALANCE

  1                  50.50
  2                 101.51
  3                 153.02
  ...
 12                 640.47
```

3.14 If you invest $1000 for one year at an interest rate of 12%, the return is $1120 at the end of the year. But if interest is compounded at the rate of 1% *monthly* (i.e. 1/12 of the annual rate), you get slightly more interest in the long run. Adapt the program Invest in Section 3.1 to compute the balance after a year of compounding interest in this way. The answer should be $1126.83. Evaluate the formula for this result separately as a check: 1000×1.01^{12}.

3.15 A plumber opens a savings account with $100 000 at the beginning of January. He then makes a deposit of $1000 at the end of each month for the next 12 months (starting at the end of January). Interest is calculated and added to his account at the end of each month (before the $1000 deposit is made). The monthly interest rate depends on the amount A in his account at the time when interest is calculated, in the following way:

$$A \leq 110\,000 : \quad 1\%$$
$$110\,000 < A \leq 125\,000 : \quad 1.5\%$$
$$A > 125\,000 : \quad 2\%$$

Write a program which displays, for each of the 12 months, under suitable headings, the situation at the end of the month as follows: the number of the month, the interest rate, the amount of interest and the new balance. (Answer: values in the last row of output should be 12, 0.02, 2534.58, 130263.78)

3.16 It has been suggested that the population of the United States may be modelled by the formula

$$P(t) = \frac{197\,273\,000}{1 + e^{-0.03134(t-1913.25)}}$$

where t is the date in years. Write a program to compute and display the population every *ten* years from 1790 to 2000. Use the intrinsic function EXP(X) to compute the exponential e^x.

Use your program to find out if the population ever reaches a "steady state", i.e. whether it stops changing.

3.17 A fruit packaging company wants a program that reads the number of apples that can be packed into one box (BOX) and the total number of apples to be packed (APPLES), and prints out the number of boxes needed (FULL) and the number of apples left over (LEFT).

(a) Write a structure plan for the problem.
(b) Write the Fortran program.

3.18 There are 39.37 inches in a metre, 12 inches in a foot, and three feet in a yard. Write a program to read a length in metres (which may have a decimal part) and convert it to yards, feet and inches. (Check: 3.51 metres converts to 3 yds 2 ft 6.19 in.)

3.19 Write some Fortran statements which will:

(a) find the length C of the hypotenuse of a right-angle triangle in terms of the lengths A and B of the other two sides;
(b) find the length C of a side of a triangle given the lengths A and B of the other two sides and the size in degrees of the included angle θ, using the cosine rule:
$$C^2 = A^2 + B^2 - 2AB \cos \theta.$$

3.20 Translate the following formulae into Fortran expressions:

(a) $\log(x + x^2 + a^2)$

(b) $(e^{3t} + t^2 \sin 4t) \cos^2 3t$

(c) $4 \arctan 1$

(d) $\sec^2 x + \cot y$

(e) $\cot^{-1} |x/a|$ (inverse cotangent)

3.21   A sphere of mass m_1 impinges obliquely on a stationary sphere of mass m_2, the direction of the blow making an angle α with the line of motion of the impinging sphere. If the coefficient of restitution is e it can be shown that the impinging sphere is deflected through an angle β such that

$$\tan \beta = \frac{m_2(1 + e) \tan \alpha}{m_1 - em_2 + (m_1 + m_2) \tan^2 \alpha}$$

Write a program to read values of m_1, m_2, e, and α (in degrees) and to compute the angle β in degrees.

4

Program Preparation

Our examples so far have been very simple logically, since we have been concentrating on the technical aspects of writing Fortran statements correctly. However, real problems are far more complex, and to program successfully we need to understand a problem thoroughly, and to break it down into its most fundamental logical stages. In other words, we have to develop a systematic procedure or *algorithm*, for solving the problem. There are a number of methods which assist in this process of algorithm development. In this chapter we outline two: flow-charts, and structure plans, which have already been mentioned briefly.

4.1 Flowcharts

This approach is rather old-fashioned, and tends to be frowned upon in certain computing circles. However, engineers often prefer this visual method, so for that reason, and for historical interest, some examples are given here.

Suppose we want to write a program to convert a temperature on the Fahrenheit scale (where water freezes and boils at 32° and 212° respectively) to the more familiar Celsius centigrade scale. The flowchart for the problem is in Figure 4.1.

The main symbols used in flowcharts are explained in Figure 4.2.

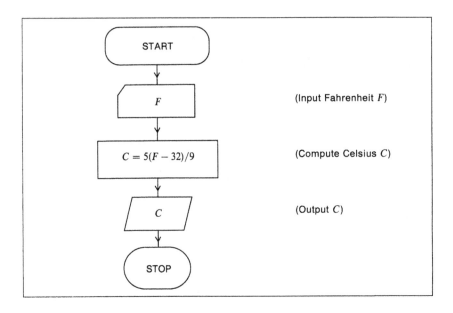

Fig. 4.1 Fahrenheit to Celsius conversion

Quadratic equation When you were at school you probably solved hundreds of quadratic equations of the form

$$ax^2 + bx + c = 0.$$

The complete algorithm for finding the solution(s) x, given any values of a, b and c, is flowcharted in Figure 4.3.

Newton's method for square rooting In Chapter 3 we wrote a program Newton to find square roots, which used a DO loop. There is no universally accepted way of flowcharting a DO loop, but one way is to use the elongated diamond to give the conditions under which the block of statements in the loop (the body of the loop) is executed, with a small circle to mark the end of the loop, as shown in Figure 4.4. Note that the contents of the boxes can be either Fortran statements or more general mathematical expressions.

4.2 Structure Plans

This is an alternative method of program preparation, which has advantages when the equivalent flowchart gets rather big. It is an example of what is called *pseudo-code*. The plan may be written at a number of levels, each of increasing complexity, as the logical structure of the program is developed. For example, a first level plan of the temperature conversion problem in Figure 4.1 above might be a simple statement of the problem:

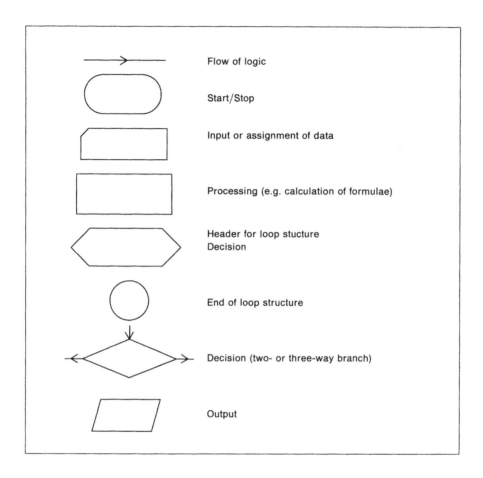

Processing (e.g. calculation of formulae)

Fig. 4.2 Flowcharting symbols

    1. Read Fahrenheit temperature
    2. Calculate and write Celsius temperature
    3. Stop.

Step 1 is pretty straightforward, but step 2 needs elaborating, so the second level plan could be something like this:

    1. Input Fahrenheit temperature (F)
    2. Calculate Celsius temperature (C):
        2.1. Subtract 32 from F and multiply by 5/9
    3. Output the value of C
    4. Stop.

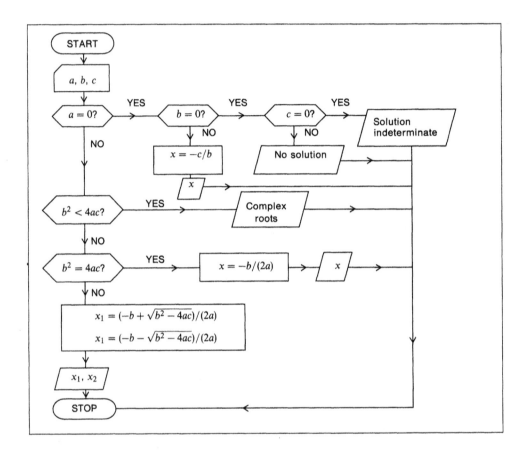

Fig. 4.3   Quadratic equation flowchart

There are no hard and fast rules about how to write flowcharts and structure plans; you should use whichever method you prefer (or even a mixture). The essential point is to cultivate the mental discipline of getting the logic of a program clear before attempting to write the program. The "top down" approach of flowcharts or structure plans means that the overall structure of a program is clearly thought out before you have to worry about the details of syntax (coding), and this reduces the number of errors enormously.

Quadratic equation   The equivalent structure plan for the solution of the quadratic equation flowcharted in Figure 4.3 is shown in Figure 4.5.

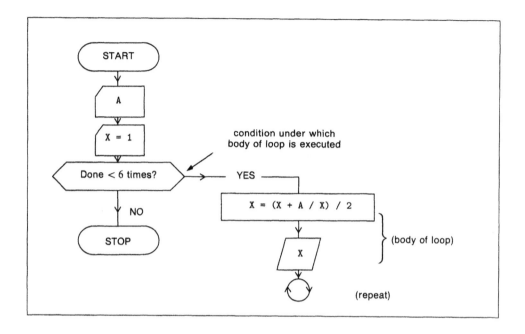

Fig. 4.4 Newton's method for square rooting

4.3 Structured Programming with Procedures

Many examples later in this book will get rather involved. More advanced programs like these should be structured by means of *procedures (subprograms)*, which are dealt with in detail in Chapter 8. A procedure is a self-contained section of code which can communicate with the main part of the program in specific ways, and which may be invoked or "called" by the main program. The main program will then look very much like a first level structure plan of the problem. For example, the quadratic equation problem may be structure planned at the first level as follows:

1. Read the data
2. Find and print the solution(s)
3. Stop.

Using a procedure (actually a *subroutine* in this example) this may be translated directly into a Fortran main program:

```
READ*, A, B, C
CALL SOLVE_QUADRATIC( A, B, C )
END
```

The details of how to code this problem are left as an exercise in Chapter 8.

```
1. Start
2. Input data (a, b, c)
3. If a = 0 then
       If b = 0 then
           If c = 0 then
               Print 'Solution indeterminate'
           else
               Print 'There is no solution'
       else
           x = -c/b
           Print x (only one root: equation is linear)
   else if b² < 4ac then
       Print 'Complex roots'
   else if b² = 4ac then
       x = -b/(2a)
       Print x (equal roots)
   else
       x₁ = (-b + √(b² - 4ac))/(2a)
       x₂ = (-b - √(b² - 4ac))/(2a)
       Print x₁, x₂
4. Stop.
```

Fig. 4.5   Quadratic equation structure plan

Summary

- An algorithm is a systematic logical method for solving a problem.
- An algorithm must be developed for a problem before it can be coded.
- A flowchart is a diagrammatic representation of an algorithm.
- A structure plan is a representation of an algorithm in pseudo-code.
- A procedure (or subprogram) is a separate collection of Fortran statements designed to handle a particular task, and which may be activated (invoked) whenever needed.

Exercises

The problems in these exercises should all be structure planned or flowcharted before being coded into Fortran.

4.1 This structure plan defines a geometric construction. Carry out the plan by sketching the construction:

1. Draw two perpendicular x- and y-axes
2. Draw the points A (10, 0) and B (0, 1)
3. While A does not coincide with the origin repeat:
       Draw a straight line joining A and B
       Move A one unit to the left along the x-axis
       Move B one unit up on the y-axis
4. Stop.

4.2 Consider the following structure plan, where M and N represent Fortran integer variables:

1. Set $M = 44$ and $N = 28$
2. While M not equal to N repeat:
    While $M > N$ repeat:
        Replace M by $M - N$
    While $N > M$ repeat:
        Replace N by $N - M$
3. Write M
4. Stop.

(a) Work through the structure plan, sketching the contents of M and N during execution. Give the output.

(b) Repeat (a) for $M = 14$ and $N = 24$.

(c) What general arithmetic procedure does the algorithm carry out (try more values of M and N if necessary)?

4.3 Write a program to convert a Fahrenheit temperature to a Celsius one. Test it on the data in Exercise 3.2.

4.4 A builder is given the measurements of five planks in feet (') and inches ("). He wants to convert the lengths to metres. One foot is 0.3048 metres, and one inch is 0.0254 metres. The measurements of the planks are: 4'6", 8'9", 9'11", 6'3" and 12'0" (i.e. the first plank is 4 feet 6 inches long). Store the data in a file.
    Write a program to display (under suitable headings) the length of each plank in feet and inches, and in metres, and to find and display the total length of planking in metres. (Answer: the total length is 12.624 metres)

4.5 Write a program to read any two real numbers (which you may assume are not equal), and write out the larger of the two with a suitable message.

4.6 Write a program to read a set of 10 numbers (from a file) and write out the *largest* number in the set.
    Now adjust the program to write out the *position* of the largest number in the set as well, e.g. if the data is

    4 7 2 9 3 -1 0 6 8 -2

(on separate lines in the file) the output should be 9 (largest number) and 4 (fourth number in the set).

4.7 Write a program to compute the sum of the series
$$1 + 1/2 + 1/3 + \ldots + 1/100.$$
The program should write the current sum after every 10 terms (i.e. the sum after 10 terms, after 20 terms, ..., after 100 terms).
    Hint: the intrinsic function MOD(N, 10) will be zero only when N is a multiple of 10. Use this in an IF statement to write the sum after every 10th term.
(Answer: 5.18738 after 100 terms)

4.8   To convert the integer variable Mins minutes into hours and minutes you would first use integer division (Mins/60 gives the whole number of hours) and then the MOD intrinsic function (MOD(Mins, 60) gives the number of minutes). Write a program which reads a number of minutes and converts it to hours and minutes.

Now write a program to convert seconds into hours, minutes and seconds. Use integer type again. Try out your program on 10 000 seconds, which should convert to 2 hours 46 minutes and 40 seconds.

4.9   Try to write the structure plans for Exercises 5.2 and 5.5 (don't try to write the programs until you've worked that far).

5
Decisions

Apart from its ability to add numbers extremely quickly, a computer's other major property is to be able to make decisions, as we saw briefly in Chapter 3. It is this facility, together with its ability to repeat statements endlessly without getting bored, which gives the computer its great problem-solving power. The fundamental decision-making construct in Fortran is the IF construct, of which the CASE construct is another form.

5.1 The IF Construct

We have seen some examples of the simple IF statement and the construct already. Further examples, which become more involved, are given in this section.

Bending moment in a beam   A light uniform beam $0 < x < L$ is clamped with its ends at the same level, and carries a concentrated load W at $x = a$. The bending moment M at any point x along the beam is given by two different formulae, depending on the value of x relative to a, viz.

$$M \; = \; W(L-a)^2[aL - x(L+2a)]/L^3 \quad (0 \le x \le a),$$
$$M \; = \; Wa^2[aL - 2L^2 + x(3L - 2a)]/L^3 \quad (a \le x \le L).$$

The following program extract computes the bending moment every metre along a 10 metre beam, with a load of 100 Newtons at a point 8 metres from the end $x = 0$:

```
INTEGER X
REAL A, L, M, W

L = 10
W = 100
A = 8

DO X = 0, L
  IF( X <= A )THEN
    M = W * (L - A) ** 2 * (A * L - X * (L + 2 * A)) / L ** 3
  ELSE
    M = W * A * A * (A * L - 2 * L * L + X * (3 * L - 2 * A)) /
    L ** 3
  END IF
  PRINT*, X, M
END DO
```

Note that X is an integer for use in the DO loop.

Top of the class   A class of students write a test, and each student's name (maximum of 15 characters) and mark is entered in a data file. Assume there are no negative marks. We want to write a program which prints out the name of the student with the highest mark, together with his/her mark. We are assuming that there is only *one* highest mark. The problem of what to do when two or more students share the top mark is discussed in Chapter 9.
   A first level structure plan for this problem could be:

1. Start
2. Find top student and top mark
3. Print top student and top mark.

Step 2 needs elaborating, so a more detailed plan might be:

1. Start
2. Initialize TopMark (to get process going)
3. Repeat for all students
           Read Name and Mark
           If Mark> TopMark then
                   Replace TopMark with Mark
                   Replace TopName with Name
4. Print TopName and TopMark
5. Stop.

The program (for a sample class of 3 students) is:

```
IMPLICIT NONE

INTEGER       I             ! student counter
REAL          Mark          ! general mark
CHARACTER*15  Name          ! general name
REAL    ::    TopMark = 0  ! top mark; can't be less than zero
CHARACTER*15  TopName        ! top student

OPEN( 1, FILE = 'MARKS' )

DO I = 1, 3
  READ( 1, * ) Name, Mark
  IF (Mark > TopMark) THEN
    TopMark = Mark
    TopName = Name
  END IF
END DO

PRINT*, 'Top student: ', TopName
PRINT*, 'Top mark:    ', TopMark
```

Work through the program by hand for a few turns to convince yourself that it works. Try it out on the following sample data (remember the apostrophes, because the names contain commas):

```
"Able, RJ" 40
"Nkosi, NX" 60
"October, FW" 13
```

ELSE IF   Recall the program Final_Mark in Chapter 3. To output the grade (1, 2+, 2–, 3 or F) of each student's final mark we might be tempted to replace the segment

```
IF (Final >= 50) THEN
...
END IF
```

with a set of simple IF statements as follows:

```
IF (Final >= 75) PRINT*, Name, CRM, ExmAvg, Final, '1'
IF (Final >= 70 .AND. Final < 75)
   PRINT*, Name, CRM, ExmAvg, Final, '2+'
IF (Final >= 60 .AND. Final < 70)
   PRINT*, Name, CRM, ExmAvg, Final, '2-'
IF (Final >= 50 .AND. Final < 60)
   PRINT*, Name, CRM, ExmAvg, Final, '3'
IF (Final < 50) PRINT*, Name, CRM, ExmAvg, Final, 'F'
```

(the logical operator .AND. is explained fully below).

While this works, it is inefficient and may waste precious computing time. There are five separate IF statements. The logical expressions in *all five* (e.g. Fin >= 75) have to be evaluated for each student, although we know that only one can be true; a student cannot get a first class pass and also fail! The following is a more efficient way of coding the problem. For good measure, we will also count how many passed in the first class, how many in the second class, and so on. The integer variables Firsts, UpSeconds, LowSeconds, Thirds and Fails represent the number of students in each of these respective classes.

```
IF (Final >= 75) THEN
   PRINT*, Name, CRM, ExmAvg, Final, '1'
   Firsts = Firsts + 1
ELSE IF (Final >= 70) THEN
   PRINT*, Name, CRM, ExmAvg, Final, '2+'
   UpSeconds = UpSeconds + 1
ELSE IF (Final >= 60) THEN
   PRINT*, Name, CRM, ExmAvg, Final, '2-'
   LowSeconds = LowSeconds + 1
ELSE IF (Final >= 50) THEN
   PRINT*, Name, CRM, ExmAvg, Final, '3'
   Thirds = Thirds + 1
ELSE
   PRINT*, Name, CRM, ExmAvg, Final, 'F'
   Fails = Fails + 1
END IF
```

This saves time because Fortran stops checking as soon as it finds a true logical expression. So if Final >= 75 is true, it won't bother to check further. The onus rests on you therefore to code the construct correctly, so that *only one* of the logical expressions is true.

Note also how indentation makes the structure easier to follow.

The IF construct in general   A more general form of the IF construct is:

```
IF (logical-expr1) THEN
     block1
ELSE IF (logical-expr2) THEN
     block2
ELSE IF (logical-expr3) THEN
     block3
...
ELSE
     blockE
END IF
```

If *logical-expr1* is true the statements in *block1* are executed, and control passes to the next statement after END IF. If *logical-expr1* is false, *logical-expr2* is evaluated. If it is true the statements in *block2* are executed, followed by the next statement after END IF. If none of the logical expressions is true, the statements in *blockE* are executed. Clearly, the logical expressions should be arranged so that only one of them can be true at a time.

There may be any number of ELSE IFs (or none at all), but there may be no more than one ELSE.

An IF construct may be optionally named as an aid to the reader (usually to clarify complicated nesting), e.g.

```
[GRADE:] IF (Final >= 50) THEN
         PRINT*, 'Pass'
       ELSE [GRADE]
         PRINT*, 'Fail'
       END IF [GRADE]
```

An ELSE or ELSE IF block may only be named if the corresponding IF and END IF blocks are named, and must be given the same name. The name must be a valid and unique Fortran name.

Note that nothing may follow the keyword THEN on the first line of the construct.

Nested IFs   When IF constructs are nested, the positioning of the END IFs is crucial, as this determines to which IFs the ELSE IFs belong. An ELSE IF or ELSE belongs to the most recently opened IF which has not yet been closed. To illustrate, consider once again programming the solution of the ubiquitous quadratic equation, $ax^2 + bx + c = 0$. It is necessary to check if $a = 0$, to prevent a division by zero:

```
Disc = B * B - 4 * A * C
Outer: IF (A /= 0) THEN
         Inner: IF (Disc < 0) THEN
                  PRINT*, 'Complex roots'
                ELSE Inner
                  X1 = (-B + SQRT( Disc )) / (2 * A)
                  X2 = (-B - SQRT( Disc )) / (2 * A)
                END IF Inner
       END IF Outer
```

What will happen if the END IF Inner is moved up 3 lines as shown below?

```
Outer: IF (A /= 0) THEN
         Inner: IF (Disc < 0) THEN
                  PRINT*, 'Complex roots'
                END IF Inner    ! Wrong place now!
                ELSE Inner
                  X1 = (-B + SQRT( Disc )) / (2 * A)
                  X2 = (-B - SQRT( Disc )) / (2 * A)
       END IF Outer
```

Well, the compiler will object because of a clash of names: ELSE Inner cannot appear after END IF Inner closes the Inner IF. However, if all the names are omitted, the segment will compile, but will make a division by zero certain if $a = 0$, since the ELSE will now belong to the *first* IF—try it.

Nesting may extend to any depth; indentation and/or naming should be carefully used in such cases to make the logic clearer.

DOs and IFs   A DO loop may contain an IF construct, and vice versa. The basic rule is that if a construct begins inside another construct, it must also end inside that construct. The following is therefore illegal:

```
DO I = 1, 10
  IF (I > 5) THEN
    ...
    END DO          ! Illegal: IF must end before DO
END IF
```

and so is this:

```
IF ( ... ) THEN
  DO I = 1, 10
    ...
    END IF          ! Illegal: DO must end before IF
END DO
```

5.2 Logical Type

So far four of the five intrinsic data types have been discussed: integer, real, character and complex. The time has come to discuss the fourth type: logical.

Logical constants   The default kind of logical type has two literal constants: .TRUE. and .FALSE. (upper- or lowercase). The value of the default kind parameter is returned in the usual way, by KIND(.TRUE.).

Your compiler may have non-default logical kinds; these may be used, for example, for storing logical arrays more compactly.

Logical expressions   We have seen logical expressions briefly in Chapter 3. They can be formed in two ways: from numeric expressions in combination with the six relational operators, or from other logical expressions in combination with logical variables and the five logical operators.

The *relational operators* and their meanings, with some examples, are as follows:

Relational Operator	Meaning	Example
.LT. or <	less than	A < 1e-5
.LE. or <=	less than or equal	B ** 2 .LE. 4 * A * C
.EQ. or ==	equal	B ** 2 == 4 * A * C
.NE. or /=	not equal	A /= 0
.GT. or >	greater than	B ** 2 - 4 * A * C > 0
.GE. or >=	greater than or equal	X >= 0

Logical operators Fortran 90 has five *logical operators*, which operate on logical expressions:

Logical Operator	Precedence	Meaning
.NOT.	1	logical negation
.AND.	2	logical intersection
.OR.	3	logical union
.EQV. and .NEQV.	4	logical equivalence and non-equivalence

The following "truth table" shows the effects of these operators on the logical expressions *lex1* and *lex2* (T = true; F = false):

lex1	lex2	.NOT. lex1	lex1 .AND. lex2	lex1 .OR. lex2	lex1 .EQV. lex2	lex1 .NEQV. lex2
T	T	F	T	T	T	F
T	F	F	F	T	F	T
F	T	T	F	T	F	T
F	F	T	F	F	T	F

The order of precedence, shown above, may be superseded with parentheses, which always have the highest precedence.
Examples:

```
(B * B == 4 * A * C) .AND. (A /= 0)
(Final >= 60) .AND. (Final < 70)
(A /= 0) .or. (B /= 0) .or. (C /= 0)
.not. ((A /= 0) .and. (B == 0) .and. (C == 0))
```

Incidentally, the last two expressions are equivalent, and are false only when $A = B = C = 0$—it makes you think, doesn't it?

Logical variables A variable may be declared with logical type in a LOGICAL statement. Logical constants or expressions may be assigned to logical variables:

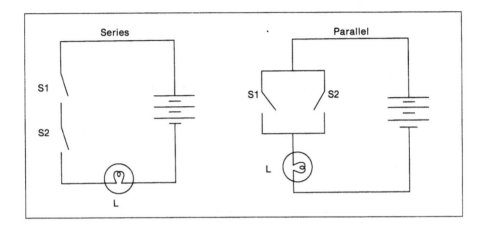

Fig. 5.1 Switching circuits

```
LOGICAL L1, L2, L3, L4, L5
REAL A, B, C
...
L1 = .TRUE.
L2 = B * B - 4 * A * C >= 0
L3 = A == 0
L4 = L1 .and. .not. L2 .or. L3
L5 = (L1 .and. (.not. L2)) .or. L3
```

(The precedence rules make L4 and L5 logically equivalent.)

The truth values of logical variables are represented by T and F in list-directed I/O.

Simulation of a switching circuit   In the following program segment the logical variables S1 and S2 represent the state of two switches (ON = true; OFF = false) and L represents the state of a light. The program simulates the circuits in Figure 5.1, where the switches are arranged either in series or parallel.

```
LOGICAL L, S1, S2
READ*, S1, S2
L = S1 .and. S2        ! series
!L = S1 .or. S2        ! parallel
PRINT*, L
```

When the switches are in series, the light will be on only if both switches are on. This situation is represented by S1.and.S2. When the switches are in parallel, the light will be on if one or both of the switches is on. This is represented by S1.or.S2.

Bit manipulation functions   Some programming languages, such as Pascal and C, have operators, called *bitwise operators*, which operate directly on the bits of their operands. These are usually discussed in the context of logical (or *Boolean*) variables. In Fortran 90 their counterparts are the bit manipulation intrinsic functions which operate on the bits of their integer arguments. These are described in Appendix C.

5.3 The CASE Construct

The CASE construct is similar to IF. It allows selection between a number of situations or cases, based on a selector. In such cases it is more convenient than IF. Consider the following program segment:

```
CHARACTER CH

DO
  READ*, CH
  PRINT*, ICHAR( CH )
  IF (CH == '@') EXIT

  IF (CH >= 'A' .and. CH <= 'Z'.or. CH >= 'a' .and. CH <= 'z')
    THEN SELECT CASE (CH)
      CASE ('A', 'E', 'I', 'O', 'U', 'a', 'e', 'i', 'o', 'u')
        PRINT*, 'Vowel'
      CASE DEFAULT
        PRINT*, 'Consonant'
    END SELECT
  ELSE
    PRINT*, 'Something else'
  END IF

END DO
```

It decides whether a character is a vowel, consonant, or something else. It stops when the symbol @ is read. This could be programmed entirely with IF, but would produce a lot more code which would be harder to read (try it).

The general form of CASE is

```
SELECT CASE (expr)
        CASE (selector1)
                block1
        CASE (selector2)
                block2
       [CASE DEFAULT
                blockD]
END SELECT
```

where *expr* must be integer, character or logical. If it evaluates to a particular *selector*, that *block* is executed, otherwise CASE DEFAULT is selected. CASE DEFAULT is optional, but there may be only one. It does not necessarily have to be the last clause of the CASE construct.

The general form of the selector is a list of non-overlapping values and ranges, of the same type as *expr*, enclosed in parentheses, e.g.

```
CASE( 'a':'h', 'i':'n', 'o':'z', '_')
```

Note that the colon may be used to specify a range of values. If the upper bound of a range is absent, the CASE is selected if *expr* evaluates to a value that is greater than or equal to the lower bound, and vice versa.

Parts of the CASE construct may be named in the same way as the IF construct.

The selection of grades in the amended Final_Mark program of Section 5.1 can also be programmed with CASE if the mark Final is converted to integer type:

```
SELECT CASE ( INT(Final) )
  CASE (75:)
    PRINT*, Name, CRM, ExmAvg, Final, '1'
    Firsts = Firsts + 1
  CASE (70:74)
    PRINT*, Name, CRM, ExmAvg, Final, '2+'
    UpSeconds = UpSeconds + 1
  CASE (60:69)
    PRINT*, Name, CRM, ExmAvg, Final, '2-'
    LowSeconds = LowSeconds + 1
  CASE (50:59)
    PRINT*, Name, CRM, ExmAvg, Final, '3'
    Thirds = Thirds + 1
  CASE DEFAULT
    PRINT*, Name, CRM, ExmAvg, Final, 'F'
    Fails = Fails + 1
END SELECT
```

There are times when CASE is more efficient than IF, since only one expression *expr* needs to be evaluated.

5.4   The GO TO Statement

It would be difficult to overestimate the damage done to languages like Fortran and Basic by the indiscriminate and thoughtless use of the GOTO statement. Proponents of the classically more structured languages, like Pascal and C, regard it as the programmer's four-letter word. (I once heard a particularly caustic critic ask why Fortran didn't have a COME FROM statement!)

GO TO is an *unconditional* branch, and has the form

GO TO *label*

where *label* is a statement label: a number in the range 1–99999 preceding a statement on the same line. Control passes unconditionally to the labelled statement. E.g.

```
    GO TO 99
    X = 67.8
99  Y = -1
```

The statement X = 67.8 is never executed, perhaps causing a ship to sink, an airplane to crash, or a shuttle launch to abort.

Novices may ask why GO TO is ever needed. Its use goes back to the bad old days when older versions of Fortran lacked the block IF construct, and had to make do with the simple IF statement. Consider the following (clear) segment of code (L1 and L2 are two defined logical variables):

```
IF (L1) THEN
   I = 1
   J = 2
ELSE IF (L2) THEN
   I = 2
   J = 3
ELSE
   I = 3
   J = 4
END IF
```

In the absence of the IF construct this must be coded as the following tangle of "spaghetti":

```
    IF (.NOT.L1) GOTO 10
       I = 1
       J = 2
       GOTO 30
10  IF (.NOT.L2) GOTO 20
       I = 2
       J = 3
       GOTO 30
20  I = 3
    J = 4
30  CONTINUE        ! Dummy statement - does nothing
```

Need we say more? except that GOTO should never be used—it will not be found in any examples in this book. It is mentioned here purely for historical and pedagogical reasons.

Summary

- The IF construct allows for the conditional execution of blocks of statements.
- The IF statement allows for the conditional execution of a single statement.
- The IF construct may have any number of ELSE IF clauses, but no more than one ELSE clause.
- The IF construct may be named.

- IF constructs may be nested.
- Logical constants, variables and expressions can only have one of two values: .TRUE. or .FALSE.
- Logical expressions may be formed from numeric expressions with relational operators <, <=, etc.
- The logical operators (.NOT., .AND., etc.) may be used to form more complex logical expressions from other logical expressions and variables.
- Fortran has bit manipulation functions which operate directly on the bits representing integers.
- The CASE construct may be used to select a particular action.
- The GOTO statement branches unconditionally, and should be avoided at all costs.

Exercises

5.1 Write a program which reads two numbers (which may be equal) and writes out the larger one with a suitable message, or if they are equal, writes out a message to that effect.

5.2 Write a structure plan and program for the following problem: read 10 integers and write out how many of them are positive, negative or zero. Write the program with an IF construct, and then rewrite it using a CASE construct.

5.3 Design an algorithm (draw the flowchart or structure plan) for a machine which must give the correct amount of change from a $10 note for any purchase costing less than $10. The plan must specify the number and type of all notes and coins in the change, and should in all cases give as few notes and coins as possible. (Define your own denominations if necessary.)

5.4 Write a program for the general solution of the quadratic equation $ax^2 + bx + c = 0$.

Use the structure plan developed in Chapter 4. Your program should be able to handle all possible values of the data a, b, and c. Try it out on the following values of a, b and c:

(a) 1, 1, 1 (complex roots);
(b) 2, 4, 2 (equal roots of −1.0);
(c) 2, 2, −12 (roots of 2.0 and −3.0).

Rewrite your program with complex types so that it can handle complex roots, as well as all the other special cases.

5.5 Develop a structure plan for the solution of two simultaneous linear equations (i.e. two straight lines). Your algorithm must be able to handle all possible situations, viz. lines which are intersecting, parallel, or co-incident. Write a program to implement your algorithm, and test it on some equations for which you know the solutions, e.g.

$$x + y = 3$$
$$2x - y = 3$$

($x = 2$, $y = 1$). **Hint**: begin by deriving an algebraic formula for the solution of the system

$$ax + by \;=\; c$$
$$dx + ey \;=\; f.$$

The program should read the coefficients a, b, c, d, e and f.

6

Loops

In Chapter 3 we introduced the powerful DO construct to execute a block of statements repeatedly. A situation where the number of repetitions may be determined in advance is sometimes called *deterministic repetition*. However, it often happens that the condition to end a repeat structure (or *loop*) is only satisfied during the execution of the loop itself. This type of repeat structure is called *non-deterministic*. Both of these (logically quite different) situations are programmed with the DO construct in Fortran 90.

6.1   Deterministic Repetition

In this section we will see how to generalize the DO construct after first considering some more examples.

Factorials! The variable in a DO loop may be used in any expression inside the loop, although its value may not be changed explicitly, (e.g. by an assignment statement as a quick and dirty way of terminating the loop early). The following program prints a list of n and $n!$ where

$$n! = 1 \times 2 \times 3 \times \ldots \times (n-1) \times n.$$

Do you trust the real or integer output, and why?

```
INTEGER ::  NFACT = 1
INTEGER N
REAL    ::  XFACT = 1

DO N = 1, 20
   NFACT = NFACT * N
   XFACT = XFACT * N
   PRINT*, N, NFACT, XFACT
END DO
```

Binomial coefficient This is widely used in statistics. The number of ways of choosing r objects out of n without regard to order is given by

$$\binom{n}{r} = \frac{n!}{r!(n-r)!} = \frac{n(n-1)(n-2)\cdots(n-r+1)}{r!},$$

$$\text{e.g.} \binom{10}{3} = \frac{10!}{3! \times 7!} = \frac{10 \times 9 \times 8}{1 \times 2 \times 3}.$$

If the form involving factorials is used, the numbers can get very big, causing the cycling problem shown in the previous example. But using the right-most expression above is much more efficient:

```
INTEGER :: BIN = 1
INTEGER K, N, R

PRINT*, 'Give values for N and R'
READ*, N, R

DO K = 1, R
   BIN = BIN * (N - K + 1) / K
END DO

PRINT*, N, 'c', R, '=', BIN
```

Limit of a sequence DO loops are ideal for computing successive members of a sequence. This example also highlights a problem that sometimes occurs when computing a limit. Consider the sequence

$$x_n = a^n/n!, \quad n = 1, 2, 3, \ldots$$

where a is any constant, and $n!$ is the factorial function defined above. The question is: what is the limit of this sequence as n gets indefinitely large? Let's take the case

$a = 10$. If we try to compute x_n directly we could get into trouble, because $n!$ gets large very rapidly as n increases, and cycling or overflow could occur. However, the situation is neatly transformed if we spot that x_n is related to x_{n-1} as follows:

$$x_n = ax_{n-1}/n.$$

There are no numerical problems now. The following program computes x_n for $a = 10$, and increasing values of n, and prints it for every tenth value of n:

```
REAL :: X = 1
REAL :: A = 10
INTEGER N

DO N = 1, 100
  X = A * X / N
  IF (MOD( N, 10 ) == 0) PRINT*, N, X
END DO
```

Complex transfer function   The response (output) of a linear system, which may be thought of as a "black box", is characterized in electrical engineering by its transfer function. An input signal with a given angular frequency (ω radians/s) is applied at one end of the box. The output from the other end is then given by the input multiplied by the absolute value of the transfer function, with its phase shifted by the phase angle of the transfer function.

Suppose a servomechanism is characterized by the transfer function

$$T(i\omega) = \frac{K(1 + 0.4i\omega)(1 + 0.2i\omega)}{i\omega(1 + 2.5i\omega)(1 + 1.43i\omega)(1 + 0.02i\omega)^2}$$

where i is the unit imaginary number $\sqrt{-1}$ (j in electrical engineering) and K is an amplification factor. $T(i\omega)$ is a complex number. If its real and imaginary parts (returned by REAL and AIMAG) are a and b respectively then its absolute value is $\sqrt{a^2 + b^2}$ and its phase angle ϕ is given by $\arctan b/a$. If the ATAN2 intrinsic function is used, the angle returned will be in the range $-\pi$ to π, so that the correct quadrant is given (which is not the case for ATAN).

The program below shows how the servomechanism responds to different input frequencies ω. This information is necessary in the design of stable feedback control devices. The initial input frequency is 0.02 radians/sec. This is multiplied by a factor (Fact) of 1.25 each time for a given number of steps. The amplification factor K is 900. The phase shift ϕ of the output is given in degrees.

Note that a named complex constant (i) is used for $\sqrt{-1}$. The complex variable iom is formed from i and Omega purely for notational convenience.

```
IMPLICIT NONE

INTEGER            N              ! counter
INTEGER         :: Steps          ! iteration count
REAL               A, B           ! Re(T), Im(T)
REAL            :: Fact = 1.25    ! scaling factor
REAL            :: K    = 900     ! amplification
REAL            :: Omega = 0.02   ! angular frequency
```

```
      REAL                  Phase                    ! phase angle
      REAL, PARAMETER    :: Pi    = 3.1415927
      COMPLEX, PARAMETER :: i     = (0, 1)     ! sqrt(-1)
      COMPLEX               iom                      ! sqrt(-1) * omega
      COMPLEX               T                        ! complex transfer function

      READ*, Steps
      PRINT 20
20    FORMAT( ' Omega', T12, 'Real T', T27, 'Im T', T42, 'Abs T', &
                       T62, 'Phase' )
      PRINT*

      DO N = 0, Steps
         iom = i * Omega
         T = (K*(1 + 0.4*iom)*(1 + 0.2*iom)) /                        &
             (iom*(1 + 2.5*iom)*(1 + 1.43*iom)*(1 + 0.02*iom)**2)
         A = REAL( T )
         B = AIMAG( T )
         Phase = ATAN2( B, A ) * 180 / Pi          ! phase degrees
         PRINT 10, Omega, A, B, ABS( T ), Phase
10       FORMAT( F7.3, T10, E11.4, T25, E11.4, T40, E11.4, T60, F7.2)
         Omega = Omega * Fact
      END DO
```

Sample output:

Omega	Real T	Im T	Abs T	Phase
0.020	-0.3024E+04	-0.4483E+05	0.4493E+05	-93.86
0.025	-0.3018E+04	-0.3578E+05	0.3591E+05	-94.82
...				
120.371	-0.1651E-01	0.1830E-01	0.2465E-01	132.07
150.463	-0.7512E-02	0.1100E-01	0.1332E-01	124.33

If you run the program you will see how the input signal is amplified at first, but is then attenuated. The phase shift starts at about $-90°$ and moves gradually to about $-180°$, after which it swings backwards and forwards across the real axis as the input frequency gets larger.

6.2   The DO in General

Try the following program segments (output is shown after each one):

```
      DO I = 2, 7, 2
         WRITE( *, '(I3)', ADVANCE = 'NO' ) I
      END DO
```

Output: 2   4   6

```
DO I = 5, 4
  WRITE( *, '(I3)', ADVANCE = 'NO' ) I
END DO
```

Output: (nothing)

```
DO I = 5, 1, -1
  WRITE( *, '(I3)', ADVANCE = 'NO' ) I
END DO
```

Output: 5   4   3   2   1

```
DO I = 6, 1, -2
  WRITE( *, '(I3)', ADVANCE = 'NO' ) I
END DO
```

Output: 6   4   2

The general form of the DO construct that we shall use is

[*name* :] DO *variable* = *expr1* , *expr2* [, *expr3*]
        block
    END DO [*name*]

where *variable* (the DO variable) is an integer variable, *expr1* , *expr2*, and *expr3* are any valid integer expressions, and *name* is the optional construct name. *expr3* is optional, with a default value of 1. The expressions *expr1* , *expr2*, and *expr3* are called the DO *parameters*.

The DO variable is initialized to *expr1* before a decision is made whether or not to loop, according to the formula below. On completion of each loop, *expr3* is added to the DO variable, again before deciding whether or not to loop. It follows that after completion of the DO construct, the DO variable will *not* have the value it had during the last execution of the block. E.g. in the first segment above, the final value of I is 8.

The number of iterations of a DO construct is given by the formula

MAX((*expr2* − *expr1* + *expr3*)/*expr3*, 0)

where MAX is the intrinsic function returning the maximum of its arguments. Since MAX returns a value which has the same type as its arguments, the value returned in this case will be the value of the expression (truncated if necessary), or zero, whichever is larger.

This formula is called the *iteration count* or the *trip count* of the DO loop. You should verify that the iteration counts for the four segments above are 3, 0, 5 and 3 respectively.

Note that it is possible for the DO block not to be executed at all. This is called a *zero-trip loop*, and will occur whenever the first argument of MAX in the formula evaluates to a non-positive quantity.

DO $I = J, K, L$

- If L is positive, the block is executed with I starting at J and increased by L every time until it has been executed for the greatest value of I *not exceeding* K.
- If $L > 0$ and $J > K$ the block is not executed at all (zero-trip count).
- If L is negative, the block is executed with I starting at J and decreased by $|L|$ every time until it has been executed for the smallest value of I *not less than* K.
- If $L < 0$ and $J < K$ the block is not executed at all (zero-trip count).

Fig. 6.1　DO parameters

The formula for the iteration count is evaluated before the block is executed for the first time. Even if the values of the DO parameters are subsequently changed inside the block, this will not affect the iteration count.

These rules are summarized in Figure 6.1.

The DO variable and parameters may be real. This feature, however, has been declared obsolescent (i.e. may be removed entirely from the next standard), so you should try very hard not to use it if you are an old Fortran addict. It gives rise to all sorts of nasty rounding errors.

6.3　DO with Non-integer Increments

There are many situations in scientific and engineering computing when one wants to make non-integer increments in a loop. Consider again the stone thrown vertically upwards in Chapter 2. Suppose it is launched at time $t = 0$ seconds, and we want to compute its position $s(t)$ between times $t = t_0$ and $t = t_1$ every dt seconds. These times are most unlikely to be integers.

One way to solve this problem is to calculate our own iteration count for the problem. The number of intervals involved is $(t_1 - t_0)/dt$. Since we want the result at each end of the interval between t_0 and t_1, we need to add 1 to this. The obvious value for our iteration count is therefore

$$(t_1 - t_0)/dt + 1.$$

Now, since this must be an integer, do we truncate it with INT or round it with NINT? To answer this we must first decide what must happen if $t_1 - t_0$ is not an exact multiple of dt. Let's say we don't want calculations made outside our specified range. That rules out NINT. Suppose $t_0 = 0$, $t_1 = 5$ and $dt = 0.4$. Our iteration count is 12.5 exactly. Rounding up with NINT would give 13, with an unwanted calculation beyond t_1. So INT must be used.

However, this also has its problems. Because of rounding error the number of intervals $(t_1 - t_0)/dt$ could easily just fall short of a whole number (like $10/0.1$ coming out as 99.9999 instead of 100), so truncating would lose one loop. Fortran 90 has a neat solution to this problem. The new intrinsic function SPACING(X) returns the absolute spacing between values near X. So the most satisfactory answer is to add SPACING(dt) to the iteration count before truncating.

The following program reads values for t_0 (TStart), t_1 (TEnd) and dt, and prints the iteration count (TRIPS) before computing and printing the stone's position every dt seconds. Note that t must be explicitly updated in the DO block now, since I is used purely as a counter.

```
REAL, PARAMETER :: G = 9.8
REAL             dT, S, T, TStart, TEnd
REAL          :: U = 60
INTEGER          I, TRIPS

READ*, TStart, TEnd, dT
TRIPS = INT( (TEnd - TStart) / dT + SPACING(dT) ) + 1
PRINT*, TRIPS
T = TStart

DO I = 1, TRIPS
  S = U * T - G / 2 * T * T
  PRINT*, I, T, S
  T = T + dT
END DO
```

A further interesting problem arises. Suppose we still want to compute $s(t)$ every dt seconds, but only want to print it every h seconds—this is a common problem in numerical analysis, where the step-length dt might be very small. Given that we want output on the first iteration, we therefore have to skip the next h/dt iterations before printing again. Because the DO variable I starts at 1 this means that we want output whenever $(I-1)$ is an exact multiple of h/dt. This can be achieved by replacing the PRINT above with

```
IF (MOD(I-1, INT( H / dT + SPACING(dT) )) == 0) PRINT*, I, T, S
```

where the same allowance has been made for rounding error, and the value of h must be input.

Note that the loop in this problem is indeed deterministic—we could determine our own iteration count in advance. Although this is the recommended way of handling non-integer increments, there is another solution which is mentioned later when we look at non-deterministic loops.

6.4 Nested DOs: Loan Repayments

If a regular fixed payment P is made n times a year to repay a loan of amount A over a period of k years, where the nominal annual interest rate is r, P is given by

$$P = \frac{rA(1 + r/n)^{nk}}{n[(1 + r/n)^{nk} - 1]}. \tag{6.1}$$

The next program uses nested DOs to print a table of the repayments on a loan of $1000 over 15, 20 or 25 years, at interest rates that vary from 10% to 20% per annum. P is directly proportional to A in Equation 6.1. Therefore the repayments on a loan of any amount may be found from the table generated by the program, by simple proportion. The WRITE statements used to make the output look neater are explained in Chapter 10. You can probably figure out how they work.

```
IMPLICIT NONE

INTEGER     I              ! counter
INTEGER  :: N = 12         ! number of payments per year
INTEGER     K              ! repayment period (yrs)
INTEGER     TRIPS          ! iteration count

REAL     :: A = 1000       ! principal
REAL        P              ! payment
REAL        R              ! interest rate
REAL        R0, R1, RINC   ! lowest, highest interest and increment

READ*, R0, R1, RINC
TRIPS = INT( (R1 - R0) / RINC + RINC/2 ) + 1
R = R0

PRINT*, "Rate       15 yrs     20 yrs     25 yrs"
PRINT*

DO I = 1, TRIPS
  WRITE( *, '(F5.2, "%")', ADVANCE = 'NO' ) 100 * R

  DO K = 15, 25, 5
    P = R/N * A * (1 + R/N) ** (N * K) / ((1 + R/N) ** (N * K) - 1)
    WRITE( *, '(F10.2)', ADVANCE = 'NO' ) P
  END DO

  PRINT*                   ! get a new line
  R = R + RINC
END DO
```

Some sample output (with input 0.1, 0.2, 0.01):

```
  Rate      15 yrs     20 yrs     25 yrs

10.00%      10.75       9.65       9.09
11.00%      11.37      10.32       9.80
  . . .

20.00%      17.56      16.99      16.78
```

Clearly, you should not use the same DO variables in nested loops (the compiler fortunately won't allow this). If the level of nesting is deeper it will probably help to name the DOs.

You can see why real DO variables and parameters should be avoided by running this program with the outer DO statement replaced by

```
DO R = R0, R1, RINC
```

and the statement R = R + RINC omitted. Rounding error makes the iteration count too small.

6.5 Non-deterministic Loops

Deterministic loops all rely on the fact that you can work out exactly what the iteration count is before the loop starts. But in the next example, there is no way *in principle* of working out the iteration count, so a different form of the DO construct is needed.

A guessing game   The problem is easy to state. The program "thinks" of an integer between 1 and 10 (i.e. generates one at random). You have to guess it. If your guess is too high or too low, the program must say so. If your guess is correct, a message of congratulations must be displayed.

A little more thought is required here, so a structure plan might be helpful:

  1. Generate random integer
  2. Ask user (assumed male) for guess
  3. Repeat until guess is correct:
          If guess is too low then
                  Tell him it is too low
          Otherwise
                  Tell him it is too high
          Ask him for another guess
  4. Polite congratulations
  5. Stop.

Before we look at the whole program let's see how the random integer is generated. The statement

```
CALL RANDOM_NUMBER( R )
```

first generates a random real R in the range $0 \leq R < 1$, i.e. [0, 1). 10 * R will be in the range [0, 10), and 10 * R + 1 will be in the range [1, 11), i.e. between 1.000000 and 10.999999 inclusive. Using INT on this will then give an integer in the range 1 to 10, as required.

If you want to play more than once, with different random numbers each time, you will need to "re-seed" the random number generator in a specific way each time you run the program. The first time you run the program, supply any integer you like for the seed. But on subsequent occasions you should use the new seed printed at the end of the previous game. Detailed discussion of this process is left to Chapter 14.

```
INTEGER                    FtnNum, MyGuess
INTEGER, DIMENSION(1) ::   Seed
REAL                       R

WRITE( *, '("Seed: ")', ADVANCE = 'NO' )
READ*, Seed(1)                   ! user supplies seed
CALL RANDOM_SEED( PUT=Seed)      ! seeds the random number generator
CALL RANDOM_NUMBER( R )
FtnNum = INT( 10 * R + 1)
WRITE( *, '("Your guess: ")', ADVANCE = 'NO' )
READ*, MyGuess

DO
  IF (MyGuess == FtnNum) EXIT
    IF (MyGuess > FtnNum) THEN
      PRINT*, 'Too high.  Try again'
    ELSE
      PRINT*, 'Too low.  Try again'
    END IF
    WRITE( *, '("Your guess: ")', ADVANCE = 'NO' )
    READ*, MyGuess
END DO

PRINT*, 'BINGO!  Well done!'
CALL RANDOM_SEED( GET=Seed)      ! get the new seed for another game
PRINT*
PRINT*, 'New seed: ', Seed(1)
```

Try it out a few times. Note that the DO loop (which now has no variables or parameters) repeats as long as MyGuess is not equal to FtnNum. There is no way of knowing in principle how many loops will be needed before they are equal, and so this new form of the DO construct is essential here. In this case looping terminates when the statement EXIT is executed. The problem is truly non-deterministic.

On reflection, you might feel the coding is a little wasteful. The section

```
WRITE( *, '("Your guess: ")', ADVANCE = 'NO' )
READ*, MyGuess
```

has to appear twice. Once, to start the loop going (or MyGuess would be undefined), and a second time in the loop itself. Change the program as indicated below and try running it (only the section with changes is reproduced):

```
...
FtnNum = INT( 10 * R + 1)
! remove two lines

DO
    WRITE( *, '("Your guess: ")', ADVANCE = 'NO' ) ! move up
    READ*, MyGuess                                 ! move up
```

```
      IF (MyGuess > FtnNum) THEN
         PRINT*, 'Too high.  Try again'
      ELSE IF (MyGuess < FtnNum) THEN        ! ELSE IF now
         PRINT*, 'Too low.  Try again'
      ELSE
         PRINT*, 'Well done!'                ! congrats here now
      END IF
   IF (MyGuess == FtnNum) EXIT                     ! move down
END DO


! remove congrats
CALL RANDOM_SEED( GET=Seed)    ! get the new seed for another game
```

The equivalent structure plan for the new version is:

1. Generate random integer
2. Repeat:
        Ask user for guess
        If guess is too low
                Tell him it is too low
        Otherwise if guess is too high
                Tell him it is too high
        Otherwise
                Polite congratulations
   Until guess is correct
3. Stop.

The essential difference is that the EXIT occurs at the *top* of the DO block in the first version, but at the *end* of the block in the second version. There is a more subtle difference, however: in the first case the condition for exiting is tested at the top; in the second case it is only tested at the end.

DO: conditional EXIT We have seen two further versions of the DO construct:

```
DO
   IF (logical-expr) EXIT
        block
END DO
```

and

```
DO
     block
   IF (logical-expr) EXIT
END DO
```

(both versions may be named).

The EXIT statement provides a means to exit from an otherwise endless loop. It may in fact go anywhere in the loop. However, it is best for it to go either at the top or at the end; the reader does not then have to search through the loop to find the exit condition.

Some purists might argue that the EXIT should always be at the top of such a non-deterministic loop, so that it is clear to a reader how a loop will end when she first encounters it. The while-do construct of languages like Pascal lends itself more readily to this convention. The way Fortran 90 is designed makes it more natural to put the EXIT at the end. However, I am sure you are old enough to decide for yourself!

There is one situation in which the EXIT *must* be at the top of the loop, and this is when a zero trip count is logically possible. An example is the original form of the guessing game above: if the user guesses the number correctly first time, there should be no executions of the DO block.

DO WHILE   A DO construct may be headed with a DO WHILE statement:

```
DO WHILE (logical-expr)
    block
END DO
```

This is logically equivalent to

```
DO
    IF (.NOT.logical-expr) EXIT
        block
END DO
```

The DO WHILE is a very compelling construction since the condition to repeat is stated clearly at the top of the loop. It may however involve optimization penalties under certain circumstances. There are many examples of its usage later.

DO: variations which are not recommended   The EXIT statement may also be used in a DO construct with a DO variable and parameters:

```
DO I = 1, N
    ...
    IF (I == J) EXIT
    ...
END DO
```

This form is most strongly not recommended! If you are tempted to try this in order to get out of a tricky situation it probably means you have not thought through the logic clearly enough. You *must* be able to state all the possible conditions for an exit unambiguously either at the top or the bottom of the loop. Some examples where this situation arises are given below.

The statement

```
CYCLE [name]
```

transfers control to the END DO statement of the corresponding construct, so if further iterations are still to be carried out the next one is initiated. Its use is not recommended—it makes the logic more difficult to see.

The DO construct may make use of a statement label, as follows:

```
DO 100 I = 1, N
    ...
100   CONTINUE
```

The CONTINUE is a dummy statement which does nothing. The construct may also end with a labelled END DO. This form is not recommended—the labels are not necessary and obscure the logic with redundant information.

Doubling time of an investment   Suppose we have invested some money which draws 10% interest per year, compounded. We would like to know how long it takes for the investment to double. More specifically, we want a statement of the account each year, *until* the balance has doubled. The English statement of the problem hints heavily that we should use a non-deterministic DO with the EXIT condition at the *end* of the loop. The structure plan and program for the problem are:

1. Start
2. Initialize balance, year, rate, interest
3. Write headings
4. Repeat
        Update balance according to interest rate
        Write year, interest, balance
    until balance exceeds twice original balance
5. Stop.

```
IMPLICIT NONE
INTEGER  Year
REAL     Interest, New, Old, Rate

PRINT*, 'Original balance:'
READ*, Old
Rate = 0.1
New = Old                    ! keep a copy of the original balance
Year = 0
PRINT*, 'Year    Interest        Balance'
PRINT*

DO
    Interest = Rate * New
    New = New + Interest
    Year = Year + 1
    PRINT*, Year, Interest, New
  IF (New > 2 * Old) EXIT
END DO
```

The condition New > 2 * Old is checked each time before another iteration. Repetition occurs only if the condition is true. The DO block must be executed at least once, since you must invest your money for at least a year for anything to happen. Consequently, the EXIT must be at the end of the DO. The output looks like this (for an opening balance of $1000):

```
Year    Interest         Balance

1    1.0000000E+02    1.1000000E+03
2    1.1000000E+02    1.2100000E+03
  . . .
7    1.7715611E+02    1.9487172E+03
8    1.9487172E+02    2.1435889E+03
```

Note that when the last iteration has been completed, the condition to EXIT is true for the first time, since the new balance ($2143.59) is more than $2000. Note also that a deterministic DO *cannot* be used here because we don't know how many iterations are going to be needed until after the program has run (although in this example perhaps you *could* work out in advance how many iterations are needed?).

If you want to write the new balance only while it is *less* than $2000, all that has to be done is to move

```
    PRINT*, Year, Interest, New
```

until it is the first statement in the DO loop (try it). Note that the starting balance of zero is written now.

The EXIT condition can be placed at the top of the original DO block if it is rephrased as follows:

```
    IF (New < 2 * Old) EXIT
```

Note that > has been replaced by <. Try this also. Either form is acceptable, although the purists might prefer the version with EXIT at the top. This condition is immediately apparent to anyone reading the program; you do not have to search for the end of the loop to find the condition to exit.

Prime numbers   Many people are obsessed with prime numbers, and most books on programming have to include a program to test if a given number is prime. So here's mine.

A number is prime if it is not an exact multiple of any other number except itself and 1, i.e. if it has no factors except itself and 1. The easiest plan of attack then is as follows. Suppose P is the number to be tested. See if any numbers N can be found that divide into P without remainder. If there are none, P is prime. Which numbers N should we try? Well, we can speed things up by restricting P to odd numbers, so we only have to try odd divisors N. When do we stop testing? When $N = P$? No, we can stop a lot sooner. In fact, we can stop once N reaches $\sqrt{P}$, since if there is a factor greater than $\sqrt{P}$ there must be a corresponding one less than $\sqrt{P}$, which we would have found. And where do we start? Well, since $N = 1$ will be a factor of any P, we should start at $N = 3$. The structure plan is as follows:

1. Read P
2. Initialize N to 3
3. Find remainder R when P is divided by N
4. Repeat until $R = 0$ or $N \geq \sqrt{P}$:
       Increase N by 2
       Find R when P is divided by N
5. If $R \neq 0$ then
       P is prime
   Else
       P is not prime
6. Stop.

Note that the exit condition is tested at the top of the loop because R might be zero the first time. Note also that there are *two* conditions under which the loop will stop. Consequently, an IF is required after completion of the loop to determine which condition stopped it. Here's the program:

```
PROGRAM Prime
! Tests if an odd integer > 3 is prime

IMPLICIT NONE
INTEGER ::  N = 3
INTEGER     P, Rem

PRINT*, 'Gimme an odd integer:'
READ*, P
Rem = MOD( P, N )

DO
  IF (Rem == 0 .OR. N >= SQRT( REAL(P) )) EXIT
    N = N + 2
    Rem = MOD( P, N )
END DO

IF (Rem /= 0) THEN
  PRINT*, P, ' is prime'
ELSE
  PRINT*, P, ' is not prime'
END IF

END
```

Try it out on the following: 4 058 879 (not prime), 193 707 721 (prime) and 2 147 483 647 (prime). If such things interest you, the largest prime number at the time of writing is $2^{756\,839} - 1$. It has 227 832 digits and takes up about 7 pages of newsprint. Obviously this program cannot test such a large number, since it's greater than the largest integer which can be represented by a Fortran intrinsic type. Ways of testing such huge numbers for primality are described in D.E. Knuth, *The Art of Computer Programming. Volume 2: Seminumerical Algorithms* (Addison-Wesley, 1981).

The DO WHILE form of the DO construct would be very convenient to use here. Step 4 of the structure plan needs to be changed to

4. While $R \neq 0$ and $N < \sqrt{P}$ repeat:

and the DO must be rephrased as

```
DO WHILE (Rem /= 0 .AND. N < SQRT( REAL(P) ))
  N = N + 2
  Rem = MOD( P, N )
END DO
```

Note that the condition is the logical negation of the condition to exit as given originally.

Reading an unknown amount of data   The next program uses DO WHILE with a special feature of the general READ statement to read an unknown amount of data from a file DATA and to find their mean:

```
REAL :: A, SUM
INTEGER :: N = 0
INTEGER :: IO = 0

OPEN( 1, FILE = 'DATA' )
SUM = 0

DO WHILE (IO == 0)
  READ (1, *, IOSTAT = IO) A
  IF (IO == 0) THEN
    SUM = SUM + A
    N = N + 1
    PRINT*, A
  END IF
END DO

PRINT*, "Mean:", SUM / N
```

This is the crudest solution to the problem: the data must be supplied one value per line in the file. More elegant solutions will be given later. IOSTAT is a *specifier* which is set to zero if the READ succeeds or to a negative value if an *end-of-file* condition occurs during the READ. It is discussed more fully later.

Taylor series for sine   You may have wondered how a computer calculates functions such as sine and cosine. Really ancient computers actually used to look up tables entered in memory, but young and upwardly mobile ones are more cunning. Mathematically, it can be shown that $\sin x$, for example, is the sum of an infinite series (called a Taylor series), as follows:

$$\sin x = x - \frac{x^3}{3!} + \frac{x^5}{5!} - \frac{x^7}{7!} + \cdots$$

We obviously can't compute the sum of an infinite series, but we can at least arrange to stop after the terms in the series are all less than some prescribed value, say 10^{-6}. It can be shown that we can always get a term less than some arbitrarily small number by going far enough in the Taylor series. As an exercise you should try to draw a flowchart or structure plan before studying the program below. The main idea is to construct each term in the series from the previous one, as described in the limit problem in Section 6.1. In constructing the denominator each time, use has been made of the fact that if k is any integer, $2k$ is even and $2k + 1$ is odd. So if $k = 0$ labels the first term (x), the second term (labelled by $k = 1$) can be obtained from the first term by multiplying it by

$$\frac{-x^2}{2k(2k + 1)}.$$

Work out the first few terms by hand as a check. The program is as follows:

```
PROGRAM Taylor
! Computes sine(x) from Taylor series

INTEGER, PARAMETER :: Pi = 3.14159278

INTEGER   :: K        = 1      ! term counter
INTEGER   :: MaxTerms = 10     ! max number of terms

REAL      :: Err      = 1e-6   ! max error allowed
REAL         Sine              ! sum of series
REAL         Term              ! general term in series
REAL         X                 ! angle in radians

PRINT*, 'Angle in degrees?'
READ*, X
X = X * Pi / 180               ! convert to radians
Term = X                       ! first term in series
Sine = Term

DO WHILE ((ABS( Term ) > Err) .and. (K <= MaxTerms))
  Term = - Term * X * X / (2 * K * (2 * K + 1))
  K = K + 1
  Sine = Sine + Term
END DO

IF (ABS( Term ) > Err) THEN                 ! why did DO end?
  PRINT*, 'Series did not converge'
ELSE
  PRINT*, 'After', K, 'terms Taylor series gives', Sine
  PRINT*, 'Fortran 90 intrinsic function: ', SIN( X )
```

```
END IF

END
```

The DO WHILE may be replaced by

```
DO
   IF ((ABS( Term ) <=  Err) .or. (K > MaxTerms)) EXIT
   ...
END DO
```

Note how the logical condition must be negated—it is now the condition to exit.

DO WHILE or EXIT at the top of the loop is appropriate here since the initial term might be small enough, in which case k will still be 1.

Note also that there are two conditions for terminating the loop. Consequently, an IF is required after the DO to establish which condition was satisfied.

You may be tempted to use a DO with parameters and an EXIT to escape if Term gets small enough:

```
DO I = 1, MaxTerms
   IF (ABS( Term ) <=  Err) EXIT
   ...
END DO
```

Although this works perfectly well, it is definitely *not recommended* (some programmers will definitely disagree!). The reasons are as follows. My objection is that all conditions for exit are not clear at the very top of the loop—after a cursory glance you might think it is a deterministic loop. But, you may argue, I am splitting hairs; after all, the second condition for exit is in the very next line. But after a few months you might introduce further conditions later in the block. The trouble is that this innocent looking structure allows for ad-hoc amendments later—at which stage the programmer might easily lose track of what all the conditions for exit are.

The principle is: *all conditions for exit should be stated clearly in one place—at the top or the end of the loop.*

6.6   Taking Stock: Modelling a Population of Gnus

Once you have mastered loops a great vista of interesting and solvable problems begins to unfold. One such problem is presented in this section.

The wildebeest (gnu) population in the Kruger National Park, South Africa, declined from about 14 000 in 1969 to 6 700 in 1975, giving rise to considerable concern (see Table 6.1). Mathematical modelling techniques were applied to this problem, as described in A.M. Starfield and A.L. Bleloch, *Building Models for Conservation and Wildlife Management* (MacMillan, 1986).

The population in year k may be divided into four biologically distinct age groups: c_k, the number of new-born calves; y_k, the number of yearlings; t_k, the number of two-year-olds; w_k, the number of adults (older than two years).

We can think of the population as a vector with four components, each measured annually (in January, when the females calve). The essence of the problem is to predict the next year's vector, given an initial population at some time. At this stage we turn to the game rangers, who tell us that yearlings do not produce young—this is the prerogative of the two-year-olds and adults. We thus have the equation modelling the dynamics of calves:

$$c_{k+1} = aw_{k+1} + a't_{k+1}, \tag{6.2}$$

where a and a' are the birth-rates (number of expected offspring per individual per year) for adults and two-year-olds respectively. It turns out that the best way to model yearling population dynamics is simply

$$y_{k+1} = bc_k, \tag{6.3}$$

where b is the overall survival-rate for calves. Obviously this year's yearlings can only come from last year's calves, so $b < 1$.

For the other two age groups life is fairly uncomplicated. Their members die of practically only one cause—lion attack. This is modelled as follows. It seems that lion are indiscriminate in their attacks on all groups except the calves. Therefore the number of yearlings taken by lion is in direct proportion to the fraction of yearlings in the total non-calf population, and so on. Of course the number taken in year k is also in proportion to the number of hunting lion in year k—call this number l_k. So we can model the number of two-year-olds and adults with

$$t_{k+1} = y_k - \frac{gl_ky_k}{y_k + t_k + w_k} \tag{6.4}$$

and

$$w_{k+1} = w_k + t_k - \frac{gl_k(t_k + w_k)}{y_k + t_k + w_k}, \tag{6.5}$$

where g is the lion kill-rate (number of gnu taken per lion per year).

The order in which these equations are computed is important. w_{k+1} and t_{k+1} must be computed *before* c_{k+1}.

After consultation with game rangers, a is estimated as 0.45, and a' as 0.15 (Starfield and Bleloch). The lion kill-rate is between 2.5 and 4 (lion have other choices on their menu), and calf survival b is between 0.5 and 0.7.

More precise values of g and b for each year were found "experimentally" by seeing which values gave a total population that agreed more or less with the annual census figures. Fitting the model to the census data was further complicated by the culling (killing by rangers) of wildebeest between 1969 and 1972, to relieve pressure on the vegetation. However, since culling is indiscriminate among the non-calf population it is easy to argue that the term gl_k in equations (6.4) and (6.5) must be replaced by $(gl_k + d_k)$, where d_k is the total number culled in year k. This number is accurately known.

The model run starts in 1969 ($k = 1$), with $c_1 = 3660$, $y_1 = 2240$, $t_1 = 1680$ and $w_1 = 6440$. These figures are from the census. Table 6.1 shows the total population predicted by the model compared with the census data. The column headed *Model 1* shows projections taking the annual culling into account, whereas *Model 2* assumes *no* culling (by setting $d_k = 0$ when running the model). Note also that a particular projection is based on the input in the previous row, e.g. if $l_1 = 500$, $d_1 = 572$, $b =$

Table 6.1   Wildebeest model data and output

Year	l_k	d_k	b	g	Census	Model 1	Model 2
1969	500	572	0.5	4	14020		
1970	520	550	0.5	4	11800	12617	13140
1971	530	302	0.5	4	10600	11233	12932
1972	540	78	0.5	4	8000	9847	12248
1973	550	0	0.7	3.5	7700	8457	11369
1974	540	0	0.7	3.5	–	7679	11239
1975					6700	6779	11120

0.5 and $g = 4$, the model predicts

$$c_2 + y_2 + t_2 + w_2 = 12617.$$

The parameters g and b are realistic. 1970–1972 were dry years in the Park, when lion killed regularly at waterholes. This justifies the higher g and lower b values. In subsequent years the lion did not kill so freely, since the improved vegetation and declining wildebeest population made the prey more difficult to find. The same factors lead to a higher calf survival-rate.

The program below implements this model. Note that two sets of variables are used to represent the age groups. C, Y, T and W represent values in year k, while NC, NY, NT and NW represent values in year $k + 1$. One might have been tempted to code the update equations as follows:

```
Y = B * C
T = Y - (G * L + D) * Y / (Y + T + W)
...
```

This, however, would mean that we would be using *next year's* Y, obtained from equation (6.3), on the righthand side of equation (6.4), instead of *this* year's. Using two sets of variables means that the set representing the current year's values must be updated at the end of each year in readiness for next year's update. Try the program out with different parameter values, to see what happens. Also try running it for longer.

```
IMPLICIT NONE

INTEGER   Year

REAL ::   A  = 0.45    ! adult birth-rate
REAL ::   Ad = 0.15    ! a-dash: 2-yr-old birth-rate
REAL ::   C  = 3660    ! calves
REAL ::   T  = 1680    ! 2-yr-olds
REAL      Tot          ! total population
REAL ::   W  = 6440    ! adults
REAL ::   Y  = 2240    ! yearlings
```

```
REAL NC, NT, NW, NY      ! next year's population
REAL L, D, B, G          ! other model parameters

DO Year = 1969, 1974
   WRITE( *, '(I4, " data: ")', ADVANCE = 'NO' ) Year
   READ*, L, D, B, G
   NY = B * C
   NT = Y - (G * L + D) * Y / (Y + T + W)
   NW = W + T - (G * L + D) * (T + W) / (Y + T + W)
   NC = A * NW + Ad * NT
   C = NC
   Y = NY
   T = NT
   W = NW
   Tot = C + Y + T + W
   WRITE( *, '(I4, " projection: ", F6.0)' ) Year+1, Tot
   PRINT*
END DO

END
```

Summary

- A DO construct with parameters should be used to program a deterministic loop, where the number of iterations (the iteration count) is known to the program (i.e. in principle to the programmer) *before* the loop is encountered. This situation is characterized by the general structure plan:

    Repeat *N* times:
        Block of statements to be repeated

  where *N* is known or computed *before* the loop is encountered for the first time, and is not changed by the block. The syntax for DO in this case is

    [*name*:] DO *variable* = *first*, *last*, *step*
                block
    END DO [*name*]

  All forms of the construct may be optionally named.
      If *step* is omitted, it defaults to 1. If *step* is negative, *variable* will be decreased as long as *first* is greater than or equal to *last*.
- DO with EXIT may be used to program a non-deterministic loop, where the iteration count is *not* known in advance, i.e. whenever the truth value of the condition for exiting is changed in the DO block. This situation is characterized by the following two structure plans:

    Repeat until *condition* is true:
        Block to be repeated (reset truth value of *condition*).

or

Repeat:
        Block to be repeated (reset truth value of *condition*)
until *condition* is true.

Note that *condition* is the condition to exit from the loop.
The syntax of these forms is

```
DO
    IF (condition) EXIT
    block
END DO
```

and

```
DO
    block
    IF (condition) EXIT
END DO
```

- A non-deterministic loop may also be programmed with a DO WHILE construct. Here the general structure plan is

While *condition* is true repeat:
        Block of statements to be repeated.

Note that *condition* is now the condition to make another iteration, *not* to exit.
The syntax for this structure is

```
DO WHILE (condition)
    block
END DO
```

This construct may incur optimization penalties.
- The DO variable and parameters should be integers.
- The DO variable should not be explicitly changed in the DO block.
- The iteration count (which may be zero) is calculated from the initial values of the parameters.
- DO constructs may be nested to any depth.
- Good programming style requires that an EXIT from a DO occurs as near to the top or the end of the loop as possible.
- The IOSTAT specifier may be used with READ to detect an end-of-file condition.

Exercises

6.1 Write a program to find the sum of the successive even integers 2, 4, ..., 200. (Answer: 10100)

6.2 Write a program which produces a table of $\sin x$ and $\cos x$ for angles x from $0°$ to $90°$ in steps of $15°$.

6.3 A person deposits $1000 in a bank. Interest is compounded monthly at the rate of 1% per month. Write a program which will compute the monthly balance, but write it only *annually* for 10 years (use nested DO loops, with the outer loop for 10 years, and the inner loop for 12 months). Note that after 10 years, the balance is $3300.39, whereas if interest had been compounded annually at the rate of 12% per year the balance would only have been $3105.85.

6.4 There are many formulae for computing π (the ratio of a circle's circumference to its diameter). The simplest is

$$\frac{\pi}{4} = 1 - 1/3 + 1/5 - 1/7 + 1/9 - \ldots \qquad \text{(E6.1)}$$

which comes from the series

$$\arctan x = x - \frac{x^3}{3} + \frac{x^5}{5} - \frac{x^7}{7} + \frac{x^9}{9} - \ldots \qquad \text{(E6.2)}$$

when $x = 1$.

(a) Write a program to compute π using series (E6.1). Use as many terms in the series as your computer will reasonably allow (start modestly, with 100 terms, say, and re-run your program with more and more each time). You should find that the series converges very slowly, i.e. it takes a lot of terms to get fairly close to π.

(b) Rearranging the series speeds up the convergence:

$$\frac{\pi}{8} = \frac{1}{1 \times 3} + \frac{1}{5 \times 7} + \frac{1}{9 \times 11} \ldots$$

Write a program to compute π using this series instead. You should find that you need fewer terms to reach the same level of accuracy that you got in (a).

(c) One of the fastest series for π is

$$\frac{\pi}{4} = 6 \arctan \frac{1}{8} + 2 \arctan \frac{1}{57} + \arctan \frac{1}{239}.$$

Use this formula to compute π. Don't use the standard function ATAN to compute the arctangents, since that would be cheating. Rather use the series (E6.2).

6.5 The following method of computing π is due to Archimedes:

1. Let $A = 1$ and $N = 6$
2. Repeat 10 times, say:
   Replace N by $2N$
   Replace A by $\sqrt{2 - \sqrt{(4 - A^2)}}$
   Let $L = NA/2$
   Let $U = L/\sqrt{1 - A^2/2}$
   Let $P = (U + L)/2$ (estimate of π)
   Let $E = (U - L)/2$ (estimate of error)

Print N, P, E

3. Stop.

Write a program to implement the algorithm.

6.6   Write a program to compute a table of the function

$$f(x) = x \sin\left[\frac{\pi(1 + 20x)}{2}\right]$$

over the (closed) interval $[-1, 1]$ using increments in x of (a) 0.2 (b) 0.1 and (c) 0.01. Use a DO with integer variable and parameters; compute the iteration count explicitly as in Section 6.3. Use your tables to plot a graph of $f(x)$ for the three cases, and observe that the tables for (a) and (b) give totally the wrong picture of $f(x)$.

6.7   The transcendental number e (2.718281828 ...) can be shown to be the limit of

$$\frac{1}{(1 - x)^{1/x}}$$

as x tends to zero (from above). Write a program which shows how this expression converges to e as x gets closer and closer to zero (use the real kind with the greatest precision available on your system).

6.8   A square wave of period T may be defined by the function

$$f(t) = \begin{cases} 1 & (0 < t < T) \\ -1 & (-T < t < 0). \end{cases}$$

The Fourier series for $f(t)$ is given by

$$\frac{4}{\pi} \sum_{k=0}^{\infty} \frac{1}{2k+1} \sin\left[\frac{(2k+1)\pi t}{T}\right].$$

It is of interest to know how many terms are needed for a good approximation to this infinite sum. Taking $T = 1$, write a program to compute and display the sum to n terms of the series for t from 0 to 1 in steps of 0.1, say. Run the program for different values of n, e.g. 1, 3, 6, etc.

6.9   If an amount of money A is invested for k years at a nominal annual interest rate r (expressed as a decimal fraction), the value V of the investment after k years is given by

$$V = A(1 + r/n)^{nk}$$

where n is the number of compounding periods per year. Write a program to compute V as n gets larger and larger, i.e. as the compounding periods become more and more frequent, like monthly, daily, hourly, etc. Take $A = 1000$, $r = 4\%$ and $k = 10$ years. You should observe that your output gradually approaches a limit. **Hint**: use a DO loop which doubles n each time, starting with $n = 1$.
   Also compute the value of the formula Ae^{rk} for the same values of A, r and k (use

the intrinsic function EXP), and compare this value with the values of V computed above. What do you conclude?

6.10 Write a program to compute the sum of the series $1 + 2 + 3 \ldots$ such that the sum is as large as possible without exceeding 100. The program should write out how many terms are used in the sum.

6.11 One of the programs in Section 6.5 shows that an amount of $1000 will double in about seven years with an interest rate of 10%. Using the same interest rate, run the program with initial balances of $500, $2000 and $10 000 (say) to see how long they all take to double. The results may surprise you.

6.12 Write a program to implement the structure plan of Exercise 4.2.

6.13 Use the Taylor series

$$\cos x = 1 - \frac{x^2}{2!} + \frac{x^4}{4!} - \frac{x^6}{6!} + \ldots$$

to write a program to compute $\cos x$ correct to four decimal places (x is in radians). See how many terms are needed to get 4-figure agreement with the intrinsic function COS.

6.14 A man borrows $10 000 to buy a used car. Interest on his loan is compounded at the rate of 2% per month while the outstanding balance of the loan is more than $5000, and at 1% per month otherwise. He pays back $300 every month, except for the last month, when the repayment must be less than $300. He pays at the end of the month, *after* the interest on the balance has been compounded. The first repayment is made one month after the loan is paid out to him. Write a program which writes out a monthly statement of the balance (after the monthly payment has been made), the final payment, and the month of the final payment.

6.15 A projectile, the equations of motion of which are given in Chapter 3, is launched from the point O with an initial velocity of 60 m/s at an angle of 50° to the horizontal. Write a program which computes and writes out the time in the air, and horizontal and vertical displacement from the point O every 0.5 seconds, as long as the projectile remains above a horizontal plane through O.

6.16 When a resistor (R), capacitor (C) and battery (V) are connected in series, a charge Q builds up on the capacitor according to the formula

$$Q(t) = CV(1 - e^{-t/RC})$$

if there is no charge on the capacitor at time $t = 0$. The problem is to monitor the charge on the capacitor every 0.1 seconds in order to detect when it reaches a level of 8 units of charge, given that $V = 9$, $R = 4$ and $C = 1$. Write a program which writes the time and charge every 0.1 seconds until the charge first exceeds 8 units (i.e. the last charge written must exceed 8). Once you have done this, rewrite the program to output the charge only while it is strictly less than 8 units.

6.17 If a population grows according to the *logistic* model, its size $X(t)$ at time t is given by the formula

$$X(t) = \frac{KX_0}{(K - X_0)e^{-rt} + X_0},$$

where X_0 is the initial size at time $t = 0$, r is the growth-rate, and K is the *carrying capacity* of the environment. Write a program which will compute and print values of $X(t)$ over a period of 200 years. Take $X_0 = 2$, $r = 0.1$ and $K = 1000$. Experiment with different values of K, and see if you can interpret K biologically.

7
Errors

Programs seldom run correctly the first time, even for experienced programmers. In computer jargon, an error in a program is called a *bug*. The story is that a moth short-circuited two thermionic valves in one of the earliest computers. This primeval (charcoaled) "bug" took days to find. The process of detecting and correcting such errors is called *debugging*. There are four types of errors:

- *compilation* errors
- *run-time* errors
- errors of *logic*
- *rounding* error.

In this chapter we deal with the sort of errors that can arise with the programming we have done so far.

7.1 Compilation Errors

Compilation errors are errors in syntax and construction, like spelling mistakes, that are picked up by the compiler during compilation, the process whereby your program is translated into machine code. They are the most frequent type of error.

The compiler prints messages, which may or may not be helpful, when it encounters such an error.

Generally, there are three sorts of compiler errors:

- ordinary errors—the compiler will attempt to continue compilation after one or more of these errors has occurred, e.g.

  ```
  missing ENDIF statements
  ```

- fatal errors—the compiler will not attempt further compilation after detecting a fatal error, e.g.

  ```
  Program too complicated - too many strings
  ```

- warnings—these are not strictly errors, but are intended to inform you that you have done something unusual which might cause problems later, e.g.

  ```
  Expression in IF construct is constant
  ```

  or that you have used an obsolescent feature, e.g.

  ```
  Non-integer DO control variables are obsolescent
  ```

(these messages are generated by the FTN90 compiler; your compiler might have slightly different messages).

There are a large number of compiler error messages, which will be listed in the user's manual that comes with your particular compiler. Since the compiler is not as intelligent as you are, the error messages can sometimes be rather unhelpful—even misleading. Some common examples are given below.

`Inappropriate use of symbol X at line N`
> The name X has been used to represent more than one object, most probably the program name as well as a variable. The duplicated occurrence will be at line N.

`Implicit type for X at line N`
> The variable X has not been declared explicitly, following an IMPLICIT NONE statement. Spelling mistakes in declared variables will be spotted in this way.

`Syntax error at line N`
> This is one of the most infuriating messages, and covers a multitude of errors, e.g.

```
G = 9,8                  !comma instead of decimal point
IF (A = 0) X = 1         != instead of == in a logical expression
IF (A == 0) THEN X = 1 !incorrect use of THEN in a simple IF ..
           !.. or incorrect placement of a statement after THEN
X = 1 + (2 * 3           !unpaired parentheses
```

One wonders why the compiler could not be a little more specific.

`Symbol X referenced but not set at line N`
This is a helpful message which warns you that no value has been assigned by the program to X. However, the line number given seems to refer to the *last* line in the program.

Curiously, however, the following coding runs without error (under FTN90):

```
IMPLICIT NONE
REAL X

X = X + 1
```

The result is garbage (1.4209760E+14 with the FTN90 compiler on one occasion) because of course X is undefined. It seems as if the compiler thinks that because X appears on the left-hand side of an assignment it must be defined!

There are many, many more compiler errors—you will probably have discovered a good number on your own by now. With experience you will gradually become more adept at spotting your mistakes.

7.2 Run-time Errors

If a program compiles successfully, it will run. Errors occurring at this stage are called run-time errors, and are invariably fatal, i.e. the program "crashes". An error message, such as

`Floating point division by zero`

or

`Floating point arithmetic overflow`

is generated. The latter is quite common. It occurs, for example, when an attempt is made to compute a real expression which is too large, or when SQRT has a negative argument, or when the argument of LOG is non-positive.

Some compilers have interactive debugging facilities, where you can, for example, step through a program line by line until you find the line where the run-time error occurs, or where you can mark a line in the code and run to that point. These facilities are extremely helpful, especially for debugging large programs; you should make a point of finding out and making use of what your compiler offers in this line.

Error interception   Fortran 90 has facilities for intercepting and handling certain run-time errors, such as input/output errors (e.g. attempting to read past the end-of-file, or from a non-existent file). These are discussed later, when we deal with advanced I/O and file handling.

7.3   Errors in Logic

These are errors in the actual algorithm you are using to solve a problem, and are the most difficult to find; the program runs, but gives the wrong answers! It's even worse if you don't realize the answers are wrong. The following tips might help you to check out the logic.

- Try to run the program for some special cases where you know the answers.
- If you don't know any exact answers, try to use your insight into the problem to check whether the answers seem to be of the right order of magnitude.
- Try working through the program by hand (or use the debugging facilities) to see if you can spot where things start going wrong.

7.4   Rounding Error

At times a program will give numerical answers to a problem which appear inexplicably different from what we know to be the correct mathematical solution. This can be due to *rounding error*, which results from the finite precision available on the computer, e.g. two or four bytes per variable, instead of an infinite number.

Run the following program extract:

```
X = 0.1

DO
   X = X + 0.001
   PRINT*, X
   IF (X == 0.2) EXIT
END DO
```

You will find that you need to crash the program to stop, e.g. with **ctrl-break** on a PC. X never has the value 0.2 *exactly*, because of rounding error. In fact, X misses the value of 0.2 by about 10^{-9}, as can be seen by printing X - 0.2 as well each time. It would be better to replace the EXIT clause with

```
IF (X > 0.2) EXIT
```

or

```
IF (ABS(X - 0.2) < 1E-6) EXIT
```

In general, it is always better to test for "equality" of two real expressions in this way, e.g.

```
IF (ABS(A - B) < 1E-6) PRINT*, 'A practically equal to B'
```

Rounding error may be reduced (although never completely eliminated) by using the real kind with higher precision than the default, e.g.

```
REAL(KIND = 2) A, B
```

Rounding error may also be reduced by a mathematical re-arrangement of the problem. If the well-known quadratic equation is written in the less familiar form

$$x^2 - 2ax + e = 0,$$

the two solutions may be expressed as

$$x_1 = a + \sqrt{a^2 - e},$$
$$x_2 = a - \sqrt{a^2 - e}.$$

If e is very small compared with a, the second root is expressed as the difference between two nearly equal numbers, and considerable significance is lost. E.g. taking $a = 5 \times 10^6$ and $e = 1$ gives $x_2 = -9.42 \times 10^{-3}$ with FTN90. However, the second root may also be expressed mathematically as

$$x_2 = \frac{e}{a + \sqrt{a^2 - e}} \approx \frac{e}{2a}.$$

Using this form with FTN90 gives $x_2 = 10^{-7}$, which is more accurate.
Rounding error is also discussed in Chapter 16.

Summary

- Compilation errors are mistakes in the syntax (coding).
- Execution (run-time) errors occur while the program is running
- Input/output errors may be intercepted at run-time.
- Debugging facilities may be used to work through a program, statement by statement.
- Logical errors are errors in the algorithm used to solve the problem.
- Rounding error occurs because the computer can store numbers only to a finite accuracy. It is reduced but not necessarily eliminated by using reals with higher precision than the default.

Exercises

7.1 The Newton quotient

$$\frac{f(x + h) - f(x)}{h}$$

may be used to estimate the first derivative $f'(x)$ of a function $f(x)$, if h is "small". Write a program to compute the Newton quotient for the function

$$f(x) = x^2$$

at the point $x = 2$ (the exact answer is 4) for values of h starting at 1, and decreasing by a factor of 10 each time. The effect of rounding error becomes apparent when h gets "too small", i.e. less than about 10^{-6}.

7.2 The solution of the set of simultaneous equations

$$ax + by = c$$
$$dx + ey = f$$

(Exercise 5.5) is given by

$$x = (ce - bf)/(ae - bd),$$
$$y = (af - cd)/(ae - bd).$$

If $(ae - bd)$ is small, rounding error may cause quite large inaccuracies in the solution. Consider the system

$$0.2038x + 0.1218y = 0.2014,$$
$$0.4071x + 0.2436y = 0.4038.$$

Show that with four-figure floating point arithmetic the solution obtained is $x = -1.714$, $y = 4.286$. This level of accuracy may be simulated in the solution of Ex. 5.5 with some statements like

```
AE = NINT( A * E * 1E5 ) / 1E5
```

and appropriate changes in the coding. The exact solution, however, which can be obtained with default precision, is $x = -2$, $y = 5$. If the coefficients in the equations are themselves subject to experimental error, the "solution" of this system using limited accuracy is totally meaningless.

7.3 This problem, suggested by R.V. Andree, demonstrates another numerical problem called *ill-conditioning*, where a small change in the coefficients causes a large change in the solution. Show that the solution of the system

$$x + 5.000y = 17.0$$
$$1.5x + 7.501y = 25.503$$

is $x = 2$, $y = 3$, using the program for Ex. 5.5 with default precision. Now change the term on the right-hand side of the second equation to 25.501, a change of about one part in 12 000, and observe that a totally different solution results. Also try changing this term to 25.502, 25.504, etc. If the coefficients are subject to experimental errors, the solution is again meaningless. One way to anticipate this sort of error is to perform a *sensitivity analysis* on the coefficients: change them all in turn by the same percentage, and observe what effect this has on the solution.

8

Subprograms and Modules

We saw in Chapter 4 that the logic of a non-trivial problem could be broken
down into separate *subprograms* (or *procedures*), each carrying out a particular,
well-defined task. It often happens that such subprograms can be used by many
different "main" programs, and in fact by different users of the same computer
system. Fortran 90 enables you to implement these subprograms as *functions* and
subroutines which are independent of the main program. Examples are procedures

to perform statistical operations, or to sort items, or to find the best straight line through a set of points, or to solve a system of differential equations.

Subprograms may be *internal* or *external*. Useful procedures may be collected together as libraries. Such collections are called *modules*. Main programs (i.e. everything we have seen so far), external subprograms, and modules are referred to as *program units*.

Basically, an internal subprogram is contained within another program unit—and therefore compiled with it, whereas an external subprogram is not—it is in fact compiled *separately*. An important difference between the two types of subprogram is that an internal subprogram may use names of entities declared by the program unit that contains it, whereas an external subprogram is not contained within another program unit.

We deal first with internal subprograms.

8.1   Internal Subprograms

There are two types of subprograms: functions and subroutines. We will first look at functions.

We have already seen how to use some of the intrinsic functions supplied by Fortran 90, such as SIN, COS, LOG, etc. You can write your own functions, to be used in the same way in a program. Before we discuss the rules in detail, we will look at some examples.

Newton's method again   Newton's method (see also Chapter 16) may be used to solve a general equation $f(x) = 0$ by repeating the assignment

$$x \text{ becomes } x - \frac{f(x)}{f'(x)},$$

where $f'(x)$ is the first derivative of $f(x)$, until $f(x)$ has come close enough to zero.

Suppose that $f(x) = x^3 + x - 3$. Then $f'(x) = 3x^2 + 1$. The program below uses Newton's method to solve this equation starting with $x = 2$, and stopping either when the absolute value of $f(x)$ is less than 10^{-6}, or after 20 iterations, say. It uses two functions: F(X) for $f(x)$ and DF(X) for $f'(x)$.

```
PROGRAM Newton
! Solves f(x) = 0 by Newton's method

IMPLICIT NONE
INTEGER  ::  Its       = 0          ! iteration counter
INTEGER  ::  MaxIts    = 20         ! maximum iterations
LOGICAL  ::  Converged = .false.    ! convergence flag
REAL     ::  Eps       = 1e-6       ! maximum error
REAL     ::  X         = 2          ! starting guess

DO WHILE (.NOT. Converged .AND. Its < MaxIts)
   X = X - F(X) / DF(X)
   PRINT*, X, F(X)
   Its = Its + 1
```

```
    Converged = ABS( F(X) ) <= Eps
END DO

IF (Converged) THEN
  PRINT*, 'Newton converged'
ELSE
  PRINT*, 'Newton diverged'
END IF

CONTAINS
  FUNCTION F(X)
  ! problem is to solve f(x) = 0
    REAL F, X
    F = X ** 3 + X - 3
  END FUNCTION F

  FUNCTION DF(X)
  ! first derivative of f(x)
    REAL DF, X
    DF = 3 * X ** 2 + 1
  END FUNCTION DF
END PROGRAM Newton
```

Note that there are two conditions that will stop the DO loop: either convergence, or the completion of 20 iterations. Otherwise the program could run indefinitely.

Rotation of co-ordinate axes   Functions are particularly useful when arithmetic expressions, which can become long and cumbersome, need to be evaluated repeatedly. A good example is the rotation of a Cartesian co-ordinate system. If such a system is rotated counter-clockwise through an angle of a radians, the new co-ordinates (x', y') of a point referred to the rotated axes are given by

$$x' = x \cos a + y \sin a$$
$$y' = -x \sin a + y \cos a$$

where (x, y) are its co-ordinates before rotation of the axes. The following functions could be used to define the new co-ordinates:

```
FUNCTION Xnew( X, Y, A )
  REAL XNew, X, Y, A
  Xnew = X * COS( A ) + Y * SIN( A )
END FUNCTION Xnew

FUNCTION YNew( X, Y, A )
  REAL YNew, X, Y, A
  YNew = - X * SIN( A ) + Y * COS( A )
END FUNCTION Ynew
```

Internal functions   Since functions and subroutines are very similar, common features are described by referring to them collectively as subprograms. Most of the following rules apply also to external subprograms, except where otherwise stated.

All internal subprograms are placed between a CONTAINS statement and the END statement of the main program. Subprograms look almost like a main program, except for their headers and END statements. Internal subprograms may not contain other subprograms, and so may not themselves have a CONTAINS statement.

The general syntax of an internal function is

FUNCTION *Name* ([*argument list*])
    [*declaration statements*]
    [*executable statements*]
END FUNCTION [*Name*]

The statement

FUNCTION *Name* (*argument list*)

is called the *function statement*, or header, or declaration. Note that if the main program has an IMPLICIT NONE statement (and sound programming style insists that it *should* have one) the function name and arguments must be declared with a type. Although this may be done in the main program, it is recommended that you declare the function name and arguments in the function body itself.

Since a value is associated with the function name, this value must be assigned to the function name in the function body. Note that when the function name appears on the left-hand side of an assignment statement, *its arguments must be omitted*, e.g.

YNew = - X * SIN(A) + Y * COS(A)

in the function YNew above. The function is said to *return* this value to the calling, or host, program. A function value may also be returned by means of a RESULT clause (see below).

An internal subprogram automatically has access to all its host's entities. Variables declared in the host program are therefore *global*, in the sense that they are available throughout the *scope* of the host program. This scope includes all internal subprograms. This can sometimes lead to serious bugs, which is why internal subprograms should only be used for fairly small tasks peculiar to their particular host. More general procedures should be written as external subprograms.

Since an internal subprogram is in a sense declared in its host, this scoping rule also implies that internal subprograms are known to each other, i.e. they may call each other.

However, if a variable is *redeclared* in a subprogram, that subprogram no longer has access to the original variable of the same name declared in the host.

Arguments   The arguments in a subprogram statement, e.g. X, Y and A in

FUNCTION YNew(X, Y, A)

are *dummy* arguments. That is, they exist only for the purpose of defining the function. They represent general variables of the same type. Consequently, the same names do not have to be used when *calling* or *invoking* the subprogram. E.g. YNew may be invoked in the host program with the statement

```
YNew( U, V, Pi/2 )
```

You can think of the values of the *actual* arguments U, V and Pi/2 being copied into the dummy arguments X, Y and A respectively. The actual arguments are said to be *passed* to the subprogram. An actual argument which is a variable name must have the same type and kind type parameters as its corresponding dummy argument. The exact way in which arguments are passed is discussed below.

You should be aware that if the value of a dummy argument is *changed* inside a function, that change is "copied back" into the corresponding actual argument in the host program, if it is a variable. This is an undesirable *side effect* in a function, and should be avoided in the interests of sound programming. If you *want* to change an actual argument, the correct vehicle is a subroutine.

Local and global variables   The next program contains an internal function Fact(N) which computes *n*! There is something wrong with it. See if you can work out by hand what the first few lines of output will be, before running it.

```
PROGRAM Factorial
IMPLICIT NONE
INTEGER I

DO I = 1, 10
  PRINT*, I, Fact(I)
END DO

CONTAINS
  FUNCTION Fact( N )
    INTEGER Fact, N, Temp
    Temp = 1
    DO I = 2, N
      Temp = I * Temp
    END DO
    Fact = Temp
  END FUNCTION
END
```

The problem is that I is a *global* variable, i.e. the name I represents the same variable inside and outside the function. Fact is first called when I = 1, which is the first value written. This value is passed to the function's dummy argument N. The same I is now given the initial value 2 by the DO loop inside Fact, but since it is greater than N, the DO loop is not executed, so I still has the value 2 when Fact returns to be printed in the main program. However, I is now incremented to 3 in the DO loop in the main program, which is the value it has when the second call to Fact takes place. In this way, Fact is never computed for an even value of I. All this is a consequence of the variable I being global.

The problem is solved by redeclaring I in the function to make it local. You should make it a rule to declare all variables used in subprograms. That way you can never inadvertently make use of a global variable in the wrong context.

If you need to get information into a subprogram from its host, the safest way to do it is through the dummy arguments. When there is a large amount of such information to be shared by many subprograms, the best solution is to declare global variables in a module, and for subprograms needing access to those variables to use the module (see Section 8.5).

The use of IMPLICIT NONE in a main program is particularly important when there are internal subprograms. It forces you to declare all local variables and dummy arguments, which makes for good programming style.

The RETURN statement   Normal exit from a subprogram occurs at its END statement. However, it is sometimes convenient to exit from other points. This may be done with the statement RETURN. Excessive use of RETURN should be avoided since it very easily leads to *spaghetti* (unstructured code).

Statement functions   In older versions of Fortran a function could be defined in a single line, e.g.

```
F(X) = X ** 3 + X - 3
```

This form is supported by Fortran 90, but is not recommended since it does not follow many of the general rules for subprograms.

Internal subroutines   Subroutines are very similar to functions. The differences are:

- No value is associated with the name of a subroutine, hence it must not be declared.
- A subroutine is invoked with a CALL statement.
- The keyword SUBROUTINE is used in the definition and the END statement.
- A subroutine need not have any arguments, in which case the name is written without parentheses, e.g.

```
CALL PLONK
```

A function without arguments must have empty parentheses, e.g. Fung().

The following program prints a line with the subroutine PrettyLine, which has two dummy arguments. Num is the number of characters to be printed; Symbol is the ASCII code of the characters to be printed.

```
IMPLICIT NONE

CALL PrettyLine( 5, 2 )

CONTAINS
   SUBROUTINE PrettyLine( Num, Symbol )
      INTEGER I, Num, Symbol
      CHARACTER*80 Line
      DO I = 1, Num
```

```
    Line(I:I) = ACHAR( Symbol )
  END DO
  PRINT*, Line
END SUBROUTINE
END
```

Character substrings, such as `Line(I:I)`, are discussed in Chapter 11.

The next example shows how dummy arguments may be used to take information back to the calling program—in this case their values are exchanged:

```
IMPLICIT NONE
REAL A, B

READ*, A, B
CALL SWOP( A, B )
PRINT*, A, B

CONTAINS
  SUBROUTINE SWOP( X, Y )
    REAL Temp, X, Y
    Temp = X
    X = Y
    Y = Temp
  END SUBROUTINE
END
```

What actually happens is that the actual arguments A and B are *passed by reference* (see Section 8.7). The effect is that the values of the actual arguments are given to the dummy arguments, and any changes made to the dummy arguments are *copied back to the actual arguments*. In this way information can be returned from the subroutine. This can have unpleasant side effects. You might inadvertently change a dummy argument inside a subprogram—after return to the calling program the corresponding actual argument will also be changed, perhaps with disastrous effects. Fortran 90 has a way of preventing this, called argument *intent*, which is discussed in Section 8.7.

Since `Temp` in the example above is declared in the subroutine it is local to it and not accessible to the main program.

The general syntax of an internal subroutine is therefore

```
SUBROUTINE Name [( argument list )]
    [declaration statements]
    [executable statements]
END SUBROUTINE [Name]
```

8.2 The Main Program

Every complete program must have one and only one *main program*, which has the form

```
[PROGRAM name]
    [declaration statements]
    [executable statements]
[CONTAINS
    internal subprograms]
END [PROGRAM [name]]
```

If the last statement ahead of the CONTAINS statement does not result in a branch (and it should not), control *passes over* the internal subprograms to the END statement, and the program stops. In other words, the internal subprograms are only executed if properly invoked by a CALL statement in the case of a subroutine, or by referencing its name, in the case of a function.

8.3 External Subprograms

An *external subprogram* resides in a separate file from the main program. It will generally perform a specific task, and is external in order to be accessible to many different calling programs. Apart from the header and END statement, a subprogram is identical in appearance to a main program:

```
SUBROUTINE name[( arguments )]
    [declaration statements]
    [executable statements]
[CONTAINS
    internal subprograms]
END [SUBROUTINE [name]]
```

or

```
FUNCTION name([ arguments ])
    [declaration statements]
    [executable statements]
[CONTAINS
    internal subprograms]
END [FUNCTION [name]]
```

Note the small but significant differences between external and internal subprograms:

- external subprograms may themselves contain internal subprograms (which will only be accessible to the host external subprogram); internal subprograms may not contain further internal subprograms
- the keyword FUNCTION or SUBROUTINE is optional in the external subprogram END statement but obligatory in the internal subprogram END statement.

Note also that, since an external subprogram resides in a separate file from the main program, it must be compiled *separately*. Under FTN90 an intermediate type of machine code, called *relocatable binary* is produced in a file with the .OBJ extension. This in turn must be linked with the calling program by means of a special program called a *linker*, finally resulting in a .EXE version of the main program. Your compiler manual will have the details of how to do this. Once it is finally debugged, an external subprogram need never be recompiled, only linked. This prevents you from wasting time in compiling it over and over, which would be the case if it was an internal subprogram.

As an example, let's rewrite the internal subroutine SWOP of Section 8.1 as an external subroutine. The main program (in one file) becomes

```
IMPLICIT NONE
EXTERNAL SWOP
REAL A, B

READ*, A, B
CALL SWOP( A, B )
PRINT*, A, B

END
```

and the external subroutine (in a separate file) is then

```
SUBROUTINE SWOP( X, Y )
  REAL Temp, X, Y
  Temp = X
  X = Y
  Y = Temp
END SUBROUTINE
```

The EXTERNAL statement is discussed below. You should now try compiling, linking and running this example.

If you want more than one external subprogram in the same file, you should use a module (Section 8.5).

The EXTERNAL statement If you accidentally used the name of an intrinsic subprogram for an external subprogram, the compiler would by default assume you were referring to the intrinsic subprogram, so your external subprogram would be inaccessible. You might think you know the names of all intrinsic subprograms, and that this problem will not present itself. However, you could have a problem when transporting your code to another installation, because the standard allows compilers to provide additional intrinsic subprograms.

To avoid this problem, the names of all external subprograms should be specified in an EXTERNAL statement, which should come after any USE (Section 8.5) or IMPLICIT statements. Naming an external subprogram like this ensures that it is linked as an external subprogram, and makes any intrinsic subprogram with the same name unavailable. This practice is strongly recommended.

8.4   Interface Blocks

If the compiler is to generate calls to subprograms correctly, it needs to know certain things about the subprogram: name, number and type of arguments, etc. This collection of information is called the subprogram's *interface*. In the case of intrinsic subprograms, internal subprograms and module subprograms the interface is always known to the compiler, and is said to be *explicit*.

However, when the compiler generates a call to an *external* subprogram this information is not available, and the subprogram interface is said to be *implicit*.

We have seen that the EXTERNAL statement in the calling program is sufficient to supply the compiler with the name of the external subprogram, and this enables it to be found and linked. However, the interface is still implicit, and in more complicated cases (such as with optional or keyword arguments, as discussed below) further information is required for a satisfactory interface. Fortran 90 has a mechanism, called an *interface block*, which enables an explicit interface to be made.

The general form of an interface block, which must be placed in the scope of the calling program, is

```
INTERFACE
     interface body
END INTERFACE
```

where the *interface body* could be an exact copy of the subprogram header, declarations of its arguments and results, and its END statement. However, the names of the arguments may be changed, and other specifications may be included (e.g. for a local variable), although *not* DATA or FORMAT statements or internal subprograms.

The calling program for the external subroutine SWOP above could be rewritten with an interface block as follows:

```
IMPLICIT NONE

INTERFACE
   SUBROUTINE SWOP( X, Y )
     REAL X, Y
   END SUBROUTINE
END INTERFACE

REAL A, B

READ*, A, B
CALL SWOP( A, B )
 . . .
```

More general access to interface blocks may be provided by means of modules.

Interface blocks are also used for *overloading* a number of subprogram names with a single "generic" name.

When to use interface blocks   It is never wrong to use an interface block for an external procedure. However, there are situations when one *must* be used. These are

---

An interface block is needed to call an external procedure in the following cases:
- when the procedure is called with a keyword and/or missing argument;
- when a procedure is called which defines or overloads an operator, or the assignment;
- when the procedure called is an array-valued function, or a character function which is neither a constant nor assumed length;
- when the procedure called has a dummy argument which is an assumed-shape array, a pointer or a target;
- when the procedure is a dummy or actual argument;
- when the procedure is called using a generic name.

Fig. 8.1 When to use an interface block

summarized in Figure 8.1. We will encounter most of these situations later; they are collected here for ease of reference.

8.5 Modules

Recall that there are three types of program unit: a main program, an external subprogram, and a *module*.

A module differs from a subprogram in two important ways:

- a module may contain more than one subprogram (called module subprograms);

- a module may contain declaration and specification statements which are accessible to all program units which use the module.

Modules are also compiled separately.

In the following example, the subroutine SWOP is placed in a module MyUtils. For the sake of illustration, the module also declares a real parameter Pi. The main program now has a statement USE MyUtils which renders the module accessible to it. The name Pi is therefore known to the main program. The amended main program is:

```
USE MyUtils

IMPLICIT NONE
REAL A, B

READ*, A
B = Pi
CALL SWOP( A, B )
PRINT*, A, B

END
```

while the module (again saved in a separate file) is

```
MODULE MyUtils
  REAL, PARAMETER :: Pi = 3.1415927

CONTAINS
  SUBROUTINE SWOP( X, Y )
    REAL Temp, X, Y
    Temp = X
    X = Y
    Y = Temp
  END SUBROUTINE SWOP
END MODULE MyUtils
```

Note that the EXTERNAL statement is now neither necesssary nor in fact correct, since SWOP is no longer an external subprogram—it is now technically a *module subprogram*.

The general form of a module is

```
MODULE name
    [declaration statements]
[CONTAINS
    module subprograms]
END [MODULE [name]]
```

It is accessed by means of a USE statement in the host program unit, which *must precede* all other statements:

```
USE module-name
```

A *module subprogram* has exactly the same form as an external subprogram, except that the FUNCTION or SUBROUTINE keyword *must* be present in the END statement. It has access to all other entities in the module, including all variables declared in it. Note that a module subprogram may contain its own internal subprograms.

We have now encountered all three types of program unit. The nesting of internal, external and module subprograms relative to these program units is illustrated in Figure 8.2.

A module may USE other modules, although it may not access itself indirectly through a chain of USE statements in different modules. No ordering of modules is required by the standard. In developing libraries of modules, however, you should try to design a hierarchy to ensure that later modules only use earlier ones.

Since a module may contain declaration statements which are accessible to all host program units, global variables may be declared in this way for use by all hosts accessing the module. This feature is particularly useful for making more complicated declarations, such as those for derived types, globally available.

In particular, interface blocks may be grouped together into modules. As an example, consider again the external subroutine SWOP of Section 8.3. Its interface could be in a module MyMod,

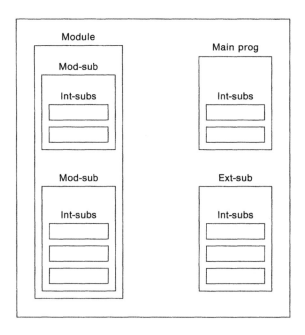

Fig. 8.2 Subprograms and program units (Mod-sub: module subprogram, Int-subs: internal subprograms; Ext-sub: external subprogram)

```
MODULE MyMod

INTERFACE
  SUBROUTINE SWOP( U, V )
    REAL U, V
  END SUBROUTINE
END INTERFACE

END MODULE
```

which may be accessed with the statement USE MyMod in the calling program.

The USE statement We have seen that the USE statement allows access to entities in a module. There are two special forms of the USE statement which affect the mode of access.

It may be inconvenient (or impossible) to use the name of a particular entity in a module. For example, two independently written modules may each have a subprogram with the same name. Or a module entity may have a long and unwieldy name. Module entities may be *renamed* for use in the host program under the new name. E.g. if the module YourMod has a subprogram or variable named YourPlonk, it may be renamed for use under the name MyPlonk as follows:

```
USE YourMod, MyPlonk => YourPlonk
```

The general form is

```
USE module-name, rename-list
```

where each item in *rename-list* is of the form

new-name => *original-name*

Any number of renames may appear in the list. This use is not really recommended, and should only be used as a last resort. It would be better to use a text editor to change the original names.

The other way in which access to a module may be affected is by the ONLY clause in the USE statement. E.g. the statement

```
USE YourMod, ONLY : X, Y
```

allows access to only the entities X and Y of the module. The items following the colon may also be renames.

Each module accessed must appear in a separate USE statement.

PUBLIC and PRIVATE attributes   As we have seen all entities in a module are accessible by default to any program unit that uses the module. However, access may be restricted by specifying a variable with the PRIVATE attribute in its declaration:

```
REAL, PRIVATE :: X
```

Alternatively, a variable or subprogram may be specified with this attribute in a separate statement:

```
PRIVATE X, SWOP
```

This means that the entities X and SWOP are not available *outside* the module. They are still accessible inside the module, however.

The PUBLIC attribute (the default) may be similarly specified.

The statement PUBLIC or PRIVATE with no entity list confirms or resets the default. So the statements

```
PRIVATE
PUBLIC SWOP
```

make all entities in the module PRIVATE by default, except for SWOP.

8.6   Scope

The *scope* of a label or name is the set of lines where that name or label may be used unambiguously. Scoping rules for labels and names are different.

Scope of labels   The only approved use of labels in this book is in FORMAT statements, which we will only discuss in detail in Chapter 10. However, labels can also be used

> A scoping unit is one of the following (Metcalf and Reid):
>
> - a derived-type definition (Chapter 12);
> - a subprogram interface body, excluding any derived-type definitions and interface bodies contained within it; or
> - a program unit or subprogram, excluding derived-type definitions, interface bodies, and subprograms contained within it.

Fig. 8.3 A scoping unit

in conjunction with the notorious GOTO statement, and to end a DO loop, although such practices are not recommended.

Each subprogram, internal or external, has its own independent set of labels. So, for example, the same label may be used in a main program and several of its internal subprograms without ambiguity. The scope of a label, therefore, is a main program or a subprogram, excluding any internal subprograms that it contains.

Scope of names The scope of a name declared in a program extends from the PROGRAM statement to the END statement, and does not extend to any external subprograms that may be invoked.

A name declared in a subprogram has scope from the subprogram's header to its END statement. It follows that a name declared in a main or external subprogram has scope in all subprograms which it contains.

The scope of a name declared in an internal subprogram extends throughout that internal subprogram only, and does not extend to other internal subprograms. It follows that the scope of a name declared in a program or subprogram does not include any internal subprograms in which it is redeclared.

The scope of the name of an internal subprogram, as well as its number and type of arguments, extends throughout the containing program or subprogram (and therefore throughout all other internal subprograms).

The scope of a name declared (where the name is that of a variable or a subprogram now) in a module extends to any program units that use the module, but obviously excludes any internal subprograms in which the name (in the case of a variable) is redeclared.

Having described the basic elements of scope, it is helpful to make the concept more precise by defining a *scoping unit* (Figure 8.3).

Some implications follow from this definition:

- Entities declared in different scoping units are always different, even if they have the same names and properties.
- Within a scoping unit, each named data object, subprogram, derived type, named construct and namelist group must have a distinct name, with the exception of generic names of subprograms.
- The names of program units are global, so program units in the same program may not have the same name, neither may they have the names of any entities declared in the program unit.

There is a separate scoping rule for the DO variable of an *implied* DO (Chapters 9 and 10); it extends only to the implied DO.

8.7 Arguments

There are a number of important properties of subprogram arguments which are summarized in this section for ease of reference.

We first look at precisely how actual arguments are passed to subprograms. This happens in two fundamentally different ways: by reference, or by value. It is necessary to understand clearly the difference between these two mechanisms.

Reference arguments   If the actual argument is a variable it is *passed by reference*. The term "variable" includes an array name, an array element, an array substring, a structure component, or a substring; all these concepts are discussed later.

What actually happens in this case is that the *address* in memory of the actual argument is passed to the subprogram, and the corresponding dummy argument is made to reside at the same memory address. In other words, the actual argument and dummy argument both refer to the same memory location. As a result, any changes made to the dummy argument are reflected in the actual argument on return to the calling program.

You can therefore think of the value of the actual argument being copied to the dummy argument on call, and the value of the dummy argument, which may have been changed, being copied back again on return.

It is bad programming style for dummy arguments of *function* subprograms to be changed in this way; if you need more than one value back from a function rewrite it as a subroutine.

Value arguments   If an actual argument is a constant or an expression more complex than a variable, it is *passed by value*.

This means that the value of the actual argument is literally copied to the dummy argument. Changes made to the dummy argument are consequently *not* reflected in the actual argument on return.

It should be noted that enclosing a variable in parentheses makes it an expression. So the first argument of

```
CALL Plonk( (X), Y )
```

is passed by value. If this is not what was intended, it can be very difficult to spot. This very subtle error can be prevented by giving dummy arguments an *intent*; this is discussed next.

Argument intent   Dummy arguments may be specified with an *intent* attribute, i.e. whether you intend them to be used as input, or output, or both, e.g.

```
SUBROUTINE PLUNK( X, Y, Z )
   REAL, INTENT(IN)    :: X
   REAL, INTENT(OUT)   :: Y
   REAL, INTENT(INOUT) :: Z
   ...
```

If intent is IN, the dummy argument may not have its value changed inside the subprogram.

If the intent is OUT, the corresponding actual argument *must* be a variable. Such a specification would prevent the last error mentioned above, since a call such as

```
CALL PLUNK( A, (B), C )
```

would generate a compiler error—(B) is an expression, not a variable.

If the intent is INOUT, the corresponding actual argument must again be a variable.

If the dummy argument has *no* intent, the actual argument may be a variable or an expression.

It is recommended that all dummy arguments be given an intent. In particular, all function arguments should have intent IN.

Intent may also be specified in a separate statement, e.g.

```
INTENT(INOUT) X, Y, Z
```

Matching type The type of an actual argument must match the type of the corresponding dummy argument. E.g. if PLONK is defined with one *real* argument the statement

```
CALL PLONK( 0 )
```

will cause an error, because the constant 0 is an integer.

Optional and keyword arguments Argument lists can get very long; sometimes not all of them are needed. Some or all of the dummy arguments may be specified with the OPTIONAL attribute (which may also be used as a statement). If the wanted arguments happen to be consecutive, starting from the first dummy argument, they are listed normally in the CALL statement. However, the wanted arguments may be scattered, in which case a *keyword argument list* must be provided, after an ordinary (positional) argument list (which may be empty). Perhaps an example will clarify the situation.

The external subroutine Plonk has six arguments, the last four of which are optional. The following main program shows the interface block required for Plonk, together with some sample calls:

```
INTERFACE
  SUBROUTINE Plonk( DumU, DumV, DumW, DumX, DumY, DumZ )
    OPTIONAL DumW, DumX, DumY, DumZ
  END SUBROUTINE
END INTERFACE
...

CALL Plonk( A, B )                              ! 1
CALL Plonk( A, B, C, D)                         ! 2
CALL Plonk( A, B, DumX = D, DumY = E, DumZ = F )  ! 3
```

In the first call, only the non-optional arguments are passed. In the second call, the first two optional arguments are required, so the list simply contains the first four arguments. However, the third call requires the last three optional arguments, so they must be supplied as a keyword argument list, the keyword in each case being the dummy argument name. There may be no further positional arguments after the first keyword argument, so the call

```
CALL Plonk( A, B, DumX = D, E, F )      ! wrong
```

would be invalid.

Note that an explicit interface in the form of an interface body must be supplied when an external subprogram has optional arguments. However, since modules provide explicit interfaces, this is not necessary in the case of module subprograms with optional arguments.

Arrays as arguments   This is more appropriate to discuss in Chapters 9 and 15, where we deal with arrays and matrices in some depth.

The SAVE attribute   Local variables in a subprogram do not normally retain their values between calls, unless they have the SAVE attribute, e.g.

```
REAL, SAVE :: Temp
```

Local variables which are *initialized* automatically have the SAVE attribute.

A dummy variable may not be specified with SAVE.

Subprograms as arguments   We have seen that actual arguments of a subprogram may be variables or expressions. A subprogram name may also be passed as an argument. This is discussed in Chapter 16, where there is an appropriate example.

8.8   Generic Subprogram Names: Overloading

You may have wondered, having seen how actual and dummy arguments must match exactly in type and number, how some of the intrinsic functions manage to accept arguments of more than one type. For example, the argument of ABS may be integer, real or even complex! The answer is to use a neat trick provided by Fortran 90: *overloading*.

Overloading is a general facility provided by many modern programming languages. In this context, it is the ability to call a number of different subprograms with the same *generic* name. In principle, subprograms, with different *specific* names, are written for different types of arguments; their specific names are then overloaded by a single generic name for all of them. The generic name is called; the compiler decides which specific name to invoke behind the scenes according to the type of the actual arguments.

Consider again the external subroutine SWOP(X, Y) of Section 8.3. It accepts only real arguments. We can make it accept integer arguments as well, in a number of ways.

One is to write two separate external subroutines, SwopReals and SwopIntegers, with real and integer arguments respectively, e.g.

```
SUBROUTINE SwopReals( X, Y )
  REAL X, Y, Temp
  Temp = X
```

```
      X = Y
      Y = Temp
   END SUBROUTINE SwopReals
```

and

```
   SUBROUTINE SwopIntegers( X, Y )
     INTEGER X, Y, Temp
     Temp = X
     X = Y
     Y = Temp
   END SUBROUTINE SwopIntegers
```

Since these are to be *external* subprograms, each must reside in a separate file and be compiled separately. The overloading can then be done in the main program, by means of an INTERFACE statement, which specifies the generic name (SWOP), and interface bodies for the two overloaded subroutines:

```
PROGRAM Main

INTERFACE SWOP
   SUBROUTINE SwopReals( X, Y )
     REAL X, Y, Temp
   END SUBROUTINE SwopReals
   SUBROUTINE SwopIntegers( X, Y )
     INTEGER X, Y, Temp
   END SUBROUTINE SwopIntegers
END INTERFACE

REAL A, B
INTEGER I, J
...

CALL SWOP( A, B )
CALL SWOP( I, J )
...
```

A specific name may be the same as the generic name if this is more convenient.

A generic name may be the same as another accessible generic name, in which case all subprograms with this generic name are invoked through it. In this way, the intrinsic functions may be extended to accept arguments of a derived type.

If you want to overload a module subprogram, the interface is already explicit, so it is incorrect to specify an interface body. Instead, you must include the statement

MODULE PROCEDURE *procedure-names*

in the interface block, where *procedure-names* are the procedures (subprograms) to be overloaded. So if the subroutines SwopReals and SwopIntegers were defined in a module, the interface block would be

```
INTERFACE SWOP
   MODULE PROCEDURE SwopReals, SwopIntegers
END INTERFACE
```

This interface block could be placed in the module itself. Try it.

We will see later how to overload intrinsic operators and the assignment in order to extend these operations to derived types.

8.9   Stubs

A large program will have many subprograms. To plan and code them all before compiling is asking for trouble. A useful trick is to use *stubs*, which define the subprogram names, but do nothing (at first). Then fill the stubs in one at a time, compiling after each fill in. That way, it's much easier to catch all the compiler errors. You can initially define the subprograms as internal, with all local variables declared, moving them out to modules as they are completed. This obviates having to recompile everything as more and more stubs are filled in. E.g.

```
PROGRAM BigOne

IMPLICIT NONE

CALL FIRST
CALL LAST

CONTAINS
   SUBROUTINE FIRST
     PRINT*, 'First here'
   END SUBROUTINE

   SUBROUTINE LAST
     PRINT*, 'Last here'
   END SUBROUTINE
END PROGRAM BigOne
```

It may not do much at this stage, but at least it compiles!

8.10   Recursion

Many mathematical functions (and more general procedures) may be defined *recursively*, i.e. in terms of simpler cases of themselves. For example, the factorial function may be defined recursively as

$$n! = n \times (n - 1)!$$

given that 1! is defined as 1.

To implement this definition as a function, it is necessary for the function to call itself. Normally in Fortran 90 this is not possible. However, if the RECURSIVE keyword is prefixed to the function header, the function may call itself. If the call is direct (i.e. the function name occurs in the body of the function definition) a RESULT clause must be added to the function header, in order to use a different (local) name for the function. This is illustrated below, where the function Factorial is defined recursively:

```
IMPLICIT NONE
INTEGER I

I = 10
PRINT*, I, Factorial(I)

CONTAINS
  RECURSIVE FUNCTION Factorial( N ) RESULT (Fact)
    INTEGER Fact, N
    IF( N == 1 ) THEN
      Fact = 1
    ELSE
      Fact = N * Factorial( N-1 )
    END IF
  END FUNCTION
END
```

The RESULT clause is needed because the name Factorial may not appear on the left-hand side of an assignment. Note that the name Factorial must *not* be declared in the INTEGER statement: the declaration of Fact is sufficient.

Recursion is an advanced topic, although it appears deceptively simple. You may wonder how the recursive Factorial function really works. It is important to distinguish between the function being *called* and *executed*. When the initial call takes place N has the value 10, so the ELSE clause in Factorial is evaluated. However, the value of Factorial(9) is not known at this stage, so a *copy* is made of all the statements in the function which will need to be executed once the value of Factorial(9) is known. The reference to Factorial(9) makes Factorial call itself, this time with a value of 9 for N. Again the ELSE clause is evaluated, and again Fortran 90 discovers that it doesn't know the value of Factorial(8). So another (different) copy is made of all the statements that will need to be executed once the value of Factorial(8) is known. And so each time Factorial is called, separate copies are made of all the statements *yet to be executed*. Finally, the compiler finds a value of N (1) for which it knows the value of Factorial, so at last it can begin to execute (in reverse order) the pile of statements which have been dammed up inside the memory.

This discussion illustrates the point that recursion should be used carefully. While it is perfectly in order to use it in a case like this, it can chew up huge amounts of computer memory and time.

It should be mentioned that a RESULT clause may be used optionally when a function is not defined recursively—in other words, it is never wrong to have a RESULT clause. Here it is shown with a non-recursive version of Factorial:

```
IMPLICIT NONE
INTEGER I

DO I = 1, 10
  PRINT*, I, Factorial( I )
END DO

CONTAINS
  FUNCTION Factorial( N ) RESULT (Fact)
    INTEGER Fact, I, N
    Fact = 1
    DO I = 2, N
      Fact = I * Fact
    END DO
  END FUNCTION
END
```

When a subroutine calls itself directly, the keyword RECURSIVE must also be used. In the example below, Factorial is rewritten as a recursive subroutine. This is a little more subtle.

```
IMPLICIT NONE
INTEGER F, I

DO I = 1, 10
  CALL Factorial( F, I )
  PRINT*, I, F
END DO

CONTAINS
  RECURSIVE SUBROUTINE Factorial( F, N )
    INTEGER F, N
    IF (N == 1) THEN
      F = 1
    ELSE
      CALL Factorial( F, N-1 )
      F = N * F
    END IF
  END SUBROUTINE
END
```

When I first wrote this program, I put N instead of N-1 by mistake as the argument in the recursive call. Consequently, the program could not end, since Factorial was always called with N having the value of 10. The "escape statement", F = 1 could never be executed. Be warned!

The subtlety in this example is working out whether to place the statement F = N * F before or after the recursive call to Factorial. Try running the program with F = N * F *before* the call to Factorial. The difference is that now

F = N * F is *executed* on each call, instead of a copy being made. As a result, the last execution sets F to 1, and this is its value on return.

There are more examples of recursive functions in the exercises. A recursive subroutine is used to implement the Quick Sort algorithm in Chapter 9.

Summary

- Large programs should be broken down into subprograms (procedures) to perform simpler tasks.
- Subprograms may be internal or external.
- External subprograms are compiled separately from the main program.
- Module subprograms are subprograms which have been collected into separately compiled modules (libraries).
- A program unit is a main program, external subprogram, or module.
- Internal subprograms are contained within program units.
- Subprograms consist of functions or subroutines.
- A function returns a value, which has a type.
- A function is invoked by referencing its name.
- No value is attached to the name of a subroutine.
- A subroutine is invoked with a CALL statement.
- Dummy arguments are used in a subprogram's declaration, actual arguments in its invocation.
- The compiler provides explicit interfaces to intrinsic, internal and module subprograms.
- An EXTERNAL statement in the calling program is sufficient to link to an external subprogram in normal circumstances.
- An interface block may always be used to provide an explicit interface to an external subprogram; there are situations when one *must* be used (Figure 8.1).
- A module may contain declarations, specification statements and subprograms.
- Entities in a module specified with the PRIVATE attribute may only be accessed within the module. Entities are public by default.
- The scope of a name or label is the set of lines where it may be used unambiguously. Scoping rules for labels and names are different.
- Actual arguments may be passed to subprograms by reference or by value. An argument passed by reference may be changed on return. Constants or expressions are passed by value. Parentheses around a variable name make it an expression.
- Dummy arguments may be specified with the INTENT attribute: IN (may not be changed in the subprogram), OUT (actual argument must be a variable so that it can be changed), or INOUT (actual argument must be a variable). All dummy arguments should be given an intent.
- Function dummy arguments should have intent IN.
- Dummy arguments may be specified OPTIONAL. Wanted arguments may be provided in a keyword argument list. External subprograms with optional arguments must have an explicit interface provided by an interface body.
- An interface may be used to overload specific subprogram names with a generic name.

- Stubs (empty subprograms) should be used when developing large programs.
- Subprograms may call themselves directly if they are declared as RECURSIVE. A recursive function must have a RESULT clause in its header to return its value.

Exercises

8.1 Write a program which uses the Newton quotient

$$\frac{f(x+h) - f(x)}{h}$$

to estimate the first derivative of $f(x) = x^3$ at $x = 1$, using successively smaller values of h: 1, 10^{-1}, 10^{-2}, etc. Use a function subprogram for $f(x)$.

8.2 Write your own Fortran function to compute the exponential function directly from the Taylor series:

$$e^x = 1 + x + \frac{x^2}{2!} + \frac{x^3}{3!} + \dots$$

The series should end when the last term is less than 10^{-6}. Test your function against the intrinsic function EXP.

8.3 Write a function Bin(N, R) which returns the binomial coefficient, $n!/r!(n-r)!$, as defined in Chapter 6.

8.4 Write a subroutine

```
QUAD( X1, X2, A, B, C, J )
   REAL INTENT(OUT)    :: X1, X2
   REAL INTENT(IN)     :: A, B, C
   INTEGER INTENT(OUT) :: J
```

which computes the roots of the quadratic equation $ax^2 + bx + c = 0$. The arguments A, B and C (which may take any values) are the coefficients of the quadratic, and X1, X2 are the two roots (if they exist), which may be equal. See Figure 4.5 for the structure plan. J is a "flag" which must be set by the procedure as follows:

$$\begin{array}{rl}
-1: & \text{complex roots (discriminant} < 0); \\
0: & \text{no solution } (a = b = 0, c \neq 0); \\
1: & \text{one root } (a = 0, b \neq 0, \text{ so the root is } -c/b); \\
2: & \text{two roots (which could be equal)}; \\
99: & \text{any } x \text{ is a solution } (a = b = c = 0).
\end{array}$$

8.5 If a random variable X is distributed normally with zero mean and unit standard deviation, the probability that $0 \le X \le x$ is given by the standard normal function $\Phi(x)$. This is usually looked up in tables, but it may be approximated as follows:

$$\Phi(x) = 0.5 - r(at + bt^2 + ct^3),$$

where $a = 0.4361836$, $b = -0.1201676$, $c = 0.937298$, $r = \exp(-0.5x^2)/\sqrt{2\pi}$, and $t = 1/(1 + 0.3326x)$.

Write a function to compute $\Phi(x)$, and use it in a program to write out its values for $0 \leq x \leq 4$ in steps of 0.1. Check: $\Phi(1) = 0.3413$.

8.6 The Fibonacci numbers are generated by the sequence

$$1, 1, 2, 3, 5, 8, 13, \ldots$$

Can you work out what the next term is? Write a recursive function F(N) to compute the Fibonacci numbers F_0 to F_{20}, using the relationship

$$F_n = F_{n-1} + F_{n-2},$$

given that $F_0 = F_1 = 1$.

8.7 The first three Legendre polynomials are $P_0(x) = 1$, $P_1(x) = x$, and $P_2(x) = (3x^2 - 1)/2$. There is a general *recurrence* formula for Legendre polynomials, by which they are defined recursively:

$$(n + 1)P_{n+1}(x) - (2n + 1)xP_n(x) + NP_{n-1}(x) = 0.$$

Define a recursive Fortran function P(N, X) to generate Legendre polynomials, given the form of P_0 and P_1. Use your function to compute P(2, X) for a few values of X, and compare your results with those using the analytic form of $P_2(x)$ given above.

9

Arrays

In real programs we often need to handle a large amount of data in the same way,
e.g. to find the mean of a set of numbers, or to sort a list of numbers or names, or
to analyse a set of students' test results, or to solve a system of linear equations. To
avoid an enormously clumsy program, where perhaps hundreds of variable names
are needed, we can use *subscripted* variables, or *arrays*. These may be regarded as
variables with components, rather like vectors or matrices. They are written in the
normal way, except that the subscripts are enclosed in parentheses after the variable
name, e.g. X(3), Y(I + 2 * N).

Fortran 90 has an extremely powerful set of array features, which Fortran 77
users will be both surprised and delighted to discover.

9.1 Mean and Standard Deviation

To illustrate the basic principles, let's compute the sample mean and standard deviation of a set of N observations. The mean is defined as

$$\overline{X} = \frac{1}{N} \sum_{i=1}^{N} X_i,$$

where X_i is the ith observation. The standard deviation s is defined as

$$s^2 = \frac{1}{N-1} \sum_{i=1}^{N} (X_i - \overline{X})^2.$$

The next program computes these two quantities from data read from the disk file DATA. The first item of data in the file is the value of N. This is followed by exactly N observations—all on separate lines.

```
IMPLICIT NONE

INTEGER                :: I, N
REAL                   :: Std = 0
REAL, DIMENSION(100)   :: X
REAL                   :: XBar = 0

OPEN (1, FILE = 'DATA')

READ (1, *) N
DO I = 1, N
  READ (1, *) X(I)
  XBar = Xbar + X(I)
END DO

XBar = XBar / N

DO I = 1, N
  Std = Std + (X(I) - XBar) ** 2
END DO

Std = SQRT( Std / (N - 1) )
PRINT*, 'Mean: ', XBar
PRINT*, 'Std deviation: ', Std
```

Try this with some sample data (each number on a separate line):

10 5.1 6.2 5.7 3.5 9.9 1.2 7.6 5.3 8.7 4.4

You should get a mean of 5.76 and a standard deviation of 2.53 (to two decimal places).

The DIMENSION(100) attribute in the type declaration statement for the array X sets aside 100 memory locations, with names X(1), X(2), ..., X(100). However, the sample data above consists of only 10 numbers, so only the first 10 locations are used. Note that the value of *N* must be read first (and must be correct), before the *N* values may be read.

After the READ is complete, the memory area where the array is stored looks like this:

X(1)	X(2)	X(3)	...	X(10)
5.1	6.2	5.7	...	4.4

Now that the data are safely stored in the array, they may be used again, simply by referencing the array name X with an element number, e.g. X(3). So the sum of the first two elements may be computed as

```
SUM = X(1) + X(2)
```

This facility is necessary for computing *s* according to the formula above—the data must all be read to compute the mean, and the mean must be computed before all the data is re-used to compute *s*.

(To be fair, there is another way of calculating the standard deviation, which doesn't require the use of an array:

$$s^2 = \frac{1}{N-1} \sum_{i=1}^{N} X_i^2 - N\overline{X}^2.$$

As an exercise, rewrite the program without an array, reading all the data into a single variable X.)

Having each data value on a separate line in the file is rather cumbersome—this is required by the separate execution of each READ (1, *) X(I) in the DO loop. Fortran allows the use of an *implied* DO to read or print all or part of an array. Simply replace the entire DO construct in the program with

```
READ (1, *) ( X(I), I = 1, N )
```

Note that the syntax requires parentheses around the implied DO.

9.2 Basic Rules and Notation

The array is our first example in Fortran 90 of a *compound object*, i.e. an object which can have more than one value. Arrays can be fairly complicated creatures. Only the basics are mentioned here; more advanced features will be introduced later.

The statement

```
REAL, DIMENSION(10) :: X
```

declares X to be an array (or *list*) with 10 real *elements*, denoted by X(1), X(2), ..., X(10). The number of elements in an array is called its *size* (10 in this case). Each element of an array is a scalar (single-valued).

Array elements are referenced by means of a *subscript*, indicated in parentheses after the array name. The subscript must be an integer expression—its value must fall within the range defined in the array declaration. So

```
X(I+1)
```

is a valid reference for an element of X as declared above, as long as (I+1) is in the range 1–10. A compiler error occurs if the subscript is out of range.

By default arrays have a *lower bound* of 1 (the lowest value a subscript can take). However, you can have any lower bound you like:

```
REAL, DIMENSION(0:100) :: A
```

declares A to have 101 elements, from A(0) to A(100). The upper bound *must* be specified; if the lower bound is missing it defaults to 1.

An array may have more than one *dimension*. The bounds of each dimension must be specified:

```
REAL, DIMENSION(2,3) :: A
```

A is a two-dimensional array. The number of elements along a dimension is called the *extent* in that dimension. A has an extent of 2 in the first dimension, and an extent of 3 in the second dimension (and a size of 6). Fortran allows up to seven dimensions. The number of dimensions of an array is its *rank*, and the sequence of extents is its *shape*. The shape of A is (2, 3), or (2 × 3) in matrix notation. A scalar is regarded as having a rank of zero. We will concentrate mainly on one-dimensional arrays in this chapter—it is more appropriate to discuss two-dimensional arrays in the context of matrices (Chapter 14).

The DIMENSION attribute is optional. It provides a default shape for variables whose names are not followed by a shape:

```
REAL, DIMENSION(5) :: A, B(2,3), C(10)      ! only A is (1:5)
INTEGER I(10), K(4,4), L(5)                 ! all different
```

An array subscript can be used as the control variable in a DO loop to generate array elements. The following code assigns the first five even integers to the ten elements of X (assumed correctly declared):

```
DO I = 1, 5
  X(I) = 2 * I
END DO
```

The same effect can be achieved in a number of different ways with an *array constructor*:

```
X = (/ 2, 4, 6, 8, 10 /)
```

or

```
X = (/ (I, I = 2, 10, 2) /)
```

A constant array may be declared in this way, with the PARAMETER attribute.

Array constructors are discussed more fully in Section 9.8.

An entire array may be read:

```
READ*, X
```

Of course, the exact number of data values must be supplied.
An entire array may be assigned a scalar value:

```
X = 1
```

This is a special case of *array assignment*, which we will encounter again later.

Reading an unknown amount of data The implied DO together with the IOSTAT specifier in READ provides a neat way of reading an unknown amount of data into an array, where only the maximum size of the array is given:

```
INTEGER, PARAMETER   :: MAX = 100
REAL, DIMENSION(MAX) :: X

OPEN (1, FILE = 'DATA')
READ( 1, *, IOSTAT = IO ) ( X(I), I = 1, MAX )

IF (IO < 0) THEN
  N = I - 1
ELSE
  N = MAX
END IF

PRINT*, ( X(I), I = 1, N )
...
```

The data may be arranged in any format in the input file. Note that I is one greater than the number of values read: it is incremented in the implied DO before the end-of-file condition is detected. Note also that on normal exit from the implied DO its value would be MAX+1.

9.3 Arrays as Subprogram Arguments

An array may be passed as an argument to a subprogram in a number of ways. The neatest way is shown in the next program, where the calculation of the mean and standard deviation is relegated to the subroutine Stats:

```
IMPLICIT NONE

INTEGER              :: I, N
REAL, DIMENSION(100) :: X
REAL                 :: Std = 0
REAL                 :: XBar = 0

OPEN (1, FILE = 'DATA')
```

```
READ (1, *) N, (X(I), I = 1, N)
CALL Stats( X, N, XBar, Std )
PRINT*, 'Mean:            ', XBar
PRINT*, 'Std deviation: ', Std

CONTAINS
  SUBROUTINE Stats( Y, N, YBar, S )
    REAL, DIMENSION(:), INTENT(IN) :: Y
    REAL, INTENT(INOUT)            :: S, YBar
    INTEGER, INTENT(IN)            :: N

    INTEGER  I

    YBar = 0; S = 0

    DO I = 1, N
      YBar = Ybar + Y(I)
    END DO

    YBar = YBar / N

    DO I = 1, N
      S = S + (Y(I) - YBar) ** 2
    END DO

    S = SQRT( S / (N - 1) )
  END SUBROUTINE
END
```

The compiler requires that the *shape* of actual and dummy arguments agree. The declaration

```
REAL, DIMENSION(:), INTENT(IN) :: Y
```

of the dummy argument makes it an *assumed-shape* array, i.e. it takes on whatever shape is imposed by the actual argument. The complete syntax for the dimension in this case is

[*lower bound*]:

The lower bound defaults to 1 if omitted. Take careful note that the shape is passed, not bounds. So in this example,

```
REAL, DIMENSION(0:), INTENT(IN) :: Y
```

would result in X(I) corresponding to Y(I-1).

If the lower bounds are the same in the declaration of the actual and dummy arguments, the correspondence will be exact.

Note that if Stats is compiled separately as an external subprogram, an explicit interface will have to be provided in the calling program, e.g.

```
INTERFACE
  SUBROUTINE Stats( Y, N, YBar, S )
    INTEGER, INTENT(IN)            :: N
    REAL, DIMENSION(:), INTENT(IN) :: Y
    REAL, INTENT(INOUT)            :: S, YBar
  END SUBROUTINE
END INTERFACE
```

9.4 Allocatable (Dynamic) Arrays

The program in Section 9.2 reads an unknown amount of data into an array. However, the maximum size of the array must be declared. In programs which have a large demand on memory this could be wasteful.

A more memory efficient solution, not possible in earlier versions of Fortran, is to use *dynamic memory*. The types of variables we have seen so far have all been *static*, although this was never mentioned. This means that when the variable is declared, the compiler assigns it to a certain address in memory (with a fixed amount of storage space), and there it stays as long as the program is running. By contrast, chunks of dynamic memory are used only when needed, *while the programming is running*, and then discarded. This is often a more efficient way of using memory.

A variable is specified as dynamic with the ALLOCATABLE attribute. In particular, a one-dimensional array may be specified thus:

```
REAL, DIMENSION(:), ALLOCATABLE :: X
```

Although its rank is specified, it has no size until it appears in an ALLOCATE statement, such as

```
ALLOCATE( X(N) )
```

When it is no longer needed, it may be deallocated:

```
DEALLOCATE( X )
```

thus freeing up the memory used.

The following program extract shows how to use *allocatable arrays*, as these beasts are called, to read an unknown amount of data, which unfortunately must be supplied one item per line because of the way READ works.

```
REAL, DIMENSION(:), ALLOCATABLE :: X, OldX
REAL      A
INTEGER   IO, N

ALLOCATE( X(0) )                  ! size zero to start with?
N = 0
OPEN( 1, FILE = 'DATA' )

DO
  READ(1, *, IOSTAT = IO) A
  IF (IO < 0 ) EXIT
```

```
      N = N + 1
      ALLOCATE( OldX( SIZE(X) ) )
      OldX = X                        ! entire array can be assigned
      DEALLOCATE( X )
      ALLOCATE( X(N) )
      X = OldX
      X(N) = A
      DEALLOCATE( OldX )
   END DO

   PRINT*, ( X(I), I = 1, N )
   ...
```

We would like to be able to increase the size of X for each value read. However, before X can be allocated with a larger size, it must be deallocated—losing all the previous data read. So another dynamic array, OldX must be used to take care of this.

Note the following important features:

- an array may have zero size—this is often convenient;
- entire arrays may be assigned;
- an array which is currently allocated may not be allocated again;
- an array which is deallocated must be currently allocated.

You may be tempted to write this as a subroutine. However, dummy arguments may not have the ALLOCATABLE attribute.

9.5 Top of the Class

The program in Chapter 5 to find the student with the highest mark in a class assumes that there is only one top student. If there could be more than one name at the top, you can use an array to make a list of the top names.

```
   IMPLICIT NONE

   INTEGER                        :: I          ! student counter
   INTEGER                        :: IO         ! value of IOSTAT
   INTEGER, PARAMETER             :: MAX = 100  ! maximum class size
   INTEGER                        :: NumTop = 1 ! must be at least 1
   REAL                           :: Mark       ! general mark
   REAL                           :: TopMark = 0 ! can't be less than 0
   CHARACTER*15                   :: Name       ! general name
   CHARACTER*15, DIMENSION(MAX) :: TopName     ! top student

   OPEN( 1, FILE = 'MARKS' )

   DO
      READ( 1, * , IOSTAT = IO) Name, Mark
```

```
    IF (IO < 0) EXIT
      IF (Mark > TopMark) THEN          ! new top mark here
        TopMark = Mark                  ! reset the top mark
        NumTop = 1                      ! only one at the top now
        TopName(1) = Name               ! here she is
      ELSE IF (Mark == TopMark) THEN    ! tie for top mark here
        NumTop = NumTop + 1             ! advance top counter
        TopName(NumTop) = Name          ! add his name to the list
      END IF
  END DO

  DO I = 1, NumTop
    PRINT*, TopName(I), TopMark
  END DO
  END
```

To understand what the program does run through it by hand (make a list of the variables, and enter their values) with the following data:

```
Botha      58
Essop      72
Jones      72
Murray     72
Rogers     90
Tutu       90
```

Then run it on the computer as a check. Note that at the end the name Murray will still be in the array, in TopName(3), but his name will not be printed because NumTop has been reset to 2.

You could try to rewrite this program with TopName as an allocatable array to save memory space.

9.6 Sorting a List: the Bubble Sort

One of the standard applications of arrays is sorting a list of numbers into, let us say, ascending order. The basic idea is that the unsorted list is read into an array. The numbers are then ordered by a process which essentially passes through the list many times, swopping consecutive elements that are in the wrong order, until all the elements are in the right order. Such a process is called a Bubble Sort, because the smaller numbers rise to the top of the list, like bubbles of air in water. (In fact, in the version shown below, the largest number will "sink" to the bottom of the list after the first pass, which really makes it a "Lead Ball" sort.) There are many other methods of sorting, which may be found in most textbooks on computer science (one of them, the Quick Sort, is given in the next section). These are generally more efficient than the Bubble Sort, but its advantage is that it is by far the easiest method to program. A structure plan for the bubble sort is as follows:

1. Initialize N (length of list)

Table 9.1 Memory during a Bubble Sort

	1st pass	2nd pass	3rd pass	4th pass
X(1):	27/13	13/9	9/5	5/3
X(2):	13/27/9	9/13/5	5/9/3	3/5
X(3):	9/27/5	5/13/3	3/9	9
X(4):	5/27/3	3/13	13	13
X(5):	3/27	27	27	27
	4 tests	3 tests	2 tests	1 test

2. Read the list X
3. Repeat $N - 1$ times with counter K:
    Repeat $N - K$ times with counter J:
        If $X_j > X_{j+1}$ then
            Swop the contents of X_j and X_{j+1}
4. Print the list X, which is now sorted.

As an example, consider a list of five numbers: 27, 13, 9, 5 and 3. They are initially read into the array X. Part of the computer memory for this problem is sketched in Table 9.1. Each column shows the list during each *pass*. A stroke in a row indicates a change in that variable during the pass as the program works down the list. The number of tests ($X_j > X_{j+1}$?) made on each pass is also shown in the table. Work through the table by hand with the structure plan until you understand how the algorithm works.

Sorting algorithms are compared by calculating the number of tests they carry out, since this takes up most of the execution time during the sort. On the Kth pass of the Bubble Sort there are exactly $N - K$ tests, so the total number of tests is

$$1 + 2 + 3 + \ldots + (N - 1) = N(N - 1)/2$$

(approximately $N^2/2$ for large N). For a list of five numbers there are therefore 10 tests, but for 10 numbers there are 45 tests. The computer time needed goes up as the square of the length of the list.

The program below uses the subroutine Bubble_Sort to sort 100 random numbers. It departs slightly from the structure plan above, which will make $N-1$ passes, *even if the list is sorted before the last pass*. Since most real lists are partially sorted, it makes sense to check after each pass if any swops were made. If none were, the list must be sorted, so unnecessary (and therefore time-wasting) tests can be eliminated. In the subroutine, the logical variable Sorted is used to detect when the list is sorted, and the outer loop is coded instead as a non-deterministic DO WHILE loop.

```
IMPLICIT NONE
INTEGER, PARAMETER  :: N = 100      ! size of list
REAL, DIMENSION(N)  :: List         ! list to be sorted
INTEGER I                           ! counter
REAL R                              ! random number
```

```
      DO I = 1, N
        CALL Random_Number( R )
        List(I) = INT( N * R + 1 )          ! random integers in range 1-N
      END DO

      PRINT 10, List                         ! print unsorted list
10    FORMAT( 13F6.0 )

      CALL Bubble_Sort( List )        ! sort

      PRINT 10, List                         ! print sorted list

      CONTAINS
        SUBROUTINE Bubble_Sort( X )
          REAL, DIMENSION(:), INTENT(INOUT) :: X     ! list
          INTEGER :: Num                             ! size of list
          REAL Temp                                  ! temp for swop
          INTEGER J, K                               ! counters
          LOGICAL Sorted                ! flag to detect when sorted

          Num = SIZE(X)
          Sorted = .FALSE.          ! initially unsorted
          K = 0                     ! count the passes

          DO WHILE (.NOT. Sorted)
            Sorted = .TRUE.                ! they could be sorted
            K = K + 1                      ! another pass
            DO J = 1, Num-K                ! fewer tests on each pass
              IF (X(J) > X(J+1)) THEN      ! are they in order?
                Temp = X(J)                ! no ...
                X(J) = X(J+1)
                X(J+1) = Temp
                Sorted = .FALSE.           ! a swop was made
              END IF
            END DO
          END DO

        END SUBROUTINE
      END
```

Bubble_Sort is written here as an internal subroutine, but will run as it stands as an external subroutine or in a module.

9.7 Sorting a List: Quick Sort

Try sorting 1000 numbers with the Bubble Sort. It takes quite a while. Sorting 10 000 numbers (a not inconceivable problem) would take about 100 times longer.

The famous Quick Sort algorithm, invented by C.A.R. Hoare in 1960, is much faster. It is based on the "divide and conquer" approach: to solve a big problem, break it down into smaller subproblems, and break each subproblem down in the same way, until they are small enough to solve. As someone has remarked, "Every problem has a smaller problem inside, waiting to get out."

How do we break our sorting problem down into manageable subproblems? Well, have a look at the following list:

Number:	19	30	14	28	8	32	72	41	87	33
Position:	1	2	3	4	5	6	7	8	9	10

The value 32 in position 6 has a special property. All the values to the left of it are less than 32, while all the values to the right of it are greater than 32. The value 32 is said to *partition* the sorting problem into two subproblems: a left subproblem, and a right subproblem. These may each be sorted separately, because no value in the left subproblem can ever get into the right subproblem, and vice versa. Furthermore, the value 32 is in the correct position in the right subproblem—it is the smallest value there.

You might think it was a lucky shot that 32 neatly partitioned the list to start with. The brilliance of the algorithm is that given any list, we can always create a partition with the left-most value, without too much difficulty.

Have a look now at a rearrangement of the list:

32	19	41	14	28	8	72	30	87	33
L	L_1							R_1	R

The extreme ends are labelled L and R. We are going to partition the list with the value 32, currently at position L. We define counters L_1 and R_1 with initial values as shown.

The idea now is to move L_1 to the right, while making sure that

every value to the left of position $L_1 \leq$ partition value

and then to move R_1 to the left, while making sure that

every value to the right of position $R_1 >$ partition value.

Doing this gets us to this situation:

32	19	41	14	28	8	72	30	87	33
L		L_1					R_1		R

What now? There seems to be a deadlock. But no, just swop the value in position L_1 (41) with the value in position R_1 (30):

32	19	**30**	14	28	8	72	**41**	87	33
L		L_1					R_1		R

We can now carry on moving L_1 and R_1, subject to the rules stated above, until we get to this scene:

32	19	30	14	28	8	72	41	87	33
L					R_1	L_1			R

However, the situation now is different. L_1 and R_1 have *crossed*, so we must have found the partition point: it is at position R_1. All that remains to be done now is to swop the values at L (32) and R_1 (8), giving us a partitioned array, with 32 as the partition:

8	19	30	14	28	**32**	72	41	87	33
L					R_1	L_1			R

We can now partition any problem with its left-most value. So the resulting subproblems can be partitioned in the same way. We simply continue partitioning subproblems, until the subproblems have only 1 member, which must be sorted!

This type of "divide and conquer" algorithm is what recursion was made for. The following program implements it recursively.

```
IMPLICIT NONE
INTEGER, PARAMETER  :: N = 100    ! size of list
REAL, DIMENSION(N)  :: List       ! list to be sorted
INTEGER I                         ! counter
REAL R                            ! random number

DO I = 1, N
  CALL RANDOM_NUMBER( R )
  List(I) = INT( N * R + 1 )      ! random integers in range 1-N
END DO

PRINT 10, List                    ! print unsorted list
```

```
10   FORMAT( 13F6.0 )

     CALL Quick_Sort( List, 1, N )       ! quick sort now

     PRINT 10, List                      ! print sorted list

     CONTAINS
       RECURSIVE SUBROUTINE Quick_Sort( X, L, R )
         REAL, DIMENSION(:), INTENT(INOUT) :: X     ! list
         INTEGER, INTENT(IN)               :: L, R ! left, right bounds
         INTEGER L1, R1                             ! etc

         IF (L < R)THEN
           L1 = L
           R1 = R

           DO
             DO WHILE (L1 < R .and. X(L1) <= X(L))  ! shift L1 right
               L1 = L1 + 1
             END DO

             DO WHILE (L < R1 .and. X(R1) >= X(L))  ! shift R1 left
               R1 = R1 - 1
             END DO

             IF (L1 < R1) CALL Swop( X(L1), X(R1) ) ! swop
             IF (L1 >= R1) EXIT                      ! crossover -
                                                     ! partition
           END DO

           CALL Swop( X(L), X(R1) )         ! partition with X(L) at R1
           CALL Quick_Sort( X, L, R1-1 ) ! now attack left subproblem
           CALL Quick_Sort( X, R1+1, R ) ! don't forget right subproblem
         END IF
       END SUBROUTINE Quick_Sort

       SUBROUTINE Swop( A, B )
         REAL, INTENT(INOUT) :: A, B
         REAL                :: Temp

         Temp = A
         A = B
         B = Temp

       END SUBROUTINE Swop
     END
```

Note that the swopping is implemented as a subroutine. If you rewrite Quick_Sort as an external subroutine, Swop could be internal to it. You should try working through the program by hand with the sample array in the figures.

Try the Quick Sort out on 1000 numbers. You should be impressed! It has been proved that Quick Sort needs approximately $N \log_2 N$ comparisons as opposed to the Bubble Sort's $N^2/2$.

You may be interested to learn that Quick Sort slows down tremendously if the list is already nearly sorted (try it on a sorted list). However, it will work just as fast in this case if you choose a value near the middle of the subproblem for the partition value, instead of the left-most value. Happy sorting!

9.8   More Array Features

Fortran 90 has some powerful new array features, which are ideally suited to numerical analysis applications. They are summarized in this section.

Array constructors   A one-dimensional constant array may be constructed from a list of element values enclosed between the separators (/ and /). E.g.

    (/ 2, 4, 6, 8, 10 /)

is an array of rank one with five elements.

The general form of an *array constructor* is

    (/ array constructor value list /)

where each *value* is either an expression, or an *implied* DO of the form

    (value list, variable = expr1, expr2 [, expr3])

The parameters of the implied DO operate in the same way as those of the DO. E.g.

    (/ 2, 4, (I, I = 4, 10, 2) /)

is the same as

    (/ 2, 4, 6, 8, 10 /)

The optional parameter *expr3* is sometimes called the *stride* in the context of an implied DO. An implied DO may be nested inside another, making

    (/ ((I, I = 1, 2), J = 1, 3) /)

the same as

    (/ 1, 2, 1, 2, 1, 2 /)

If the list is empty, a zero-sized array is constructed. The scope of the implied DO variable is restricted to the implied DO—it will not affect the value of another variable of the same name elsewhere in the scoping unit of the constructor.

A constant array of rank greater than one can be constructed from an array constructor using the RESHAPE intrinsic function. E.g.

    RESHAPE(SOURCE = (/ 1, 2, 3, 4, 5, 6 /), SHAPE = (/ 2, 3 /))

forms the (2×3) matrix

$$\begin{bmatrix} 1 & 3 & 5 \\ 2 & 4 & 6 \end{bmatrix}.$$

Array sections A subarray, called a *section*, may be referenced by specifying a range of subscripts, e.g.

```
X(I:J)       ! rank one array of size J-I+1
Y(I, 1:J)    ! rank one array of size J (e.g. the Ith row of a ..
             ! .. matrix with J columns)
X(2:5, 8:9)  ! rank one array of size 4+2
```

An array section is technically an array, and may appear in statements where an array is appropriate, although its individual elements may not be referenced directly. So we can't write X(I:J)(2) to reference the second element of the section X(I:J). Rather write X(I+1) (since the first element is naturally X(I)).

One or both of the bounds in a section may be omitted, and a stride other than 1 may be used:

```
A(J, :)      ! the whole of row J
A(J, 1:K:3 ) ! elements 1, 4, 7, ... of row J
```

A section subscript may even be a one-dimensional array, of integer type. E.g., the coding

```
REAL, DIMENSION(10) :: A = (/ (I, I = 2, 20, 2) /)
INTEGER, DIMENSION(5) :: B = (/ 5, 4, 3, 2, 1 /)
PRINT*, A(B)
```

produces the output

```
10.00  8.00  6.00  4.00  2.00
```

A subscript of this nature is called a *vector subscript*. The elements of a vector subscript may be in any order. E.g.

```
A( (/ 3, 5, 1, 2 /) )
```

is a section of A with elements A(3), A(5), A(1), and A(2), in that order. Some of the values in the vector subscript may be repeated. This is called a *many-one section*, since more than one element of the section is mapped onto a single array element. E.g.

```
A( (/ 3, 5, 1, 5 /) )
```

is a section with both elements 2 and 4 referencing A(5).

A many-one section may not appear on the left of an assignment statement. If an array section with a vector subscript is an actual argument of a subprogram, it is regarded as an expression, and it may not be changed by the subprogram. It may therefore not have intent OUT or INOUT.

Initializing arrays with DATA   All or part of an array may be initialized in a DATA statement. There are a number of possibilities, e.g.

```
REAL, DIMENSION(10)  :: A, B, C(3,3)
DATA A / 5*0, 5*1 /                    ! first 5 zero, last 5 one
DATA B(1:5) / 4, 0, 5, 2, -1 /         ! section 1:5 only
DATA ((C(I,J), J= 1,3), I=1,3) / 3*0, 3*1, 3*2 / ! by rows
```

Array expressions   An intrinsic operator may operate on an array as well as a scalar, to produce an *array expression*.

When a unary intrinsic operator acts on an array, it acts on each element of the array. E.g. -X reverses the sign of each element of the array X.

When a binary intrinsic operation is applied to a pair of arrays of the same shape (identical rank and extents), the operation is applied to the corresponding elements of the operands. The result of the operation is an array of the same shape. One of the operands may be a scalar, in which case it is used in the operation on each element of the array operand (the scalar is considered to have been "broadcast" to an array of the same shape as the array operand). E.g., given the declaration

```
REAL, DIMENSION(10)  :: X, Y
```

the following are examples of array expressions:

```
X + Y          ! result has elements X(I) + Y(I)
X * Y          ! result has elements X(I) * Y(I)
X * 3          ! result has elements X(I) * 3
X * SQRT( Y )  ! result has elements X(I) * SQRT( Y(I) )
X == Y         ! result has elements .TRUE. if X(I) == Y(I),
               ! .. and .FALSE. otherwise
```

Note that when an array is the argument of an *elemental* intrinsic function, the function operates on each element of the array.

Two arrays of the same shape are *conformable*. A scalar is conformable with any array.

Note that binary operations apply to corresponding positions in the extent, not to corresponding subscripts. E.g.

```
X(2:5) + Y(4:7)
```

has element values

$$X(I) + Y(I+2), \quad I = 2, 3, 4, 5.$$

Array assignment   An array expression (this includes a scalar expression) may be assigned to an array variable of the same shape. Each element of the expression is assigned to the corresponding element of the target array. Again, correspondence is by position within the extent, rather than by subscript value. E.g.

```
REAL, DIMENSION(10)  :: X, Y
REAL, DIMENSION(5,5) :: A, C
X = Y                  ! both rank one with same size
```

```
Y = 0                  ! Y full of zeroes
X = 1 / X              ! replace each element of X
                       !   with its reciprocal
X = COS( X )           ! replace each element of X with its cosine
X(1:5) = Y(4:8)        ! both rank one with size 5
A(I, 1:J) = C(K, 1:J)  ! row K of matrix C assigned to row I of
                       !   matrix A
```

These facilities are extremely useful in numerical procedures such as Gauss reduction.

If the expression on the right of an array assignment refers to part of the array on the left, the expression is fully evaluated *before* the assignment begins. E.g.

```
X(1:3) = X(2:4)
```

results in each element of $X(I)$, I = 1, 2, 3 having the value that $X(I+1)$ had before the assignment began.

The WHERE construct   The WHERE construct may be used to perform an operation on only certain elements of an array, e.g.

```
WHERE (A > 0)
  A = LOG( A )     ! log of all positive elements
ELSEWHERE
  A = 0            ! all non-positive elements set to zero
END WHERE
```

The ELSEWHERE clause is optional. The construct is analogous to IF-THEN-ELSE.

The expression in parentheses after the keyword WHERE is a *logical array expression*, and may simply be a logical array. It is sometimes called a *mask*.

There is a corresponding WHERE statement:

```
WHERE (A /= 0) A = 1 / A ! replace non-zero elements by reciprocals
```

Array-valued functions   A function may be array-valued. If it is an external function, it needs an interface block.

Array handling intrinsic functions   There are a number of intrinsic functions which relate specifically to arrays. The complete list is in Appendix C. A sample is given here.

ALL(X) returns the value .TRUE. only if all the elements of the logical array X are true.

ANY(X) returns the value .TRUE. if any element of the logical array X is true. Otherwise it returns .FALSE.

SUM(X) and PRODUCT(X) return the sum and product of the elements of the integer, real or complex array X respectively.

In all these cases X can be an array expression, e.g.

```
INTEGER, DIMENSION(5,5) :: A
REAL X(3), Y(3)
 ...
```

```
IF (ANY(A > 0)) A = 1    ! if any element > 0 replace all by 1
IF (ALL(A == 0)) A = -1  ! if all elements = 0, replace all by -1
Dot = SUM( X * Y )       ! scalar product of X and Y
```

Summary

- Arrays are useful for representing and processing large amounts of data.
- An array is a collection of subscripted variables with the same name.
- Members of an array are called elements.
- The number of elements in an array is its size. The size may be zero.
- Upper and lower bounds of array subscripts are specified with the DIMENSION attribute in the array type specification statement.
- An array subscript may not fall outside the bounds specified by DIMENSION.
- An array subscript may be any valid numeric expression (rounded if necessary).
- The number of dimensions of an array is its rank. An array may have up to seven dimensions. A scalar has a rank of zero.
- The number of elements along a dimension of an array is the extent of the dimension.
- The sequence of the extents of an array is its shape.
- An array may be passed as an actual argument to a subprogram. The dummy argument must have the same shape. If the corresponding dummy argument is an assumed-shape array it will take on the shape of the actual argument.
- A dynamic variable (which may be an array) is specified with the ALLOCATABLE attribute and may be allocated memory while a program is running. The memory may be deallocated later.
- A dummy argument may not be allocatable.
- A rank-one array constant may be formed with an array constructor.
- An implied DO may be used in an array constructor.
- An array section is a subarray.
- A section subscript given by a rank-one integer expression is a vector subscript.
- Arrays with the same shape are conformable.
- A section is conformable with any array of the same shape.
- A scalar is conformable with any array.
- Array expressions may be formed from conformable arrays.
- Array expressions may be assigned to conformable arrays.
- When an elemental intrinsic function takes an array argument, the function is applied to each element of the array.
- The WHERE construct controls operations on array elements according to a logical mask.

Exercises

9.1 If Num is an integer array with the attribute DIMENSION(100) write the lines of coding which will

(a) put the first 100 positive integers $(1, 2, ..., 100)$ into the elements Num(1), ..., Num(100);

(b)　put the first 50 positive even integers $(2, \ldots, 100)$ into the elements `Num(1)`, ..., `Num(50)`;

(c)　assign the integers in *reverse* order, i.e. assign 100 to `Num(1)`, 99 to `Num(2)`, etc.

9.2　Write some statements to put the first 100 Fibonacci numbers (1, 1, 2, 3, 5, 8, ...) into an array `F(1)`, ..., `F(100)`.

9.3　Salary levels at an educational institution are (in thousands of dollars): 9, 10, 12, 15, 20, 35 and 50. The number of employees at each level are, respectively, 3000, 2500, 1500, 1000, 400, 100, 25. Write a program which finds and writes:

(a)　the average salary level;

(b)　the number of employees above and below the average level;

(c)　the average salary earned by an individual in the institution.

9.4　Write a program which reads 10 numbers into an array, and prints the mean, and the number in the array furthest in absolute value from the mean.

9.5　Develop a structure plan for the problem of writing all the primes less than 1000 (1 and 2 are generally regarded as primes, and will probably have to be dealt with separately). Write the program. **Hint**: use an array to store the primes as they are found.

9.6　In an experiment N pairs of observations (X_i, Y_i) are made. The *best straight line* that may be drawn through these points (using the method of *Least Squares*) has intercept A on the x-axis and slope B, where

$$B = (S_1 - S_2 S_3/N)/(S_4 - S_2^2/N),$$
$$A = S_3/N - S_2 B/N,$$

and $S_1 = \sum X_i Y_i$, $S_2 = \sum X_i$, $S_3 = \sum Y_i$, $S_4 = \sum X_i^2$.
The *correlation coefficient* R is given by

$$R = \frac{NS_1 - S_2 S_3}{\sqrt{NS_4 - S_2^2}\sqrt{NS_5 - S_3^2}},$$

where $S_5 = \sum Y_i^2$. ($R = 1$ implies a perfect linear relationship between X_i and Y_i. This fact can be used to test your program.) All the summations are over the range 1 to N. The observations are stored in a text file. It is not known how many observations there are. Write a program to read the data and compute A, B and R. **Hint**: you don't need arrays!

9.7　If a set of points (X_i, Y_i) are joined by straight lines, the value of Y corresponding to a value X which lies on a straight line between X_i and X_{i+1} is given by

$$Y = Y_i + (X - X_i)\frac{(Y_{i+1} - Y_i)}{(X_{i+1} - X_i)}.$$

This process is called *linear interpolation*. Suppose no more than 100 sets of data pairs are stored, in ascending order of X_i, in a text file. Write a program which will compute an interpolated value of Y given an arbitrary value of X keyed in at the keyboard. It is assumed that X is in the range covered by the data. Note that the data must be sorted into ascending order with respect to the X_i values. If this were not so, it would be necessary to sort them first.

10

Advanced Input and Output

So far we have concentrated on writing programs to solve various problems without paying too much attention to how the output looks. In this chapter we will see how to use FORMAT specifications to produce neater output. We will also look at data transfer involving files.

10.1   Rabbit Breeding the Fibonacci Way

To make the exercise more interesting, we will write a program to model a rabbit population using the following assumptions:

(1)   We start with one new-born male/female pair.

(2)   A new-born pair produce a male/female pair after two months.
(3)   Male/female pairs of age two months and older produce a male/female pair every month.

If we represent the number of male/female pairs after n months by the variable F_n, some scratching around with a pencil and paper soon reveals that F_n takes the following values:

Month n	1	2	3	4	5	6	7	8
Population F_n	1	1	2	3	5	8	13	?

The sequence $\{F_n\}$ is called the *Fibonacci* sequence. We want to write a program that computes the total population for up to, say, 12 months. Note that this model does not allow for deaths; this possibility is discussed in Chapter 15. It can be shown that each term in the sequence is the sum of the previous two, i.e.

$$F_n = F_{n-1} + F_{n-2}.$$

We therefore need to have three variables in the program, Fn, Fn_1 and Fn_2, which need to be updated each month (assuming that we are not going to use an array). An interesting feature of the Fibonacci sequence is that

$$\lim_{n \to \infty} \frac{F_n}{F_{n-1}} = (1 + \sqrt{5})/2 = 1.6179\ldots$$

We will also compute this ratio, to verify that it has a limit (in fact, the limit is the same whatever the first two values in the sequence are).

The program below uses FORMAT statements to control the layout of the output, to give you an idea of what can be done. The details are then discussed.

```
! Rabbit breeding the Fibonacci way

IMPLICIT NONE
INTEGER Month
REAL Fn, Fn_1, Fn_2

! Format specifications
10   FORMAT( 'Month', T12, 'Population', T27, 'Ratio' /     &
         5('-'), T12, 10('-'), T27, 5('-') / )
20   FORMAT( I3, T12, F7.1, T27, F6.4 )

! Now the executables
Fn_1 = 1
Fn_2 = 1
PRINT 10                          ! heading

DO Month = 3, 12
   Fn = Fn_1 + Fn_2
   PRINT 20, Month, Fn, Fn / Fn_1
```

```
      Fn_2 = Fn_1
      Fn_1 = Fn
   END DO

   END
```

Output:

```
Month        Population    Ratio
-----        ----------    -----

  3              2.0       2.0000
  4              3.0       1.5000
...
 12            144.0       1.6180
```

Briefly, we have replaced PRINT* with PRINT *n*, where *n* is the *label* (in the range 1–99999) of a FORMAT statement, which specifies how the output is laid out.

The first FORMAT statement prints the headings. T12 tabulates to column 12, before printing any further output. The slash (/) starts a new record (line feed). The 5 (as in 5('–')) repeats what follows immediately. Incidentally, the best way to get your headings right is to put them in *after* you have got the rest of the output looking as you want it.

The second FORMAT statement controls the output of the variables. I3 prints an integer over 3 columns. F7.1 prints a real over 7 columns with one decimal place. F6.4 prints a real over 6 columns with 4 decimal places.

FORMAT statements, which are non-executable in the sense that they don't actually initiate any action, are usually grouped together for ease of reference, e.g. at the beginning of a program.

10.2   The PRINT Statement

The general form of the PRINT statement is

   PRINT *fmt* [,*list*]

where *fmt* may be one of the following:

- a statement label referring to a FORMAT statement with the format specifications in parentheses, e.g.

   ```
      PRINT 10, X
   10 FORMAT( 'The answer is: ', F6.2 )
   ```

- an asterisk as in the list-directed I/O we have been using up to now, e.g.

   ```
      PRINT*, 'The answer is: ', X
   ```

- a character expression or constant which evaluates to a format specification in parentheses, e.g.

```
PRINT "( 'The answer is: ', F6.2 )", X
```

The quantities in *list* may be constants, expressions, variables, or implied DO lists of the form

(do-list, variable = expr1, expr2 [,expr3])

where items in *do-list* may themselves be implied DO lists.

READ can be used in the same way as PRINT, except that the quantities in the list must be variables.

10.3 Formatting Features

In this section we discuss the details of format control for input and output.

Edit descriptors *Edit descriptors*, such as F7.1 in the program above, specify exactly how a quantity should appear on output, or in preparation for input. More technically, they specify how a value represented internally by the computer should be converted into a (readable) character string on an output device or file, or converted from a character string on an input device or file.

There are three categories of edit descriptors: data, character string, and control.

Data edit descriptors In the descriptions below, the symbols w, m, d and e all represent integer constants, while b represents a blank.

In all cases involving numeric output, if the specified field width is too narrow it is filled with asterisks.

Integer values are converted by the I edit descriptor. The usual form is Iw, where w specifies the field width. The value is right justified in this field, which must allow room for a leading minus sign.

An alternative form for output is I$w.m$, which ensures that a minimum of m digits is printed, with leading zeros if necessary. E.g. I6.3 prints −99 as bb−099.

Binary, octal and hexadecimal values are also converted by the Bw, Ow and Zw edit descriptors respectively. The minimum number of digits m may also be specified. For input, the leading letter (B, O or Z) and the delimiters must be omitted. E.g.

```
READ '(B4)', I
```

will convert the input string 1111 into the decimal value 15.

Real values are converted by the F, E, EN or ES edit descriptors.

The F (fixed point) descriptor has the form F$w.d$, where w defines the total field width (including a possible sign and the decimal point), and d defines the number of digits after the decimal point (rounded if necessary). E.g. −12.345 is printed under F8.2 as bb−12.35. On input, if the input string has a decimal point, the value of d is ignored. E.g. b1.2345b is read under the descriptor F8.2 as 1.2345.

If the input string has no decimal point, the rightmost d digits are taken as the decimal part. E.g. b−12344 is read under F7.2 as −123.45.

There are two other forms of input possible under the F descriptor. If the input is in standard scientific notation, or if the E is omitted from the standard form and the exponent is signed, the *d* specifier is again ignored. E.g. 12.345E-2 (or 12.345-2*b*) is read under F9.1 as 0.12345.

The E edit descriptor has two forms. For both of them, the rules for input are the same as those for the F descriptor. On output, E*w.d* produces a mantissa (significand) of *d* digits with an absolute value less than 1 over a field of *w*. This must include room for a possible sign, the decimal point, and an exponent of four characters, consisting either of E followed by a sign and two digits, or of a sign and three digits. The form with E is not used if the magnitude of the exponent is greater than 99. E.g. 1.234×10^{23} is written under E10.4 as *b*.1234E+24 or *b*.1234+024.

The other form of the E descriptor is E*w.d*E*e*, where *e* determines the number of digits to appear in the exponent field. This form is mandatory for exponents with a magnitude greater than 999. E.g. 1.234×10^{1234} is written under E12.4E4 as *b*.1234E+1235.

The EN (*engineering*) edit descriptor is the same as the E descriptor except that on output the exponent is divisible by three, the mantissa is greater than or equal to 1 and less than 1000, and the scale factor (see below) is ignored. E.g. 0.00217 is written under EN9.3 as 2.170E-03 or 2.170-003.

The ES (*scientific*) edit descriptor is the same as the EN descriptor except that the mantissa is less than 10.

Complex values may be controlled by pairs of F, E, EN, or ES edit descriptors. The real and imaginary parts may have different descriptors, which may be separated by character string and control edit descriptors.

Logical values are controlled by the L edit descriptor in the form L*w*. On output T or F will appear in the right-most position of the field *w*. On input, optional blanks are optionally followed by a decimal point, followed by T or F (upper- or lowercase), optionally followed by additional letters. This curious arrangement is simply to allow the strings .TRUE. or .FALSE. to be input.

Character values are controlled by the A edit descriptor in one of two forms—A or A*w*. In the form A, the width of the I/O fields is determined by the length of the character variable or expression in the I/O list. E.g. if NAME is declared

```
CHARACTER NAME*7
```

then 7 characters are output, and 7 characters are input.

In the second form (A*w*), the *w* left-most characters are printed, on output. If necessary, the output field is blank-filled from the left.

The rules for input under the second form are a little strange. Suppose *len* is the length of the variable being read. If *w* is less than *len*, the left-most *w* characters are read, padded with blanks on the right. E.g. under A5, the input string NAPOLEON is read into NAME (as declared above) as NAPOL*bbb*.

However, and this is the strange bit, if *w* is greater than *len*, the *right-most len* characters are read. So under A8, for example, the string NAPOLEON is read into NAME as APOLEON. One would have expected the left-most characters to be read.

Finally, there are the *general* G*w.d* and G*w.d*E*e* edit descriptors, which may be used for any of the intrinsic data types. These descriptors are useful for printing values whose magnitudes are not well-known in advance. Where possible values are output under the equivalent F descriptor; otherwise the equivalent form with E is used.

The character string edit descriptor   A character constant (a string of characters enclosed in apostrophes or quotes) may be output by embedding it in a format specification, as we have already seen, e.g.

```
      PRINT 10
   10 FORMAT( 'Fortran 90 is the language for me' )
```

For completeness, we should mention the obsolescent H edit descriptor. It was named in honour of Hollerith, who invented punch cards to process a census in the United States during the last century. An output character string (without delimiters) may be preceded by an nH descriptor, where the integer constant n is the number of characters in the string, e.g.

```
   10 FORMAT( 24HWe must count carefully! )
```

The drawback is that you must count the number of characters in the string; it is very easy to make a mistake.

Control edit descriptors   These edit descriptors enable you to position output precisely, start a new record, skip columns on input, etc.

Embedded blanks   in input fields are treated either as zeros, or as nulls (the default). The default is overridden by the BN (blanks null) and BZ (blanks zero) edit descriptors. The new mode holds for the rest of the format specification, or until explicitly changed. E.g. the input string 1b31b3 is read under (BN, I3, BZ, I3) as the two values 13 and 103.

There are three descriptors which control the *leading* sign of a negative value on output. A leading minus is printed by default. The SP (sign print) edit descriptor causes leading positive signs to be printed. The SS (sign suppress) descriptor suppresses leading plus signs while SP is in effect, and the S descriptor restores the default option. E.g. the value 99 written three times under (SP, I3, SS, I3, S, I3) appears as +99b99b99. A sign descriptor holds for the rest of the format specification, unless changed by another sign descriptor.

Scale factors   of the form kP may be applied to input of real quantities under the E, F, EN, ES and G edit descriptors. k is an integer constant specifying the scale factor. Any quantity *without an exponent field* is *reduced* by a factor 10^k. E.g. 1.0 is read under (2P, F3.0) as 0.01. Quantities with an exponent are not affected.

A scale factor also affects output under E, F or G editing. Under F, a scale factor kP *multiplies* the output by a factor 10^k. Under E editing, and under G when the E option is taken, the exponent of the output is reduced by k, while the mantissa is multiplied by 10^k.

A scale factor holds for the rest of the format specification, or until another scale factor is encountered.

Tabulation   in input or output fields is possible in four ways. Tn causes tabulation to position n of the current I/O record. TRn (or nX) tabulates n positions to the right of the current position, and TL*n* tabulates *n* positions to the left of the current position (where in all cases tabulation can never go to the left of position 1).

On input, tabulation can be used to skip past data, or to re-read data. E.g. under (I1, 2X, I1) the input string 1234 is read as the two values 1 and 4.

On output, tabulation can be used in the conventional way, or for (partial) replacement. E.g. under (I3, TL2, I3) the values 911 and 999 are output as 9999.

A **new record** may be started at any point in a format specification by the slash (/) edit descriptor. It may have a *repeat count*, so /// is the same as 3/. It only needs to be separated by a comma from a preceding descriptor if it has a repeat count.

Colon editing stops format control if there are no more items in an I/O list. In particular, it is useful in preventing unwanted character strings from being printed. E.g. the statements

```
    PRINT 10, (X(I), I = 1, N )
10  FORMAT( 'X1:', I2 : ' X2:', I2 : ' X3:', I3 )
```

produce the output

```
    X1: 1
```

when N has the value 1. Without the colons, the output would have been

```
    X1: 1 X2:
```

Note that the colons do not need to be separated from neighbours by commas.

Repeat counts The data edit descriptors described above, as well as the new record (slash) descriptor, may all be preceded by a *repeat count* in the form of an integer constant. A repeat count may be applied to a group of edit descriptors enclosed in parentheses, and may be nested, e.g.

```
    3(2F6.2, 2(I2, 3I3))
```

If a format specification without any items in parentheses is completed before the I/O list is exhausted, a new record begins, and the format specification is repeated. Further records begin in the same way until the I/O list is exhausted. E.g. the following code prints an array of 100 elements, 20 elements per line:

```
    PRINT 10, (X(I), I = 1, 100)
10  FORMAT( 20I3 )
```

Similarly, on input, a new record is taken from the input file each time the specification is repeated. *Any excess input data on the record is ignored.* E.g. the code

```
    READ 10, I, J
10  FORMAT( I1 )
```

reads two values, 1 and 3, from the input records

```
12
34
```

A format specification without parentheses may therefore be thought of as a template of how the compiler sees the entire I/O record.

However, if a format specification contains items in parentheses, when the format is exhausted a new record is taken and format control reverts to the left parenthesis corresponding to the *second last* right parenthesis— including a possible repeat count outside the parentheses. This is called *reversion*. E.g. in

```
10    FORMAT( F5.0, 2(F6.1, 3(F7.2) ), F8.3 )
```

new records start at 2(F6.1, ...

Carriage control   Fortran's formatted output statements were originally designed for line printers. For output to such devices, the first character of each record is used for *carriage control* (an old-fashioned word from the days of mechanical typewriters). There are four options:

b (blank)	start a new line
+	remain on same line (overprint)
0	skip a line
1	advance to the beginning of a new page

A blank in the first column effectively means no action is taken, so it is good practice to make sure a blank is sent as the first character, e.g. by starting all format specifications with T2 (begin writing in position 2). Otherwise, for example, printing an integer under FORMAT(I3) will cause a page throw every time the integer is in the range 100–199!

These conventions will not necessarily work on a dot-matrix printer connected to a PC. However, a combination of OPEN and WRITE with the CHAR() intrinsic function can be used to send any special control characters to the printer. The following code sends a form feed character (new page):

```
    OPEN( 1, FILE = 'prn' )
    WRITE( 1, 10 ) CHAR( 12 )
10  FORMAT( A1 )
```

The control character is not restricted to the first position in the output record; it can be anywhere. In this way you can send any of your printer's special printing codes.

10.4 **Formatted** READ

The form of the READ statement we have used so far is

READ *fmt* [*,list*]

where *fmt* is a label, asterisk or character string, as in PRINT.

There is a more general form, which allows input from files, and which can intercept errors and end-of-file conditions gracefully, without causing the program to crash. It is

READ ([UNIT=]*u*, [FMT=]*fmt* [,IOSTAT=*ios*] [,ERR=*errorlabel*] [,END=*endlabel*]) [*list*]

The only obligatory items are the format specifier *fmt*, as described above, and the *unit* specifier *u*.

A unit is an I/O device, such as a printer, terminal, or disk drive, for example, which may be connected by the compiler to your program. Such a unit may have a *unit number* attached to it, which is usually in the range 1–99, for the duration of a program.

We have seen the only two situations where a unit number is not required. The PRINT normally expects to output to the terminal, and the first form of READ above normally expects to read from the terminal. In such cases, the terminal is called the standard I/O unit. Your system may allow you to change the standard unit.

The unit specifier *u*, when it is required, may be of three forms: an integer expression, an asterisk (which implies the standard input unit), or a character variable in the case of an internal file (see below).

The remaining specifiers are optional, and may be in any order. If IOSTAT is specified, *ios* must be an integer variable. After execution of READ *ios* has different (system-dependent) negative values depending on whether an end-of-record or end-of-file condition occurred, a positive value if an error was detected, or the value of zero otherwise. The presence of IOSTAT prevents a crash if an exception occurs.

Further details are given in Appendix B.

10.5 **Formatted** WRITE

The general form of the WRITE statement for formatted output is

WRITE ([UNIT=]*u*, [FMT=]*fmt* [,IOSTAT=*ios*] [,ERR=*errorlabel*]) [*list*]

The specifiers have the same meanings as in the READ statement.

The output device may be selected during program execution. You may be developing a large program which will eventually spew vast amounts of data out on the printer. To save time (and paper) while writing the program, you may want to be able to specify while the program is running where the output should go. The following code should help (PRN and CON are the names of the PC printer and terminal respectively):

```
CHARACTER OutputDevice*3
PRINT*, 'Where do you want the output ("prn" or "con")?'
```

```
OPEN( 1, FILE = OutputDevice )
WRITE( 1, * ) 'Output on designated device'
```

10.6　Internal Files

It was mentioned above that the unit specifier in READ or WRITE could be an *internal file*. This is basically a character variable (or array) which may be written to or read from. E.g.

```
CHARACTER(50) CAPTION
...
WRITE( CAPTION, 10 ) YEAR
10  FORMAT( 'Sales figures for the financial year: ', I4 )
```

CAPTION could then be used as a caption in a graphical display.

Internal files provide a general means of converting numeric data to strings, and vice versa. READ may be used to reverse the above process. In the code below, the string "1984" is converted to an integer with the value 1984.

```
CHARACTER (30) STRING
STRING = "1984"
READ( STRING, 10 ) NYEAR
10  FORMAT( I4 )
```

10.7　External Files

Output from a program may be sent to an *external file* (e.g. residing permanently on a disk), and input may also be fetched by a program from such a file. This powerful facility provides a means of keeping records which may need to be updated, examined and analysed.

There is a certain amount of jargon that needs to be overcome before we can proceed. In Fortran, a file is said to *exist* if a program *is able to access it*. Existence is therefore a relative term, defined from the point of view of the program attempting access. A file which exists for a program may or may not be empty, and it may or may not be *connected* to that program. A file is connected by association with a unit number known to the program. This connection is usually made by an OPEN statement, but certain files may be automatically *pre-connected*.

A file may be thought of as a stream of data, arranged into *records*. The records are all either formatted, or *unformatted*. Files may be accessed *sequentially*, or *directly*; normally a particular file is restricted to one mode of access. If access is direct, all records must have the same length; this is not necessary under sequential access.

In the rest of this chapter we outline the main file handling facilities of Fortran 90. More substantial examples follow in later chapters.

File positioning　A file has a *current position*, which may be

- within a record;
- between records;
- ahead of the first record (the *initial point*);
- after the last record (the *terminal point*).

Sequential files   A sequential file may be thought of as a continuous tape, where records are located sequentially along the tape. If the file is formatted, the records may be of varying length, i.e. the record length does not need to be specified.

A sequential file may be read only from the beginning. This makes the access time slower than for a direct access file, since to find something near the end of a sequential file, you have to read every record from the beginning. You also cannot replace or remove a record directly, as you can with direct access files. However, sequential files are helpful in situations where you might need to access the file with a word processor—in this context the file would be a text (or ASCII) file. We have seen sequential files in action in reading data from disk files.

The following example shows how to update a sequential file. It reads a line of text from the file, and asks you if you want to delete the line. If you don't want to delete the line, it is written to a temporary (SCRATCH) file. The original file is then deleted, a new empty file of the same name is created, and finally the contents of the temporary file is copied back. It sounds cumbersome, because it is cumbersome. Manipulation of sequential files usually is. Try the program out on a text file with a few names in it, which you can set up with your text editor.

```
CHARACTER(80) Name, FileName, Ans
WRITE( *, '(A)', ADVANCE = 'NO' ) "Name of file to be updated: "
READ*, FileName

OPEN( 1, FILE = FileName )
OPEN( 2, STATUS = 'SCRATCH' )

IO = 0
DO WHILE (IO == 0)
  READ( 1, *, IOSTAT = IO ) Name
  IF (IO == 0) THEN
    PRINT*, Name
    WRITE( *, '(A)', ADVANCE = 'NO' ) "Delete (Y/N)? "
    READ*, Ans              ! could be upper or lowercase
    IF (Ans /= 'Y' .AND. Ans /= 'y') WRITE( 2, * ) Name
  END IF
END DO

REWIND( 2 )                      ! back to the beginning of SCRATCH
CLOSE( 1, STATUS = 'DELETE' )    ! delete original
OPEN( 1, FILE = FileName )       ! recreate original

IO = 0
DO WHILE (IO == 0)
  READ( 2, *, IOSTAT = IO ) Name
  IF (IO == 0) WRITE( 1, * ) Name
```

```
END DO

CLOSE( 1 )                      ! keep
CLOSE( 2 )                      ! delete
END
```

Note that the two DO WHILE loops make use of the IOSTAT specifier to avoid an attempted READ past the end of the file.

The OPEN statement has the form

```
OPEN( [UNIT = ]u, speclist )
```

where *u* is the file unit number, and *speclist* is a list of specifiers, many of which are optional, and may be in any order. The unit number must appear first, unless it is specified with UNIT=. The specifiers are character expressions or constants. If character expressions are used, trailing blanks are ignored. Except for the FILE specifier, lowercase letters are converted to uppercase.

You also need to know that the OPEN statement can be executed on a unit number which is already connected to a file. This is to enable the properties of a connection to be changed, and is only allowed with certain specifiers, for example, the BLANK specifier which sets the default for the interpretation of blanks to nulls or zeros.

Some of the more common specifiers are described below; you should consult Appendix B for all the gory details.

The FILE specifier is a character expression which gives the name of the file. If this specifier is omitted (and the unit is not already connected) the STATUS specifier must appear with the value SCRATCH.

If SCRATCH is specified for the STATUS specifier (as above on unit 2), a temporary file is created. It ceases to exist when the unit is closed, or when the program terminates. If NEW is specified, the file must not already exist. If OLD is specified it must already exist. If REPLACE is specified, the file is created if it does not exist; if it does exist, it is deleted, and a new file is created with the same name.

The simple form of the OPEN statement used in the program above connects a file for sequential access (the default mode of access), with formatted records (the default for sequential access). These properties may be changed by the ACCESS and FORM specifiers, as we shall see below.

New data may be written at the *end* of a sequential file by setting the POSITION specifier to APPEND.

Errors (e.g. attempting to open a non-existent file with status OLD) may be intercepted with the IOSTAT and ERR specifiers. This avoids a crash; you can program a more graceful response.

A sequential file may be repositioned to its initial point with the statement

```
REWIND u
```

The statement

```
BACKSPACE u
```

positions a sequential file before the current record if it is positioned within a record, or before the preceding record if it is positioned between records. This statement is costly in computer overheads and should be avoided.

The end of a sequential file is marked by a special record called the *endfile* record. Most computer systems will automatically write this record at the end of a sequential file. However, if you are in doubt, you can write an endfile record explicitly with

ENDFILE *u*

A file is disconnected with a CLOSE statement. It can take the form

CLOSE([UNIT =]*u* [, STATUS = *st*])

where the STATUS may be specified as KEEP or DELETE. A file may therefore be erased on disconnection, as in the example above. The default value is KEEP, unless the file has status SCRATCH, in which case the default (and only) value is DELETE. All connected units are automatically closed when a program terminates normally (even if there are no CLOSE statements), and a CLOSE on an unconnected unit does not cause an error. However, you should make a point of closing all your files (and no others!), since it shows that you know what you are doing.

Unformatted I/O A file's records may be *unformatted*. The advantage of this is that they take up much less storage than formatted records. E.g. the largest integer available under the FTN90 compiler (2 147 483 647) takes up only 4 bytes on an unformatted record (since it can be represented with 32 bits), but 10 bytes on a formatted record (the number of characters required to represent it).

A sequential file is formatted by default, so the FORM specifier must be used if it is to be unformatted, as in the next example, which writes an integer array and reads it back.

```
INTEGER, DIMENSION(10) :: A = (/ (I, I = 1,10) /)
OPEN( 1, FILE = 'TEST', FORM = 'UNFORMATTED' )
WRITE (1) A
REWIND (1)
A = 0      ! just to be sure !
READ (1) A
PRINT*, A
CLOSE (1)
END
```

Note that to read the file it must be rewound, since it is sequential (by default).

Each READ and WRITE transfers exactly one record. The file created in this example therefore has one record, containing an array of 10 integers.

When output is to a sequential file a record of sufficient length is created. On input, the number of items in the input list must not exceed the number of values in the record.

Direct access files In the case of *direct* or *random* access files, a particular record may be read and/or rewritten, unlike the case with sequential access files, where records may not in general be replaced. Records may also be added at the end of a direct access file without rewriting the whole file. Direct access files are unformatted by default, and all their records must be the same length. This record length must be specified with the RECL specifier in the OPEN statement. Record length is generally the number of bytes occupied by the item written to the file, but may be system dependent. The INQUIRE statement may be used to find the record length (see below). The following example reads a list of names from the keyboard, writes them to a direct access file, reads them back, and finally replaces the third record.

```
CHARACTER (20) NAME
INTEGER I
INQUIRE (IOLENGTH = LEN) NAME
OPEN( 1, FILE = 'LIST', STATUS = 'REPLACE', ACCESS = 'DIRECT', &
         RECL = LEN )

DO I = 1, 6
  READ*, NAME
    WRITE (1, REC = I) NAME           ! write to the file
END DO

DO I = 1, 6
  READ( 1, REC = I ) NAME             ! read them back
  PRINT*, NAME
END DO

WRITE (1, REC = 3) 'JOKER'           ! change the third record

DO I = 1, 6
  READ( 1, REC = I ) NAME             ! read them back again
  PRINT*, NAME
END DO

CLOSE (1)
END
```

Note that a direct access file behaves like an array. In fact, if memory is in short supply, data can easily be handled with a direct access file, rather than in an array. If the file is stored on a RAM (virtual) disk there is practically no difference in access time.

The record number is given by the REC specifier in the READ and WRITE statements, which otherwise have the same forms as for sequential files.

The INQUIRE statement   This statement may be used to ascertain the status and attributes of connected files, and unit numbers, and the record length of an output list. It has three forms: INQUIRE by output list (as above), INQUIRE by unit, and INQUIRE by file.

Inquiry by output list has the form

INQUIRE (IOLENGTH = *length*) *output list*

This form may be used to establish the length of the unformatted record of an output list.

An example of inquiry by unit number is

INQUIRE ([UNIT =]*u*, EXIST = *allowed*)

The logical variable *allowed* will be assigned the value .TRUE. if unit number *u* is an allowed unit number for your system, and .FALSE. otherwise.

The existence of a file may be established similarly:

INQUIRE (FILE = *filename*, EXIST = *allowed*)

You can use the EXIST specifier to avoid accidentally overwriting or deleting an existing file.

The number of the record most recently read or written is returned with the NEXTREC specifier.

Further details are in Appendix B.

10.8 Non-advancing I/O

Normally READ and WRITE transfer complete records. This can be a nuisance. A new feature of Fortran 90 is *non-advancing* I/O, whereby a file is left positioned *within* the current record.

We have seen the use of non-advancing WRITE in giving screen prompts:

```
WRITE (*, '(A)', ADVANCE = 'NO') 'Enter a number: '
READ*, Number
```

Non-advancing READ can also be useful, for example, in reading individual characters from a text file. The following program counts the number of characters in a text file:

```
CHARACTER (1) ch
INTEGER IO, Num
OPEN( 1, FILE = 'TEXT' )
IO = 0
Num = 0

DO WHILE (IO /= -1)        ! EOF
  READ (1, '(A1)', IOSTAT = IO, ADVANCE = 'NO') ch
  IF (IO == 0) Num = Num + 1            ! genuine character read
END DO

PRINT*, Num
CLOSE (1)
END
```

Under FTN90 the IOSTAT specifier returns −1 when the end-of-file is encountered, as opposed to −2 for end-of-*record*.

Non-advancing I/O is not available with list-directed I/O.

10.9 Miscellaneous

For completeness, two further topics need to be mentioned here: list-directed I/O, and NAMELIST.

List-directed I/O   As we have seen, this takes the form

```
READ*,  list
PRINT* [, list]
```

Data in the input list may be separated by commas, slashes or at least one blank (*separators*). The real and imaginary parts of complex constants must be enclosed in parentheses.

Character constants enclosed in delimiters ('apostrophes' or "quotes") may be spread over more than one record. Delimiters may be omitted if the character constant does not contain a blank, comma, or slash; if it is contained within one record; if the first character is not a delimiter; and if the leading characters are not numeric followed by an asterisk.

The reason for the last proviso is that a data value which is to be repeated n times may be given a repeat count $n*$. E.g. 6*0 means the value zero is to be read six times.

If there is no data value between successive separators, the corresponding input item is left undefined (under the FTN90 compiler—although the standard requires that it is left *unchanged*). E.g. the code

```
CHARACTER (20) Name
A = 3; B = 3; C = 3; D = 3;
READ*, Name, A, B, C, D
PRINT '(A, 4F6.2)', Name, A, B, C, D
```

under the FTN90 compiler, with input

```
"fortran 90", 2*, 2*7
```

gives the output

```
fortran 90              2.20  2.20  7.00  7.00
```

(2.2 is a garbage undefined value).

NAMELIST   This is a curious facility which can be used to name a group of items for I/O purposes. It allows you to omit input data for some items in the group. The group of items is named in a NAMELIST statement (MYOUT in the example below). The group name may either be specified with the NML specifier in READ or WRITE, or it may replace the format specifier. An input record must be prefaced by & followed by the group name. Data values may be omitted (in which case the record must end with a slash), and do not have to be in the order specified in the NAMELIST statement. Items not specified in the input record are left unchanged. E.g.

```
INTEGER, DIMENSION(4) :: A = 7
NAMELIST/MYOUT/A, X, Y
```

```
X = 1
Y = 1
READ( *, MYOUT )
WRITE( *, NML = MYOUT )
```

Input:

```
&MYOUT A(1:2) = 2*1 Y = 3/
```

Output:

```
&MYOUT A = 1 1 7 7, X =   1.0000000, Y =   3.0000000/
```

The array section A(3:4) and the variable X are left unchanged.

Summary

- A record can be thought of as a line of input/output.
- Format specifies the layout of a record.
- Format may be specified by a labelled FORMAT statement, by an asterisk (list-directed I/O), or by a character string.
- The PRINT statement generally only handles output to the screen.
- Implied DO lists may appear in I/O lists.
- The WRITE statement can handle output to a file or printer.
- The READ statement handles input from a file or the keyboard.
- I/O may be list-directed, formatted or unformatted.
- Format is controlled by edit descriptors.
- The OPEN statement connects a file to a unit number, to enable transfer of data.
- The INQUIRE statement obtains information about files, unit numbers and record lengths of output lists.
- Various specifiers, such as IOSTAT, END, and ERR may be used in I/O statements to intercept and handle end-of-file conditions and possible errors.
- Data may be transferred directly to or from a character array, in the form of an internal file.
- Disk files are examples of external files.
- Files consist of records, which may be formatted or unformatted.
- Files are accessed sequentially (the default) or directly (random access).
- Under sequential access, records are formatted by default, and their length may vary.
- New records may be appended to a sequential file (added on at the end), but existing records may not be rewritten.
- Under direct access, records are unformatted by default, must all be the same length, and this record length must be specified in the OPEN statement.
- Under direct access, existing records may be rewritten, and new records may be appended.
- Direct access is generally more efficient than sequential access.
- If non-advancing I/O is specified, incomplete records may be transferred by READ or WRITE.

Exercises

10.1 Give the output of the following two program segments (indicate blanks and new lines carefully):

```
(a)  10   FORMAT (1X, 'M=', I3, 'N=', I4, 3X, 'X=', F6.1 / T3, E11.4)
          M = 117
          N = -27
          X = -0.1235E2
          Y = 1234.567
          PRINT 10, M, N, X, Y

(b)  10   FORMAT (I3, 1X, F6.2, F5.3, I2)
     20   FORMAT (T2, I2, F8.2 / T3. F3.1, I4 )
          READ 10, N, X, Y, J
          PRINT 20, J, X, Y, N

     Data: 0146729.123.61035
```

10.2 Show how each of the following values will be printed with the edit descriptors shown (assume that carriage control has been taken care of):

(a) −738 (I4)   (b) +738 (I3)
(c) 38.136 (F7.2)   (d) −100.64 (F6.1)
(e) 9876.545 (E10.4) (f) −0.000044009 (E9.2)

10.3 Write a program which will count all the non-blank characters in a text file of any size.

10.4 (a) Write a program which sets up a direct access file where each unformatted record contains a one-dimensional integer array of size 10, say. Write some test data to the file, and read it back to make sure it got there.

(b) Write a separate program which will add one extra record of the same length to the end of the file created in part (a).

10.5 Write a program which will read a positive integer (of any size), find its binary code, and print the binary code on one line with no blanks between the digits. **Hint**: after finding each binary digit, store it in a different element of an allocatable array.

11
Handling Characters

We have seen some simple examples of the use of the intrinsic character type. Armed with the further weapons of arrays and more advanced I/O facilities we can now tackle more interesting problems involving characters, or *strings* as they are often called.

11.1 Characters

To recap, a *character constant* is a string of characters enclosed in delimiters, which are either 'apostrophes' or "quotes". The delimiters are not part of the string.

Character variables may be declared in the following ways:

```
CHARACTER ALPHA            ! length of 1
CHARACTER (15) Name        ! length of 15
CHARACTER Word*5           ! length of 5
```

Assignment is done as follows:

```
Name = "Bonaparte, N"
```

11.2   Bar Charts and Frequency Distributions

The first example utilizes an array and the A edit descriptor for printing characters.

Suppose we want to analyse the results of a test written by a class of students. We would like to know how many students obtained percentage marks in the range 0–9, 10–19, ..., 90–99. Each of these ranges is called a *decile*, numbered from zero for convenience. We also need to cater for the bright sparks who get 100 (the eleventh "decile"). Suppose the numbers of students who get marks in these ranges are as follows:

```
1   0   12   9   31   26   49   26   24   6   1
```

i.e. 12 obtained marks in the range 20–29. We need an array F(0:10), say, with 11 elements, where each element stores the number of students with marks in that particular range, e.g. F(2) should have the value 12. The following program prints a bar chart of the *frequency distribution* F, where each asterisk represents one student in that range:

```
      INTEGER, DIMENSION(0:10) :: F = (/ 1, 0, 12, 9, 31, 26, 49, &
                                26, 24, 6, 1 /)

10    FORMAT( I3, ' - ', I3, '  (', I3, '):', 60A1 )
20    FORMAT( '100', 6X, '  (', I3, '):', 60A1 )

      DO I = 0, 10
        IF (I < 10) THEN
            PRINT 10, 10 * I, 10 * I + 9, F(I), ('*', J = 1, F(I))
        ELSE
            PRINT 20, F(I), ('*', J = 1, F(I))
        END IF
      END DO

      END
```

Output:

```
 0 -   9 (  1):*
10 -  19 (  0):
20 -  29 ( 12):************
30 -  39 (  9):*********
40 -  49 ( 31):*******************************
50 -  59 ( 26):**************************
60 -  69 ( 49):*************************************************
70 -  79 ( 26):**************************
```

```
80 -  89  ( 24):************************
90 -  99  (  6):******
100       (  1):*
```

Note the absence of asterisks for the 10–19 decile. This is because F(1) has the value zero, so that the implied DO in the PRINT statement has a zero trip count when I has the value 1.

Of course, in a real situation, the frequencies will not be presented to you neatly on a plate. You are more likely to have a list of the actual marks. You should adapt the program to read a sample set of marks, in the range 0–100, and to convert them into frequencies. The basic mechanism is

```
READ( ... ) MARK
K = INT( MARK / 10 )         ! K is the decile
F(K) = F(K) + 1              ! another mark in the Kth decile
```

11.3 Sorting Words

Characters may be compared in IF statements; this is the basis of alphabetic sorting. Each computer system has a *collating sequence* which specifies the intrinsic ordering of the available character set. The Fortran 90 standard requires only that

- A < B < C ... < Y < Z
- 0 < 1 < 2 ... < 8 < 9
- blank < A and Z < 0, or blank < 0 and 9 < A

If lowercase letters are available, there are the further requirements that

- a < b < c ... < y < z
- blank < a and z < 0, or blank < 0 and 9 < a

Note that the standard does not insist on how the lowercase characters are to be ordered relative to uppercase.

There are two intrinsic functions that relate a character to its position in the collating sequence (or more simply, its code). ICHAR('A') returns an integer code for its character argument, e.g. 65, say, in this case. CHAR(90) returns the character coded by its integer argument, e.g. Z, say.

Furthermore, the standard requires that access be provided to the ASCII (American Standard Code for Information Interchange) collating sequence, in which Z < a (see Appendix D). There are two further intrinsic functions, which specifically relate a character to its ASCII code: IACHAR and ACHAR.

However, some computers make use of the EBCDIC collating sequence (Extended Binary Coded Decimal Interchange Code—pronounced "ebsadik"). In EBCDIC, unfortunately, the lowercase characters come *before* the uppercase ones, so z < A. This has implications for word sorting, since we normally require that

bOnApArTe < NaPoLeOn

whatever the case of the characters.

One way out is always to use ASCII code, but this may be inefficient on some computer systems. A more general solution is to write a subroutine to convert lowercase alphabetic letters to uppercase, based on ICHAR and CHAR, which do not rely on the ASCII code. The subroutine ToUpper in the next program does this. It uses ICHAR('A') and ICHAR('a') to determine the "distance" between the upper- and lowercase letters (assuming all the letters of one case to be contiguous, i.e. to have consecutive codes). It then adds this distance to all the lowercase letters in the word—carefully avoiding uppercase letters and all non-letters. To test it, the program reads two words from the keyboard (e.g. NAPOLEON and bonaparte), prints them in "ascending" order as they are, converts them both to uppercase, and prints them in order again.

```
IMPLICIT NONE
CHARACTER (10) Word1, Word2

READ*, Word1
READ*, Word2

IF (Word1 < Word2) THEN
   PRINT*, Word1, Word2
ELSE
   PRINT*, Word2, Word1
END IF

CALL ToUpper( Word1 )
CALL ToUpper( Word2 )

IF (Word1 < Word2) THEN
   PRINT*, Word1, Word2
ELSE
   PRINT*, Word2, Word1
END IF

CONTAINS
   SUBROUTINE ToUpper( String )
      CHARACTER (LEN = *) String
      INTEGER I, Ismall, IBIG
      Ismall = ICHAR( 'a' )
      IBIG = ICHAR( 'A' )

      DO I = 1, LEN( String )
        IF (String(I:I) >= 'a' .AND. String(I:I) <= 'z') THEN
          String(I:I) = CHAR( ICHAR( String(I:I) ) + IBIG - Ismall )
        END IF
      END DO

   END SUBROUTINE
END
```

Note that an individual character may be referenced as a substring (String(I:I)) and that a character dummy argument in a subprogram may be declared with an asterisk to have an *assumed length*. The intrinsic function LEN returns the actual length of the argument.

The Bubble Sort of Chapter 9 can easily be amended to sort words alphabetically. Suppose we have up to 100 words each of 10 letters or less (they can be read from a text file). List must now be declared in the main program as follows:

```
CHARACTER (10), DIMENSION (100) :: List
```

The corresponding dummy argument in the subroutine BUBBLE_SORT must be declared as

```
CHARACTER (*), DIMENSION(:), INTENT(INOUT) :: X
```

The variable TEMP in the subroutine must be declared CHARACTER (10) (alternatively, it could be passed as an argument and declared with an assumed length). Finally, you should incorporate ToUpper if the words will be of mixed case.

Note incidentally, that blanks in words are significant, so that

```
Mc Bean < McBean
```

since the blank precedes the letters.

11.4 Graphs without Graphics

The following example shows how easily a simple graph can be drawn on the text screen (it could also be written to a file, or the printer). It makes use of an internal file and character substrings to draw a sine graph over one period. This technique can only draw graphs with no more than one plotting symbol per line of output. A more general graphing procedure is discussed in Chapter 15.

```
      CHARACTER (70) Line
      REAL, PARAMETER :: Pi = 3.1415927
      REAL dx, X
      INTEGER N, Trips
10    FORMAT( A70 )

      dx = Pi / 20
      Trips = INT( 2*Pi/dx + dx/2 ) + 1
      X = 0

      PRINT "(' X', T37, 'SIN(X)')"           ! heading
      PRINT*

      DO I = 1, Trips
        WRITE( Line, '(F4.2)' )X               ! Line is an internal file
        N = NINT( 25 * (1 + SIN(X)) ) + 15
        Line(40:40) = ':'
        Line(N:N) = '*'
```

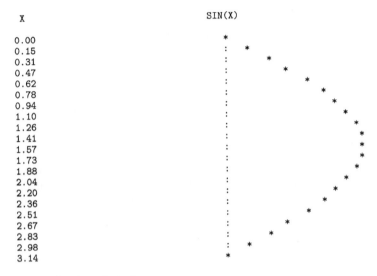

Fig. 11.1 Graph on the text screen

```
      PRINT 10, Line
      X = X + dx
   END DO

   END
```

Part of the output is shown in Figure 11.1.

11.5 Word Count and Extraction

When the authorship of a piece of prose is uncertain it sometimes helps to calculate the average number of words per sentence, and the standard deviation of this statistic. A first-year class of mine once found that with samples of about 700 lines, G.K. Chesterton is easily distinguishable from Lord Macaulay, the former having a significantly shorter mean sentence length, with a larger standard deviation. One of the exercises at the end of the chapter invites you to write a program to compute the average sentence length of a sample of text. An important part of the problem is to detect, extract and count whole words in the text. The next program reads a text file of any length, prints out one word per line (to indicate that whole words have been extracted), counting them as it does so.

It is assumed that words are separated by at least one blank—a word is defined as a string of one or more non-blank characters. So punctuation marks, like commas and full stops will not be counted as separate words, as long as they are not preceded by blanks. However, punctuation marks are filtered out before printing a word.

The most important part of the problem is to detect complete words. This takes time to think out. It often helps to think how you would explain the problem (not even the answer) to someone who didn't know the first thing about it. Imagine a stream of characters coming past you. How would you know when a complete word had passed? Surely, when a non-blank changes to a blank—it's the *change* from non-blank to blank that signals the end of a word. Realizing this will give you the Aha! experience that problem solvers rave about. So the essence of the problem is to read the text one character at a time, keeping a record of the *previous* character (OldCh) in order to compare it with the *current* character (Ch). If the previous character is non-blank when the current one is blank, we've found another word.

The rest is just mopping up. OldCh must be initialized to a blank, to start the ball rolling. If the last character in the text is a non-blank, the above argument will not catch the last word, so it's necessary to check for this after completion of the DO WHILE loop.

Non-advancing READ must be used to get one character at a time. The IOSTAT specifier returns a value of −1 under FTN90 when the end-of-file is encountered.

The intrinsic function INDEX is used to determine whether the current character is alphabetic. In the form used here it has two arguments. The first is a character constant LETTER, consisting of all the upper- and lowercase letters. The second is the current character Ch. INDEX returns the position of Ch in LETTER if it occurs there, or zero otherwise.

```
IMPLICIT NONE
CHARACTER OldCh, Ch
CHARACTER :: BL = " "
CHARACTER (*), PARAMETER :: LETTER = &
        "ABCDEFGHIJKLMNOPQRSTUVWXYZabcdefghijklmnopqrstuvwxyz"
INTEGER   :: WORDS = 0
INTEGER   :: IO = 0

OPEN( 1, FILE = 'TEXT' )
OldCh = BL

DO WHILE (IO /= -1)                       ! check for EOF
  READ (1, '(A1)', IOSTAT = IO, ADVANCE = 'NO') Ch
  IF (IO == 0) THEN                  ! protect against EOR and EOF
    IF (Ch == BL .AND. OldCh /= BL) THEN   ! arrival of blank ...
      WORDS = WORDS + 1                     ! ... signals end of
                                            !     word
      PRINT*                                ! new line
    ELSE IF (INDEX( LETTER, Ch ) /= 0) THEN! Ch must be a letter
      WRITE (*, '(A1)', ADVANCE = 'NO') Ch ! part of word
    END IF
    OldCh = Ch
  END IF
END DO

IF (OldCh /= BL) THEN ! if last char actually read is non-blank ..
  WORDS = WORDS + 1   ! ... count another word
```

```
   PRINT*                    ! new line
END IF

PRINT*
PRINT*, 'No of words: ', WORDS
END
```

11.6   General Information

Character substrings   Suppose the following character variable has been declared:

```
CHARACTER (80) TEXT
```

Individual characters in TEXT may be referenced using a *substring* notation, e.g.
TEXT(I:J) references a substring of TEXT from the Ith character to the Jth one. If
I is greater than J, the substring is empty. The colon is obligatory, but there are
default values of the subscripts, e.g.

```
TEXT(:J)                  ! same as TEXT(1:J)
TEXT(J:)                  ! same as TEXT(J:80)
TEXT(:)                   ! same as TEXT(1:80) or TEXT
```

A substring may be formed from a character constant, e.g.

```
"NAPOLEON"(3:6)
```

returns POLE.
   Following are some examples of substring expressions and assignments:

```
TEXT = "abcdefghijk"
TEXT(1:3) = "XY"          ! returns "XY defghijk"
                          ! (blank at 3rd position)
TEXT(5:5) = "*"           ! returns "XY d*fghijk"
                          ! (replaces 5th character)
TEXT(5:) = TEXT(6:)       ! returns "XY dfghijk"
                          ! (deletes 5th character)
TEXT(8:7)                 ! returns "" (null)
```

To *insert* a character at position I, each character beyond I must be moved up one
position first, in a DO loop:

```
CHARACTER (80) :: LINE = "abcdefghijklm"
I = 5

DO J = LEN_TRIM( LINE ), I, -1
  LINE( J+1:J+1 ) = LINE(J:J)
END DO

LINE(I:I) = "*"      ! returns "abcd*efghijklm"
```

The intrinsic function LEN_TRIM returns the length of its string argument with trailing blanks removed (otherwise J+1 goes out of range in the loop). Incidentally, can you see why the DO loop has to work backwards?

If substring ranges overlap in an assignment, the original values are always used on the right-hand side, e.g.

```
TEXT(1:8) = "NAPOLEON"
TEXT(3:5) = TEXT(1:3)     ! returns "NANAPEON" (not in FORTRAN 77)
```

Substrings may be passed by reference to subprograms, i.e. changes to them in the subprogram are reflected on return. However, this means that in a call such as

```
CALL JUNK( NAME(1:5), NAME(3:9) )
```

the characters common to both actual arguments, i.e. NAME(3:5), may not be changed through either corresponding dummy argument in the subprogram.

An array of characters may be declared:

```
CHARACTER (80), DIMENSION(60) :: LINE
```

Then the Ith character of the array element LINE(J) is referenced as

```
LINE(J)(I:I)
```

Note that the array subscript *precedes* the substring subscripts.

Assumed character length We have already seen that a dummy character argument may be declared with an assumed length. A named character constant (parameter) may also be declared with an assumed length, if you can't be bothered to count the number of characters. E.g.

```
SUBROUTINE JUNK( Word )
  CHARACTER (*), INTENT(IN) :: Word
  CHARACTER (*), PARAMETER :: Message = "Can't open file"
```

Concatenation The *concatenation* operator (//) is the only intrinsic operator for character expressions, e.g.

```
CHARACTER (5)  :: Initials = "JK"
CHARACTER (20) :: Surname = "Smith"
CHARACTER (7)  :: RegNo = "123456K"
CHARACTER (9)  :: UserId
UserId = Initials(1:1) // Surname(1:1) &
                    // RegNo  ! returns "JS123456K"
```

Embedded format Character expressions may be used to construct format specifications during program execution. The next code fragment reads an integer, and prints it out as an ordinal number with the correct suffix, e.g. 23 is output as 23rd, while 24 is output as 24th:

```
CHARACTER (2), DIMENSION(0:9) &
                        :: SUFF = (/ 'th', 'st', 'nd', &
             'rd', 'th', 'th', 'th', 'th', 'th', 'th' /)
CHARACTER (10) :: FMT = "(I5, '??')"
READ*, N
LastDigit = MOD( N, 10 )
FMT(7:8) = SUFF( LastDigit )    ! replace ?? appropriately
PRINT FMT, N
```

Character array constructors The elements of a character array in a constructor must all have the length specified by the length parameter. Pad with blanks if necessary:

```
CHARACTER (6), DIMENSION(3) :: Primary = (/ "RED   ", "BLUE  ", &
                                            "YELLOW" /)
```

Character handling intrinsic functions Fortran 90 has a number of new intrinsic functions relating to strings of characters, which greatly enhance its string-handling capabilities, putting it on a par with languages such as Pascal and C. A brief description of what they can do is given here; details are in Appendix C.

ADJUSTL adjusts left to return a string with leading blanks removed and inserted as trailing blanks. ADJUSTR adjusts right.

INDEX returns the starting position of the first (or last) occurrence of a substring in a string.

LEN returns the length of a string.

LEN_TRIM returns the length of a string without its trailing blanks.

REPEAT returns a string formed from multiple concatenations of a string, e.g. REPEAT("X", 3) returns XXX.

SCAN returns the position of the left- or rightmost character of one string which appears in another.

TRIM returns a string with all its trailing blanks removed.

VERIFY returns zero if each character in one string appears in another string, or the position of the left- or rightmost character of one string which does not appear in another string. E.g.

```
CHARACTER (*), PARAMETER :: LETTER = &
            "ABCDEFGHIJKLMNOPQRSTUVWXYZabcdefghijklmnopqrstuvwxyz"
CHARACTER (10) Word
IF (VERIFY( Word, LETTER ) == 0) PRINT*, 'It''s a word!'
```

The intrinsic subroutine DATE_AND_TIME(DATE, TIME, ZONE, VALUES) returns the date and time in various forms.

Recall that a number can be converted to its string representation and vice versa by writing to or reading from an internal file.

Summary

- The set of available characters is ordered into one or more collating sequences.

- Fortran 90 provides access to the ASCII collating sequence.
- Character variables may be compared and ordered on the basis of the collating sequence.
- Character substrings may be referenced.
- Character expressions may be concatenated.
- Character constants and dummy arguments may be declared with an assumed length, using an asterisk.
- Fortran 90 has a powerful set of character handling intrinsic functions.
- Format specifications may be constructed at runtime, using character variables.

Exercises

11.1 Write a program which reads some text (e.g. one line into a variable CHARACTER (80) LINE) and counts the number of blanks in it.
Extend it to remove the blanks.

11.2 Write a program which reads a sentence (ending in a full stop) and prints it backwards, without the full stop.
You might like to extend your program to check whether a sentence is a palindrome, i.e. one which reads the same backwards as forwards, such as REWARD A TOYOTA DRAWER (someone who draws Toyotas, presumably), or Napoleon's classic lament, ABLE WAS I ERE I SAW ELBA. Assume there is no punctuation, and remove all the blanks first.

11.3 A formula, called Zeller's Congruence, may be used to compute the day of the week, given the date (within a certain range of dates). The formula is

$$f = ([2.6m - 0.2] + k + y + [y/4] + [c/4] - 2c) \text{ modulo } 7,$$

where the square brackets denote the integer part and

- m is the month number, with January and February taken as months 11 and 12 of the preceding year, so March is then month 1, and December month 10;
- k is the day of the month;
- c is the century number;
- y is the year in the century;
- $f = 0$ means Sunday, 1 means Monday, etc.

E.g. 23rd August 1963 is represented by $m = 6$, $k = 23$, $c = 19$, $y = 63$; 1st January 1800 is represented by $m = 11$, $k = 1$, $c = 17$, $y = 99$.

Write a program to read the date in the usual form (e.g. 27 3 1993 for 27th March 1993) and write the given date and the day of the week (in words) on which it falls. **Hint:** use an array of characters for the days of the week. Test your program on some known dates, like today's date, or your birthday, or 7th December 1941 (Sunday).

The formula will not work if you go too far back. Shakespeare and Cervantes both died on 23rd April 1616. Shakespeare died on a Tuesday, but Cervantes died on a Saturday! This is because England had not yet adopted the Gregorian calendar and was consequently ten days behind the rest of the world. The formula will also not work if you go too far forward.

11.4   Write a program which will read a number in binary code of arbitrary length (e.g. 1100—no blanks between the digits) and write its decimal value (12 in this case). **Hint:** read the number as a string, and use an internal file to read the individual characters as integers.

11.5   Write a program to convert the contents of a text file to uppercase. You can try it out on the following text if you like:

> Roses are red
> violets are blue
> I'm schizophrenic
> and so am I.

11.6   Write a program which reads some text from a file, removes all the blanks, and prints it out in five-letter groups, separated by blanks. E.g. the text

> Twas brillig and the slithy toves
> did gyre and gimble in the wabe ...

should be printed as

```
Twasb rilli gandt hesli thyto vesdi dgyre andgi mblei nthew abe
```

11.7   Student numbers at the University of Cape Town are constructed from the first letter and next two *consonants* of the student's surname, the first three letters of her first name (padded from the right with Xs if necessary, in both cases), followed by a three-digit number, left-filled by zeros if necessary, to distinguish students for whom these six characters are the same. E.g. Napoleon Onaparte could get the student number ONPNAP001, while Charles Wu could get WXXCHA001.

Write a program which reads a student's surname and first name, in some convenient way, and prints out her student number (you can assume the suffix 001 for everyone).

11.8   Sometimes it is convenient to "pack" character and numeric data into strings. Such strings need to be "unpacked" again. Write a program to read a line of text containing a student's surname and initials, terminated by a comma, and followed by two marks, separated by at least one blank, e.g.

```
Smith JR, 34.6    78.9
```

The program should unpack the string into a character variable for the name and initials, and two real variables for the marks.

11.9   Write a program to read text from a file and compute the average number of words per sentence, and its standard deviation. Assume that sentences end with full stops, which occur nowhere else.

11.10   Languages exhibit a characteristic frequency distribution of single letters if a large enough sample of text is analysed. For example, in Act III of *Hamlet* the blank has a frequency of 19.7%, "e" 9.3%, "o" 7.3%, while "z" occurs only 14 times out of 35224 characters. (The blank is important because it gives an indication of word length.) Write a program to determine the letter frequency of a sample of text in a text file. Assume that blanks only occur singly (otherwise you must first reduce all multiple blanks to single blanks).

11.11   Write a program which will read a person's name and address from a disk file and use the data to write a "form letter" with a special offer to paint his house. The data in the file should be in the form

```
Jones
31
Campground Rd
```

If this data is used, the program output should be as follows:

```
Dear Mr Jones
We will paint your house with Sloshon at half price!
You can have the smartest house in Campground Rd.
The Jones family will be able to walk tall again.
Your neighbours at number 33 will be amazed!
```

The items in italics are read (or derived) from the data in the file.

11.12   Read up about the intrinsic subroutine DATE_AND_TIME in Appendix C. Use it to write a function TIS which returns the time in seconds (including milliseconds) elapsed since midnight.

Such a function could be used to time accurately operations in a program, e.g. sorting.

12

Derived Types: Structures

So far we have restricted ourselves to the five intrinsic data types of Fortran 90. We have seen how to use simple variables and arrays of these types to solve a variety of problems. We may, however, soon discover situations where it would be very convenient to handle more complicated collections of data as single units. Arrays, for example, are restricted in that all their elements must be of the same type.

One of the major advances of Fortran 90 over previous versions is that you now have the freedom to design data types of your own. Such data types are called *derived*. In this chapter we will discuss derived data types, which may be used to define *structures*.

12.1 Structures

As an example, let's consider the problem of maintaining student records. We have often used examples where we have processed, say, a student's name and some marks. In a real situation, additional information would be needed: address, registration and telephone numbers, and maybe even date of birth and gender. You can define a type to encapsulate all this data for one person as follows:

```
TYPE First_Year
   CHARACTER (20) Name                        ! includes initials, etc.
   CHARACTER (20), DIMENSION(4) :: Address ! 4 lines for address
   CHARACTER (10) Telephone
   CHARACTER (9) RegNo     ! e.g. SHKWIL001 as in Ex. 12.7
   LOGICAL Female          ! .TRUE. for female, .FALSE. for male (!)
   INTEGER BirthDate       ! e.g. 461121
   REAL, DIMENSION(20) :: Marks   ! Marks
END TYPE
```

This is called the *definition* of the *derived type* First_Year. A variable of this type is declared as follows

```
TYPE (First_Year) Student
```

and is called a *structure*. In this case it has seven *components*: Name, Address, etc. Note that the seventh component is a real array, for up to 20 marks. The components are referenced with the *component selector* (%). E.g.

```
Student % Birthdate = 461121
```

The components may appear in any expression where a variable of the same type (as the component) would be appropriate.

We can even declare an array of our derived type:

```
TYPE (First_Year), DIMENSION (100) :: Class
```

Since an array section may end with a structure component, the statement

```
Class % Female = .FALSE.
```

will then, for example, set the whole class' gender to male.

To illustrate some more of the properties of structures, let's define a simpler derived type:

```
TYPE Student_Type
   CHARACTER (20) NAME
   REAL Mark
END TYPE
```

Derived types have literal constants, e.g.

```
Student_Type( "Smith, JR", 49 )
```

The order of components must follow their order in the definition. Although individual components may be assigned using the component selector, as above, all the components may be assigned from the constant using a *structure constructor*, either in an initialization, or in an ordinary assignment:

```
TYPE (Student_Type) :: Student1 = Student_Type( "Bloggs", 50 )
```

A variable of a derived type may appear in an I/O list, as long as there is an appropriate format specification for each component:

```
PRINT '(A20, F6.0)', Student1
```

A variable of a derived type may be assigned to another variable of the same type:

```
Student2 = Student1
```

All the components of Student2 are replaced by the corresponding components of Student1.

Defined assignments (overloading) We have just seen that the intrinsic assignment operator (=) is automatically available for derived types. We can, however, *redefine* the assignment operator, by *overloading* it. This feature of Fortran 90, as well as general operator overloading, which is present in object-oriented programming languages like C++, will astonish Fortran 77ers. It may take a little getting used to.

Suppose, as a simple illustration, we want to redefine the assignment for Student_Type in two ways. First, we would like a short-hand way of assigning a name directly, without using the component selector, or a constructor, e.g.

```
Student = "Smith, JR"
```

on the understanding that *no value is assigned to the mark*.

Second, we would like to extract the name directly from the variable, again without using the component selector, e.g.

```
StuName = Student
```

where StuName is a character variable.

What this amounts to is a redefinition of the assignment operator to handle mixed types—character and derived—in the same way that the intrinsic assignment operator can already handle mixing of certain types.

For the first case, we need a subroutine Student_From_Name, say, with two dummy arguments, which are of type Student_Type and character. The order of dummy arguments is important, and must be the same as the order in which the types appear in the assignment to be redefined. This subroutine should assign Student % Name explicitly to the character argument.

For the second case, we need a subroutine Name_From_Student, say, with dummy arguments of type character and Student_Type (reverse order now). This subroutine should assign its character argument to Student % Name.

The most efficient way to handle this is to set up a module with the Student_Type definition and the two subroutines:

```
MODULE StudentMod

TYPE Student_Type
   CHARACTER (20) NAME
   REAL Mark
END TYPE
```

```
INTERFACE ASSIGNMENT(=)
  MODULE PROCEDURE Name_From_Student, Student_From_Name
END INTERFACE

CONTAINS
  SUBROUTINE Name_From_Student( String, Student )
    CHARACTER (*) String
    TYPE (Student_Type) Student
    String = Student % Name
  END SUBROUTINE

  SUBROUTINE Student_From_Name( Student, String )
    CHARACTER (*) String
    TYPE (Student_Type) Student
    Student % Name = String
  END SUBROUTINE
END MODULE
```

An interface block, using the keyword ASSIGNMENT, is required to overload the assignment operator with these two subroutines. It is shown here in the module, although it could also be in the main program.

A complete main program is then:

```
USE StudentMod

TYPE (Student_Type) :: Student = Student_Type( "Bloggs", 50 )
CHARACTER (20) StuName

Student = "Smith, JR"    ! assigns only the name in one direction
StuName = Student        ! assigns only the name in the
                         ! other direction

PRINT '(A20, F6.0)', Student
PRINT*, StuName
END
```

Note that subroutines are needed to redefine the assignment operator. Other operators are redefined with functions, as we shall see now.

Assignment for intrinsic types may not be redefined.

Defined operators (overloading) Operators may be defined for derived types in a similar, although not identical, way.

Consider the following example, adapted from the FTN90 *Reference Manual*. The module IntegerSets defines a type SET (similar to the set type of Pascal). Variables of this type can be constructed from the integers with the function BuildSet. A set membership operator (.IN.) is defined (e.g. I.IN.S1 returns TRUE if the integer I is a member of the set S1). The * operator is overloaded with the operation of set intersection (so that, for example, S1*S2 returns elements which are members of both S1 and S2). *Overloading* in this context means that the operator retains its original intrinsic meaning when the operands are intrinsic types (integer, real or complex in this case), but that it has a new meaning when the operands are of the derived type.

```
MODULE IntegerSets

IMPLICIT NONE
INTEGER, PARAMETER :: MaxCard = 100

TYPE SET
  PRIVATE
  INTEGER Cardinality
  INTEGER, DIMENSION( MaxCard ) :: Members
END TYPE SET

INTERFACE OPERATOR (.IN.)
  MODULE PROCEDURE MemberOf
END INTERFACE

INTERFACE OPERATOR (*)
  MODULE PROCEDURE Intersect
END INTERFACE

CONTAINS

FUNCTION BuildSet( V )
  TYPE (SET) BuildSet
  INTEGER V(:)
  INTEGER J
  BuildSet % Cardinality  = 0
  DO J = 1, SIZE( V )
    IF (.NOT.(V(J) .IN. BuildSet)) THEN
      IF (BuildSet % Cardinality < MaxCard) THEN
        BuildSet % Cardinality = BuildSet % Cardinality + 1
        BuildSet % Members( BuildSet % Cardinality ) = V(J)
      ELSE
        PRINT*, 'Maximum set size exceeded - adjust MaxCard'
        STOP
      END IF
    END IF
  END DO
END FUNCTION BuildSet

FUNCTION Card( S )
! returns cardinality of S
  INTEGER Card
  TYPE (SET) S
  Card = S % Cardinality
END FUNCTION Card
```

```
FUNCTION Intersect( S1, S2 )
  TYPE (SET) Intersect, S1, S2
  INTEGER I
  Intersect % Cardinality = 0

  DO I = 1, S1 % Cardinality
   IF (S1 % Members(I) .IN. S2) THEN
     Intersect % Cardinality = Intersect % Cardinality + 1
     Intersect % Members(Intersect % Cardinality) = S1 % Members(I)
   END IF
   END DO

END FUNCTION Intersect

FUNCTION MemberOf( X, S )
  LOGICAL MemberOf
  INTEGER X
  TYPE (SET) S
  MemberOf = ANY( S % Members(1 : S % Cardinality) == X)
END FUNCTION MemberOf

SUBROUTINE PrtSet( S )
  TYPE (SET) S
  INTEGER I

  PRINT '(20I4)', (S % Members(I), I = 1, S % Cardinality)
END SUBROUTINE PrtSet

END MODULE
```

A sample main program, with output, follows:

```
USE IntegerSets

TYPE (SET) S1, S2, S3

S1 = BuildSet( (/ 1, 2, 3, 4, 5 /) )
S2 = BuildSet( (/ 2, 4, 6, 8 /) )
S3 = S1 * S2

WRITE (*, "('S1:    ', I3, ' ELEMENTS: ')", &
  ADVANCE = 'NO') Card( S1 )
CALL PrtSet( S1 )
WRITE (*, "('S2:    ', I3, ' ELEMENTS: ')", &
  ADVANCE = 'NO') Card( S2 )
CALL PrtSet( S2 )
WRITE (*, "('S1*S2: ', I3, ' ELEMENTS: ')", &
  ADVANCE = 'NO') Card( S3 )
```

```
CALL PrtSet( S3 )

END
```

Ouput:

```
S1:      5 ELEMENTS:    1   2   3   4   5
S2:      4 ELEMENTS:    2   4   6   8
S1*S2:   2 ELEMENTS:    2   4
```

There are a number of very important points to note.

- The PRIVATE statement makes the components of the derived SET type inaccessible outside the module. This means it is possible to change the type definition without having to change any code that uses it.
- The function Card allows the cardinality of a set to be accessible outside the module.
- To define a binary operator on a derived type a function must be defined that specifies how the operator works. The only novelty is being able to replace the conventional statement

```
      S3 = Intersect( S1, S2 )
```

with the much more natural syntax

```
      S3 = S1 * S2
```

This is achieved by associating the function name with the operator token in an interface block, using the keyword OPERATOR:

```
      INTERFACE OPERATOR (*)
         MODULE PROCEDURE Intersect
      END INTERFACE
```

A function defining a unary operator would obviously have only one argument.
- The defined operator token (i.e. a sequence of characters) may be any one of the tokens used for the intrinsic operators, or a sequence of up to 31 letters enclosed in decimal points, such as .IN. above.
If an intrinsic token is used, the number of arguments and priority is the same as for the intrinsic operation. Otherwise, defined unary (binary) operators have the highest (lowest) priority.
An operation that is defined on intrinsic types cannot be redefined. For example, since the operation X * Y is defined intrinsically for arrays, the operator * cannot be redefined as a scalar product. You must either use a different token, or define a new type.
- In this example, the set is implemented as a fixed length array. It could however just as easily be represented by a linked list, which would not require the module to be recompiled.

Structure-valued functions   Note incidentally, from the previous example, that a function may be *structure-valued*, i.e. it may return the value of a derived type.

We will see further examples of derived types, assignment and operator overloading, and structure- and array-valued functions in Chapter 15.

The TYPE statement   The general form of a derived type definition is

```
TYPE [[, access] ::] typename
    [PRIVATE]
    component definitions
END TYPE [typename]
```

By default a type and all its components are accessible (PUBLIC access).

The *access* qualifier PRIVATE or the PRIVATE statement may only appear if the type is defined in a module. If the type is specified as PRIVATE then both the type name, the structure constructor for the type, and all its components are accessible only in the host module. If the PRIVATE statement appears in the definition, all the components are accessible only in the host module.

The advantage of a public type with PRIVATE components is that changes may be made to the type definition without affecting the code which accesses it. If the derived type is only used internally by the module, the access qualifier should be PRIVATE, preventing unintentional use of its name outside the module.

Objects and sub-objects   The time is right for a few more definitions.

We have seen that components of derived type may be arrays. E.g. the type First_Year defined at the beginning of the chapter has a component

```
REAL, DIMENSION(20) :: Marks   ! Marks
```

Arrays of derived type may also be declared, e.g.

```
TYPE (First_Year), DIMENSION (100) :: Class
```

An element of this array, say Class(17), is regarded in Fortran 90 as a *scalar*, because it is in a sense a single structure, although it has a component which is an array (it could even have a component which is another derived type).

An entity which is not part of a bigger entity has a name and is called a *named object*. Its *sub-objects* have *designators* consisting of the name of the object followed by one or more qualifiers, e.g. Class(3:6), Class(5) % BirthDate.

Consequently, in Fortran 90 the term *array* now means any object that is not scalar, including an array section, or an array-valued component of a structure. The term *variable* now means any named object that is not specified to be a constant, and any part of such an object, including array elements, array sections, structure components and substrings.

12.2   A Database: Student Records

In this section we combine the elegance of Fortran 90 derived types with direct access files to build a program to illustrate the basic principles of setting up, displaying, and updating a database.

Suppose we want to set up a database of student records (by *record* we mean the information relating to each student). For simplicity let's record each student's name (including initials), and one integer mark (in practice this is more likely to be an array of marks). The obvious vehicle for this is a derived type, similar to that defined in the previous section:

```
TYPE StudentRecord
   CHARACTER (NameLen)   Name
   INTEGER               Mark
END TYPE StudentRecord
```

We need a collection of subroutines to read and write variables of this type to and from a direct access file. The program template follows. Details of the subroutines are filled in below. For ease of presentation the subroutines are internal. This also makes it easier for you to run and develop the program. Consequently, the file is opened once, at the beginning of the program, and closed only at the end. In a real application, the subroutines would probably be in a module, with some global declarations, such as the type definition, the file name, etc. In that case, each subroutine which handles the file should open and close it.

The program outline is:

```
PROGRAM Student_Records
IMPLICIT NONE

INTEGER, PARAMETER :: NameLen = 20

TYPE StudentRecord
   CHARACTER (NameLen)   Name
   INTEGER               Mark
END TYPE StudentRecord

TYPE (StudentRecord) Student
INTEGER               EOF, RecLen, RecNo
LOGICAL               IsThere
CHARACTER (NameLen)   FileName
CHARACTER             Ans
CHARACTER (7)         FileStatus
CHARACTER (*), PARAMETER :: NameChars = &
          " abcdefghijklmnopqrstuvwxyzABCDEFGHIJKLMNOPQRSTUVWXYZ"

INQUIRE (IOLENGTH = RecLen) Student
WRITE (*, "('File name: ')", ADVANCE = "NO")
READ*, FileName
INQUIRE (FILE = FileName, EXIST = IsThere)

IF (IsThere) THEN
  WRITE (*, "('File already exists. Erase and recreate (Y/N)? ')", &
            ADVANCE = "NO")
  READ*, Ans
```

```
  IF (Ans == "Y") THEN
    FileStatus = "REPLACE"              ! erase and start again
  ELSE
    FileStatus = "OLD"                 ! update existing file
  END IF
ELSE
 FileStatus = "NEW"                    ! it isn't there, so create it
END IF

OPEN (1, FILE = FileName, STATUS = FileStatus, &
       ACCESS = 'DIRECT', RECL = RecLen)
Ans = ""                              ! make sure we get started

DO WHILE (Ans /= "Q")
  PRINT*
  PRINT*, "A: Add new records"
  PRINT*, "D: Display all records"
  PRINT*, "Q: Quit"
  PRINT*, "U: Update existing records"
  PRINT*
  WRITE (*, "('Enter option and press ENTER: ')", ADVANCE = "NO")
  READ*, Ans
  SELECT CASE (Ans)
    CASE ("A", "a")
      CALL AddRecords
    CASE ("D", "d")
      CALL DisplayRecords
    CASE ("U", "u")
      CALL UpDate
  END SELECT
END DO

CLOSE (1)

CONTAINS
  SUBROUTINE AddRecords
    ...
  SUBROUTINE DisplayRecords
    ...
  SUBROUTINE ReadIntCon( Num )
    ...
  SUBROUTINE StripBlanks( Str )
    ...
  SUBROUTINE UpDate
    ...
END
```

The length of the component Name of StudentRecord is declared as a named
constant NameLen because this value is used in a number of other declarations.

The basic variable in the program is Student, of type StudentRecord. An INQUIRE statement determines its record length for the subsequent OPEN statement.

The user is asked for the file name of the database. Another INQUIRE statement determines whether or not the file exists. A value is set for the STATUS specifier in the OPEN statement, depending on whether the file is to be replaced, updated or created, after which the file is opened. If the value of STATUS has been correctly set, the OPEN must succeed; otherwise you need to cater for error recovery with the IOSTAT and/or ERR specifiers.

Next, a menu is presented. The ideal construct for this is DO WHILE. The user enters a single letter response. A CASE construct selects the appropriate subroutine. An important point to note here is that the response may be in lower- or uppercase. Since other responses will be required in the program, it makes sense to write a function to convert the response to uppercase, say, before testing it. I tried to include such a function,

```
FUNCTION ChToUpper( Ch )
  ! converts a single lowercase character to uppercase
  ! leaves all other characters unchanged
  CHARACTER  Ch, ChToUpper
  ChToUpper = Ch
  SELECT CASE (Ch)
    CASE ( "a":"z" )
      ChToUpper = CHAR( ICHAR(Ch) + ICHAR("A") - ICHAR("a") )
  END SELECT
END FUNCTION ChToUpper
```

but a bug in the FTN90 compiler caused a run-time error when it was included in the database program (although it ran successfully on its own in a test program).

When the user quits, the database file is closed.

Now for the subroutines. AddRecords adds new records, either at the end of an existing database, or at the beginning of a new one.

```
SUBROUTINE AddRecords
  RecNo = 0
  EOF = 0                        ! remember to initialize

  DO WHILE (EOF == 0)
    READ( 1, REC = RecNo+1, IOSTAT = EOF )
    IF (EOF == 0) THEN         ! read succeeded, so ...
      RecNo = RecNo + 1        ! ... only increment RecNo here
    END IF
  END DO

  RecNo = RecNo + 1                              ! next record to write
  Student = StudentRecord( "a", 0 )        ! satisfy DO WHILE
  DO WHILE ((VERIFY( Student % Name, NameChars ) == 0))
    PRINT*, "Name (any non-letter/non-blank to end): "
    READ "(A20)", Student % Name
    IF (VERIFY( Student % Name, NameChars ) == 0) THEN
```

```
          PRINT*, "Mark: "
          CALL ReadIntCon( Student % Mark )
          WRITE (1, REC = RecNo) Student
          RecNo = RecNo + 1
        END IF
      END DO
    END SUBROUTINE AddRecords
```

Fortran 90 unfortunately has no way of determining the number of records in a file, other than by reading past all of them. The first DO WHILE sets RecNo to the number of records in the file. Note that a READ with no input list skips past a record; this saves time.

EOF must be initialized to zero on entry to the subroutine, because it is a global variable, so it will usually have a non-zero value from the last time the end-of-file was encountered. This provides a good reason for declaring EOF *locally*—to force you to initialize it correctly.

A DO WHILE loop accepts students' names from the keyboard. In this example, it is assumed that names will consist only of letters or blanks (e.g. between the surname and initials). So any character other than a letter or a blank will end the loop. VERIFY ensures that only a genuine name is written to the file.

Remember that READ* assumes that a string without delimiters is terminated by a blank, so if you want to read blanks as part of the string you must either use a formatted READ or enclose the string in delimiters.

Both components of Student are written to record number RecNo by the single WRITE statement—after which RecNo must be incremented.

If you ever have to write a program of this nature which *other* people will use, you will soon discover that most of your programming effort will go into anticipating and trapping *their* stupid mistakes. In particular, a crash must be avoided if the user makes an invalid response. The short subroutine ReadIntCon makes use of the IOSTAT specifier to intercept a READ error:

```
    SUBROUTINE ReadIntCon( Num )
      INTEGER Err, Num
      Err = 1                          ! remember to initialize
      DO WHILE (Err > 0)
        READ (*, *, IOSTAT = Err) Num
        IF (Err > 0) PRINT*, "Error in mark - re-enter"
      END DO
    END SUBROUTINE ReadIntCon
```

DisplayRecords uses a DO WHILE construct to read and display the file contents. The end-of-file is detected by the IOSTAT specifier:

```
    SUBROUTINE DisplayRecords
      RecNo = 1
      EOF = 0                          ! remember to initialize
      DO WHILE (EOF == 0)
        READ (1, REC = RecNo, IOSTAT = EOF) Student
        IF (EOF == 0) THEN
```

```
        PRINT "(A20, I3)", Student                  ! READ succeeded
      END IF
      RecNo = RecNo + 1
    END DO
  END SUBROUTINE DisplayRecords
```

The subroutine UpDate takes care of updating a student's record (in this example, only his single mark may be changed, but obviously this can be extended to correcting spelling in his name, etc.):

```
  SUBROUTINE UpDate
    CHARACTER (NameLen) Item, Copy
    LOGICAL Found
    Found = .false.
    EOF = 0                          ! remember to initialize
    PRINT*, "Update who?"
    READ "(A20)", Item
    CALL StripBlanks( Item )
    RecNo = 1
    DO WHILE (EOF == 0 .AND. .NOT. Found)
      READ (1, IOSTAT = EOF, REC = RecNo) Student
      IF (EOF == 0) THEN
        Copy = Student % Name
        CALL StripBlanks( Copy )  ! leave his name as is
        IF (Item == Copy) THEN
          Found = .true.                           ! found him
          PRINT*, 'Found at recno', RecNo, ' Enter new mark:'
          CALL ReadIntCon( Student % Mark )        ! new mark
          WRITE (1, REC = RecNo) Student           ! rewrite
        ELSE
          RecNo = RecNo + 1
        END IF
      END IF
    END DO
    IF (.NOT. Found) THEN
      PRINT*, Item, ' not found'
    END IF
  END SUBROUTINE UpDate
```

UpDate asks for the name of the student whose mark is to be changed, and then searches for that student. The logical variable Found will be set to TRUE if the student is found. Initially, it must be set to FALSE. You may be tempted here to have an initialization expression in its declaration, e.g.

```
  LOGICAL :: Found = .false.
```

However, this automatically gives LOGICAL the SAVE attribute, i.e. *its value is retained between calls to* UpDate. This would give it the value TRUE on entry again after a successful search, making it impossible to execute the DO WHILE.

The name to be searched for is read into Item. You may want to build in some embellishments here to facilitate getting an exact match with the name in Student % Name. For example, all the characters in Item and Student % Name could be converted to uppercase before searching. In this example, all blanks are removed by StripBlanks:

```
SUBROUTINE StripBlanks( Str )
  CHARACTER (*) Str
  INTEGER I
  I = 1
  DO WHILE (I < LEN_TRIM( Str ))   ! null str won't matter
    IF (Str(I:I) == " ") THEN
      Str(I:) = Str(I+1:)          ! don't increase I yet
    ELSE
      I = I + 1
    END IF
  END DO
END SUBROUTINE StripBlanks
```

There is only one subtlety in this routine. If a blank is found in position I, it is removed with the substring operation

```
Str(I:) = Str(I+1:)
```

However, I must not be incremented, since another blank might have moved up into position I. It must therefore be tested again. Only when a blank is not found may I be safely incremented. LEN_TRIM returns the length of Str. As blanks are removed this value will of course be reduced.

To keep matters simple, the searching procedure is the crudest one possible—read each record in the file from the beginning, until either a match is found, or the end-of-file is reached. If a match is found update the mark and rewrite that record. If no match is found, report so. More sophisticated searching procedures are discussed below—you can build them into this program if you like.

Once UpDate has found a match, the user enters the corrected mark, and the record is rewritten.

You can easily add other features to this basic skeleton, e.g. printing names and marks, analysing the marks, deleting a name, etc. You could also extend the database to include an array of marks.

Practically the only disadvantage of using a direct access file, as opposed to a text file, is that the record length is fixed. So if you wanted to allow for an array of, say, 20 marks, the record length must be increased, even though you may never use the extra space. One way out is to create a new direct access file each time a new set of marks is entered, with room for only one additional mark, and to rename it with the original name.

12.3   A Binary Search

We have seen already how to sort numbers and words. Items are usually sorted only so that we can subsequently search through them for a particular item. An obvious (and easy) method of searching is to go through the (sorted) list of items one by one comparing them with the search item. The process stops either when the search item is found, or when the search has gone past the place where the item would normally be. This is called a *linear* search. Its disadvantage is that it can be very time consuming if the list is long. A much more cunning method is the *binary* search.

Suppose you want to find the page in a telephone directory that has a particular name on it. A linear search would examine each page in turn from page 1 to determine whether the name is on it. This could clearly take a long time. A binary search is as follows. Find the middle of the directory (by consulting the page numbers), and tear it in half. By looking at the last name in the left-hand half (or the first name in the right-hand half), determine which half the required name is in. Throw away the unwanted half, and repeat the process with the half that contains the name, by halving it again. After a surprisingly low number of halvings, you will be left with one page containing the required name. Although this can be a little heavy on telephone directories, it illustrates the principle of a binary search quite well.

The method is very efficient. For example, my local directory has 1243 pages with subscribers' names and numbers. Since the method halves the number of pages each time, the number of halvings (or *bisections*) required to find a name will be the smallest power of 2 that exceeds 1243, i.e. 11, since

$$2^{10} = 1024 < 1243 < 2^{11} = 2048.$$

The smart way to find the maximum number of bisections N required is to observe that N must be the smallest integer such that $2^N > 1243$, i.e. such that $N > \log_2 1243$. In the worst possible case, the required name would be the last one in the directory. A linear search would involve examining all 1243 pages, whereas a binary search requires you to look at only 11 pages!

Suppose our student database file contains NumRecs records altogether, sorted so that the names are in alphabetical order. We would like to search for a given student (e.g. in order to be able to view his marks, and change them if necessary). A binary search through the file must try to find the record number (Mid) of the required student's name (Item). The lower and upper bounds of the record numbers for the search are Lo and Hi respectively. Mid is the average of these two values. Successive bisections change the value of either Lo or Hi, keeping the alphabetical position of Item between these bounds each time. Since each bisection takes the integer part of Mid, the starting value of Hi must be 1 more than the last record number, or the last student can never be found. The maximum number of bisections required, NumBis, is found as described above. This requires computing a logarithm to the base 2 in terms of the natural logarithm. The formula for this is $\log_2 a = \log_e a / \log_e 2$.

The coding for the binary search is as follows:

```
SUBROUTINE BinSearch( NUnit, Item, Posn )
! Binary Search for string Item through all StudentRecord ...
! ... records on NUnit.
! Record number of match returned in Posn, which is zero ...
! ... if no match found.

  CHARACTER (*) Item
  INTEGER Count, EOF, Hi, Lo, Mid, NumBis, NumRecs, NUnit, Posn
```

```
LOGICAL Found
TYPE (StudentRecord) Student

EOF = 0                          ! find the number of records NumRecs
NumRecs = 0
DO WHILE (EOF == 0)
  READ( NUnit, REC = NumRecs+1, IOSTAT = EOF )
  IF (EOF == 0) THEN
    NumRecs = NumRecs + 1
  END IF
END DO

NumBis = INT( LOG(REAL(NumRecs)) / LOG(2.0) ) + 1 ! no of
                                            ! bisections
Count = 0                                   ! counter
Found = .false.
Posn = 0                                    ! not found yet
Lo = 1                                      ! first record
Hi = NumRecs + 1                            ! last record + 1
DO WHILE (.NOT. found .AND. Count /= NumBis)
  Mid = (Hi + Lo) / 2
  READ (NUnit, REC = Mid) Student
  Student % Name = TRIM( Student % Name )
  IF (Item == Student % Name) THEN
    Found = .true.
  ELSE IF (Item < Student % Name) THEN
    Hi = Mid
  ELSE
    Lo = Mid
  END IF
  Count = Count + 1
END DO
IF (Found) Posn = Mid
END SUBROUTINE
```

You can add this subroutine to the program Student_Records of the last section, and implement it from the subroutine UpDate with the following template:

```
CALL BinSearch( 1, Item, RecNo )
IF (RecNo > 0) THEN
  PRINT*, Item, ' found at record', RecNo
  ... update record RecNo ...
ELSE
  PRINT*, Item, ' not found'
END IF
```

STUDENT.REC			MARKS.KEY	
Record	Name	Mark	RecNum	KeyField
1	Jack	23	3	89
2	Ann	34	4	76
3	Bill	89	2	34
4	Jim	76	1	23

Fig. 12.1 A file (STUDENT.REC) and its keyed file (MARKS.REC)

12.4 Keyed Files

This section is a little involved; if you are new to programming, you might like to come back to it later.

An obvious extension to the program Student_Record in Section 12.2 is to sort a particular offering into order of merit, and to save the sorted file. If the records in the data file are long (i.e. an array of offerings in the Mark component), this can be both time-consuming (because of all the swopping involved) and risky (disk errors are more likely to occur during the rewrite of a large file). The concept of a *keyed file* provides a neat solution to both these potential problems.

For ease of reference, let's call the database file STUDENT.REC. Suppose we want to sort the Mark component in the file. We really only need the Mark component (the *key field*) of each student, plus a *reference field* to point to the student's name in the original file STUDENT.REC once the key field has been sorted. We therefore create a *key file*, MARKS.KEY, the records of which will be structure variables of type Key:

```
TYPE Key
   INTEGER      RecNum
   INTEGER      KeyField
END TYPE Key
```

The component KeyField has the mark to be sorted, while the component RecNum gives the position (record number) of the student with that mark in STUDENT.REC. Now a sort need only be performed on the much smaller file MARKS.KEY. Figure 12.1 shows the contents of both files after sorting MARKS.KEY. The RecNum field gives the names of the students in order of merit: 3 (Bill), 4 (Jim), 2 (Ann) and 1 (Jack).

The program KeyTest below reads STUDENT.REC and creates the key file MARKS.KEY. It also copies the records of the key file into the array KeyArr, which is passed to the subroutine Key_Sort. This is an amendment of the Bubble Sort subroutine in Chapter 9 (only amended lines are shown). After sorting, KeyArr is written back to MARKS.KEY. The sorted key file is then used with the original database, STUDENT.REC to write the names of the students and marks, in order of merit.

```
PROGRAM KeyTest
IMPLICIT NONE
```

```
INTEGER, PARAMETER :: NameLen = 20
INTEGER, PARAMETER :: MaxStu = 100

TYPE Key
   INTEGER     RecNum
   INTEGER     KeyField
END TYPE Key

TYPE StudentRecord
   CHARACTER (NameLen)  Name
   INTEGER              Mark
END TYPE StudentRecord

TYPE (Key)          KeyVar
TYPE (KEY), DIMENSION (MaxStu) :: KeyArr
TYPE (StudentRecord) Student
INTEGER             EOF, Num, RecNo, TotRecs
INTEGER             KeyLen, StuLen
INTEGER       ::    KeyFile = 1    ! unit for key file
INTEGER       ::    StuRecFile = 2 ! unit for StudentRecord file

INQUIRE (IOLENGTH = StuLen) Student
OPEN (StuRecFile, FILE = 'student.rec', STATUS = 'OLD', &
                  ACCESS = 'DIRECT', RECL = StuLen)
INQUIRE (IOLENGTH = KeyLen) KeyVar
OPEN (KeyFile, FILE = 'marks.key', STATUS = 'REPLACE', &
              ACCESS = 'DIRECT', RECL = KeyLen)
RecNo = 0                          ! create the key file
EOF = 0
DO WHILE (EOF == 0)
  READ (StuRecFile, REC = RecNo+1, IOSTAT = EOF) Student
  IF (EOF == 0) THEN
    RecNo = RecNo + 1              ! total number of records
    KeyVar % RecNum = RecNo
    KeyVar % KeyField = Student % Mark
    WRITE (KeyFile, REC = RecNo) KeyVar
    KeyArr(RecNo) = KeyVar        ! and copy into array
  END IF
END DO

TotRecs = RecNo       ! total number of records

CALL Key_Sort( KeyArr, TotRecs )

DO Num = 1, TotRecs   ! write sorted array back to key file
  WRITE (KeyFile, REC = Num) KeyArr(Num)
END DO
```

```
PRINT*, 'Order of merit using the key file:'
PRINT*

DO Num = 1, TotRecs    ! use sorted keyfile to write order of merit
   READ (KeyFile, REC = Num) KeyVar    ! read key file for RecNum
   READ (StuRecFile, REC = KeyVar % RecNum) Student   ! read RecNum
   PRINT '(A20, I3)', Student              ! print merit list
END DO

CLOSE (1)
CLOSE (2)

CONTAINS
   SUBROUTINE Key_Sort( X )
      TYPE (KEY), DIMENSION (:), INTENT(INOUT) :: X    !list
      TYPE (KEY)  Temp                 ! temp for swop
      ...

          IF (X(J) % KeyField < X(J+1) % KeyField) THEN
      ...
   END SUBROUTINE
END
```

If a key file is set up with names as the key field, it can be sorted on the names (with slight adjustments to Key_Sort). A binary search for a name can then be conducted on the key file, with reference to the original database for that student's mark(s), if necessary.

12.5 Hashing

The program in this section does not use derived types; however, it arises naturally from the earlier discussion of searching.

One problem with a binary search is that the items must be *sorted*. This means that if additional items are added to the list, the entire list must be resorted before a search can be conducted. The method discussed in this section does *not* require the items to be sorted, and is one of the most efficient methods of searching: hashing. If you are a programming novice, you might like to skip this section and come back to it later.

Suppose we have an array Names, as in Figure 12.2. Take the first element Ann, and perform some operation on the characters in the name to produce a positive integer, e.g. add up the ASCII codes of the characters. This process is called *hashing*, it is done by a *hash function*, and the resultant integer is called the *hashed index*—let's call it K. Now set up a second array Index, and store in Index(K) Ann's position in Names, i.e. 1. Suppose K has the value 43. Then Index(43) will have the value 1, as in Figure 12.2. (The name Ann is inserted for clarity.) Now take some other item in Names, e.g. Tony, and hash it with the same hash function (whatever it is). Suppose the hashed index is 1. Then take Tony's position in Names, which is 4, and store it in Index(1), as in the figure. Obviously K is going to have to be

Names		Index	
(1)	Ann	(1)	4 (Tony)
(2)	Jack	(2)	−100 (empty)
(3)	Bill	...	
(4)	Tony	(42)	−100 (empty)
(5)	David	(43)	1 (Ann)
...		...	

Fig. 12.2   Hashing

reduced modulo the length of the array Index, e.g. if Index has indices from 1 to 53, say, and K turns out to be 4575, it must be reduced by the operation

```
K =  MOD(K, 53)+ 1
```

to put it in the range 1–53.

   We continue this process for all the items in Names. You might have thought of an objection by now. It is most unlikely that the hash function will produce a *unique* value of K for each item in the list. So when setting up the hashed list in Index, a particular hashed position might be found to be occupied already (the elements of Index should be initialized to some negative value, say −100, to indicate that they are all unoccupied at first). This is called a *collision*. There are various ways of dealing with collisions. One is to use the next position, but this causes *clumping* of the hashed list, which is inefficient. A more imaginative solution to the problem of collisions is to use *double hashing*.

   At this stage we need a little more notation. Let's rather call the original hash value H. For best results, the length of the Index array needs to be a prime number. Let's call it Mn. So K is in fact given by

```
K = MOD( H, Mn) + 1
```

For double hashing, choose another prime Mn2, which is slightly less than Mn. If position K is occupied, look in position K + InK where

```
InK =  MOD( H, Mn2)
```

Continue increasing K like this (modulo Mn) until an unoccupied position is found.

   When we have finished we will have a hashed list in Index. To find a particular item, hash it and "probe" at K, K + InK, ..., until either an unoccupied position (not found) or a match is found.

   For the best results, the total number of items in Names should not exceed 0.75Mn.

   The program Hash below demonstrates hashing on a list of names in the sequential file NAMES, which is set up separately. The file is read into the array Names, which is hashed into Index by the subroutine Place and the function Find. Items supplied by the user are then searched for with Find. If the item is found, it is displayed with its position in Names. If it is not found, Find returns minus the position it would occupy in Index if it was there.

   Mn and Mn2 are taken as 103 and 89 respectively, and the actual hashing function used, at the beginning of Find, computes the sums of the squares of the ASCII codes of the characters in the item. Different hashing functions could be used, depending on the nature of the list to be searched. Some experimentation might be necessary on a dummy list to find a hashing function which causes the least clumping (this reduces the number of probes needed to find an item).

```fortran
PROGRAM Hash
IMPLICIT NONE

INTEGER, PARAMETER :: Mn = 103          ! prime for hashing
INTEGER, PARAMETER :: Mn2 = 89          ! prime for double hashing
INTEGER, PARAMETER :: NameLen = 20      ! length of names
INTEGER H                               ! hash value
INTEGER EOF, I
INTEGER N  ! length of list:
           ! should be about 0.75Mn for best results
INTEGER, DIMENSION (Mn) :: Index        ! hashed list
CHARACTER (NameLen), DIMENSION(Mn) :: Names = ''  ! list of names
CHARACTER (NameLen), Item               ! name to search for

OPEN (1, FILE = 'NAMES')
EOF = 0
I = 1

DO WHILE (EOF == 0)                     ! read list of names
  READ (1, '(A20)', IOSTAT = EOF) Item
  IF (EOF == 0) THEN
    Names(I) = TRIM( Item )
    I = I + 1
  END IF
END DO

N = I - 1
Index = -100                 ! all positions initially unoccupied

DO I = 1, N               ! construct hash list
  CALL Place( I, Index, Names )
END DO

Item = ''                 ! now look for Items
DO WHILE (Item /= '#')
  PRINT*, 'Search for?'
  READ*, Item
  Item = TRIM( Item )
  H = Find( Index, Names, Item )
  IF (H > 0) THEN
    PRINT*, Names(H), ' found in element', H, ' of Names'
  ELSE
    PRINT*, H, ' (not found)'
  END IF
END DO
```

```
CONTAINS
  FUNCTION Find( Index, Names, Item )
  ! Hashes Item to integer K, which is increased by InK if
  ! necessary, until either an unused position (Index(K) = -100)
  ! or a match (Item = Names(Index(K))) is found.  If no match
  ! is found, Index(K) is returned.

    INTEGER F, Find, H, I, InK, K
    INTEGER, DIMENSION(:) :: Index
    CHARACTER (*), DIMENSION(:) :: Names
    CHARACTER (*) Item
    H = 0
    DO I = 1, LEN_TRIM( Item )                    ! hash it
      H = H + IACHAR( Item(I:I) ) * IACHAR( Item(I:I) )
    END DO

    K = MOD( H, Mn ) + 1
    InK = MOD( H, Mn2 )

    ! now we look until we find an unused position or a match
    F = -1
    DO WHILE (F == -1)
      IF (Index(K) == -100) THEN
        F = -K
      ELSE IF (Item == Names( Index(K) )) THEN
        F = Index(K)
      END IF
      K = MOD( K+InK, Mn ) + 1
    END DO
    Find = F
  END FUNCTION Find

  SUBROUTINE Place( J, Index, Names )
  ! Place is used to set up the hashed list Index from the list of
  ! items Names.  The item in Names(J) is hashed to the integer K.
  ! The item's position J in Names is placed in Index(K).
  ! A positive value should never be returned to Place by Find,
  ! a match is not being sought from Place.  A positive value means
  ! a duplicate item in Names.
    INTEGER J, K
    INTEGER, DIMENSION(:) :: Index
    CHARACTER (*), DIMENSION(:) :: Names
    K = Find( Index, Names, Names(J) )
    IF (K > 0) THEN ! position occupied - we should never get here!
      PRINT*, Names(J), ' already known at hash position', K
      PRINT*, 'New simple position', J, ' will be inaccessible'
    ELSE
      K = -K
```

```
        Index(K) = J
      END IF
    END SUBROUTINE Place
  END
```

Dealing with additional items is simple. Just add them on at the end of the disk file, and rehash the enlarged array Names!

Summary

- The TYPE statement defines a derived data type.
- A derived type may have components of different types (including arrays and other structures).
- A variable of a derived type is called a structure.
- Structure components are referenced with the component selector %.
- Arrays of structures may be declared.
- A structure may be initialized with a structure constructor, either in an initialization expression, or in an assignment.
- A structure may appear in an I/O list, as long as there is an appropriate format specification for each component.
- Structures of the same type may be assigned to each other. All corresponding components are assigned.
- The assignment operator may be redefined for derived types by overloading it, using an INTERFACE ASSIGNMENT block.
- New operators may be defined for derived types from a sequence of characters enclosed in decimal points (such as .IN.), or intrinsic operators may be overloaded, using an INTERFACE OPERATOR block.
- A function may be structure-valued.
- A derived type appearing in a module may be declared PRIVATE. The type and all its components are then only accessible in the module. If the PRIVATE statement appears in the definition, the type name is accessible outside the module, although the components are not.
- An entity not part of a bigger entity is called an object.
- An array is any object that is not a scalar (single-valued).
- A variable now means any named object not a constant, and any part of such an object.

Exercises

12.1 Extend the Student_Records program in Section 12.2 to compute and display the average mark as part of the subroutine DisplayRecords.

12.2 As a project extend the Student_Records program in Section 12.2 to accept further marks (offerings) for each student.

One way to do this is to set aside the maximum space required when defining the type StudentRecord by declaring the component Mark as an array. The user will then need to indicate which offering is being entered. This is wasteful of disk and memory space if fewer offerings are actually required. You may like to think of alternative solutions.

13

Pointer Variables

Warning: if you are an old confirmed Fortran 77 user, this chapter could damage your health!

13.1 Introduction

The implementation of *pointer variables*, or simply *pointers*, brings Fortran at last into the league of languages like Pascal and C.

Run the following program segment:

```
REAL, TARGET :: R = 13
REAL, POINTER :: P
P => R
R = 2 * P
PRINT*, P, R
```

You will see that P and R both have the same value: 26. P should be thought of as an *alias* of its *target* R, i.e. just another name for R. What happens to R therefore also happens to P. In this case P is the pointer. It must be specified with the POINTER attribute, and the type of the variable for which it is going to be an alias. Furthermore, the variable for which P is to be an alias must be declared with the TARGET attribute. The TARGET attribute is conferred on all the sub-objects of an object which is thus specified.

The *pointer assignment statement* above

```
P => R
```

should be thought of as "make P an alias of R", or "make P *point to* R". (If you have encountered pointers in other languages, note that a Fortran 90 pointer is not an address—it is in fact the reference variable of C++.) The pointer assignment above can be illustrated as follows:

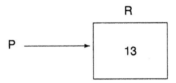

Now consider the following code:

```
REAL, TARGET :: R = 13
REAL, POINTER :: P1, P2
P1 => R
P2 => P1
PRINT*, P1, P2, R
END
```

Try to work out the result before running it. The second pointer assignment,

```
P2 => P1
```

makes P2 an alias of P1. But P1 is already an alias of R, so P2 is also an alias of R:

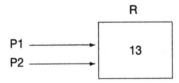

Pointer assignment versus ordinary assignment   Consider the following code:

```
REAL, TARGET :: R1 = 13
REAL, TARGET :: R2 = 17
REAL, POINTER :: P1, P2
P1 => R1
P2 => R2
```

It produces this situation:

However, if the ordinary (as opposed to pointer) assignment statement

    P1 = P2

is executed next, the situation is as follows:

Note that this assignment has exactly the same effect as

    R1 = R2

since P1 is an alias of R1 and P2 is an alias of R2.
  To sum up:

- Pointer assignments, such as P => Q, set up the pointer P as an alias of its target Q.
- A reference to a pointer variable (e.g. in an assignment or expression) is in fact a reference to its target variable.

Pointer assignment changes a current alias. The statement

    P2 => P1

following the code above changes the target of P2 to that of P1, so that P1 and P2 are now both aliases of R1:

Pointer states Any pointer in a program is always in one of the following three states:

- It may be *undefined*—all pointers are in this state at the beginning of a program.
- It may be *null* (see the NULLIFY statement below)—this means that it is not the alias of any object.
- It may be *associated* (see the ASSOCIATED intrinsic function below)—this means that it is the alias of some object.

The NULLIFY statement   As just mentioned, a pointer is undefined at the beginning of a program. However, it is sometimes convenient for a pointer to be "pointing to nothing", or "not pointing to anything". This is the null state, and is achieved by the statement

```
NULLIFY( P1 )
```

where P1 is a pointer. The null state may be tested for with the ASSOCIATED intrinsic function; this is useful when manipulating linked lists (see below). It may also be assigned to another pointer with a pointer assignment (=>). On the other hand, if two pointers have the same target, nullifying one does not nullify the other.

The ASSOCIATED intrinsic function   If this function has one pointer argument, as in

```
ASSOCIATED( P1 )
```

it returns TRUE if P1 is an alias of an object, and FALSE if it is not (i.e. null). Note that P1 *must be defined* to use this function correctly.

ASSOCIATED may have a second argument. If the second argument is a target, it returns TRUE if the first argument is an alias of the second argument. If the second argument is also a pointer, it must be defined. TRUE is returned if both pointers are null, or if they are both aliases of the same object.

Arguments with the TARGET attribute   Pointers associated with an actual argument that has the TARGET attribute do not become associated with the corresponding dummy argument, but remain associated with the actual argument. If a dummy argument has the TARGET attribute, any pointer associated with it becomes undefined on return.

Dynamic variables: ALLOCATE and DEALLOCATE   We came across dynamic memory in Chapter 9, where we saw that storage can be allocated to an array at run time. More generally, a dynamic variable (not necessarily an array) may be created as follows:

```
REAL, POINTER :: P1
ALLOCATE( P1 )
```

This makes the pointer P1 an alias of an area of memory able to store a real variable. Note that no value is assigned at this stage. However, since P1 is an alias, it may now be used as any other real variable can be, e.g.

```
P1 = 17
PRINT*, P1
```

The memory pointed to by P1 can be released by the statement

```
DEALLOCATE( P1 )
```

This returns P1 to the undefined state it had at the beginning of the program.
Both ALLOCATE and DEALLOCATE have an optional specifier STAT, e.g.

```
ALLOCATE( P1, STAT = AlloStat )
```

The integer variable AlloStat will zero only if memory was successfully allocated or deallocated.

When an array is specified with the ALLOCATABLE or POINTER attribute its bounds must be undefined:

```
REAL, DIMENSION(:), POINTER :: X
INTEGER, DIMENSION(:,:), ALLOCATABLE :: A
```

Danger! The ability to create dynamic memory brings greater versatility and freedom to programming, but also requires greater responsibility. In particular there are two potential sources of disaster which need to be studiously avoided.

The first is the *dangling pointer*. Consider the following:

```
REAL, POINTER :: P1, P2
ALLOCATE( P1 )
P1 = 13
P2 => P1
```

P1 and P2 both reference the same dynamic variable. If now the statement

```
DEALLOCATE( P1 )
```

is executed, it is clear that P1 is disassociated, and the dynamic variable to which it was pointing destroyed. What is not so clear, however, is that P2 is also affected, since the object it was aliasing has disappeared. A reference to P2 will probably not cause a program crash, but it will produce unpredictable results.

The second problem is that of *unreferenced storage*. Consider the following:

```
REAL, DIMENSION(:), POINTER :: X
ALLOCATE( X(2000) )
```

If X is nullified or set to point somewhere else, without first deallocating it, there is no way to refer to that block of memory, and so it cannot be released. The solution is to deallocate a dynamic object before modifying a pointer to it.

Array-valued functions Sometimes one may want to set up a function to return an array of varying size, but a function may not be declared with the ALLOCATABLE attribute. However, a function may be declared with the POINTER attribute, and this can achieve the same effect. The function Vector below returns its array argument with elements sorted in ascending order.

```
IMPLICIT NONE
INTEGER, DIMENSION(10) :: X = (/ 3, 6, 9, -1, 56, 4, 6, 0, 0, 8 /)

PRINT '(20I3)', Vector( X )

CONTAINS
  FUNCTION Vector( A )
    INTEGER, DIMENSION(:), POINTER :: Vector
    INTEGER, DIMENSION(:) :: A
```

```
      INTEGER I, J, T
      ALLOCATE( Vector(SIZE(A)) )     ! allowed because Vector points
      Vector = A
      DO I = 1, SIZE(A)-1
        DO J = I+1, SIZE(A)
          IF (Vector(I) > Vector(J)) THEN
            T = Vector(J)
            Vector(J) = Vector(I)
            Vector(I) = T
          END IF
        END DO
      END DO
    END FUNCTION Vector
  END
```

A problem with this example is that there seems to be no way (under FTN90 version 1.12) of deallocating `Vector`.

Arrays of pointers   If you have been brought up on an exclusive diet of Fortran, it may never have occurred to you to want to think about an *array* of pointers. But this could be useful if you wanted, for example, to set up an array of dynamic variables. Now there is no direct way of declaring an array of pointers in Fortran 90. The obvious declaration (which is not allowed) would be

```
REAL, DIMENSION(100), POINTER :: X     ! illegal
```

This, however, would mean that X is a pointer to an array of 100 real elements, not an array of 100 pointers. As we have seen, the correct syntax for the above declaration is

```
REAL, DIMENSION(:), POINTER :: X
```

This is more flexible, and allows you to allocate the array size at runtime:

```
ALLOCATE( X(N) )
```

The solution to our problem is to create a type with a pointer component, and then to declare arrays of that type.

Representation of a triangular matrix   For example, each row of a lower-triangular matrix may be represented by a dynamic array of increasing size. Run the following example, which is adapted from Metcalf and Reid:

```
TYPE ROW
  REAL, DIMENSION(:), POINTER :: R
END TYPE

INTEGER, PARAMETER :: N = 4
TYPE (ROW), DIMENSION(N) :: S, T    ! arrays of type ROW,
                                    ! i.e. matrices
```

```
DO I = 1, N
   ALLOCATE (T(I) % R(1:I))        ! allocate storage for each
                                   ! row of T
END DO

DO I = 1, N
   T(I) % R(1:I) = 1               ! assign values to matrix T
END DO

S = T                             ! array assignment

DO I = 1, N
   S(I) % R(:I) = 2               ! assign values to matrix S
END DO

DO I = 1, N
   PRINT*, T(I) % R(:I)          ! print matrix T
END DO
```

You may be surprised to find that T has taken the value of S. This is because the assignment

```
S = T
```

involves structures whose components are pointers. The rule is that *pointer assignment* occurs for the pointer components. The above assignment is therefore equivalent to the pointer assignments

```
S(I) % R => T(I) % R
```

for all the components. Since all the components of S and T are pointers, this effectively makes S an alias of T, which is why T takes the same value as S in the above example.

Note that this representation uses only half the storage of conventional two-dimensional arrays.

Sorting structures   We saw in Chapter 12 how to use a key file to sort structure variables on a particular component, in order to reduce the amount of swopping involved. An alternative approach is to use an "array" of pointers, set up as an array of structures with a pointer component, as described above.

The following program, which is discussed below, reads four records from a direct access file. Each record holds a structure variable with two components: a student's name and a mark. We want to sort the students into an order of merit.

```
IMPLICIT NONE

INTEGER, PARAMETER :: NameLen = 20
INTEGER, PARAMETER :: MaxStu = 100

TYPE KeyPointer
   TYPE (StudentRecord), POINTER :: Key
```

```
END TYPE KeyPointer

TYPE StudentRecord
   CHARACTER (NameLen)   Name
   INTEGER               Mark
END TYPE StudentRecord

TYPE (KeyPointer), DIMENSION(:), ALLOCATABLE :: Pointers

TYPE (StudentRecord), DIMENSION(MaxStu), TARGET :: Student
INTEGER             I, TotRecs
INTEGER             StuLen
INTEGER          :: StuRecFile = 2 ! unit for StudentRecord file

INQUIRE (IOLENGTH = StuLen) Student(1)
OPEN (StuRecFile, FILE = 'student.rec', STATUS = 'OLD', &
                  ACCESS = 'DIRECT', RECL = StuLen)
TotRecs = 4
ALLOCATE( Pointers(TotRecs) )
DO I = 1, TotRecs
  READ (StuRecFile, REC = I) Student(I)
  Pointers(I) % Key => Student(I)    ! aliases to each Student(I)
END DO

CALL BUBBLE_SORT( Pointers )

PRINT*, 'Order of merit using pointers:'
PRINT*

DO I = 1, TotRecs
  PRINT '(A20, I3)', Pointers(I) % Key    ! print merit list
END DO

CLOSE (2)

CONTAINS
  SUBROUTINE BUBBLE_SORT( X )
    TYPE (KeyPointer), DIMENSION (:), INTENT(INOUT) :: X    !list
    TYPE (KeyPointer)  Temp         ! temp for swop
    ...
      DO J = 1, SIZE(X) - K       ! fewer tests on each pass
        IF (X(J) % Key % Mark < X(J+1) % Key % Mark) THEN
        ...
  END SUBROUTINE
END
```

Pointers is an array of type KeyPointer, which has a single component, pointing to StudentRecord. It has the ALLOCATABLE attribute so that a dynamic array may be created. We could have declared `Pointers` with the `POINTER` attribute; however, we do not need this attribute for the array—only for the component.

Since we want to set up `Pointers` as aliases of the array `Student`, `Student` must have the `TARGET` attribute.

The `ALLOCATE` statement sets up a dynamic array `Pointers` with four elements (in this case). The `I`th record from the file is read into `Student(I)`, which is aliased by `Pointers(I) % Key`. The array `Pointers` is passed to the subroutine `BUBBLE_SORT`. Only the lines which differ from the version in Chapter 9 are given here. Note that the number of elements in `Pointers` does not have to be passed; this is obtained directly with `SIZE`.

The sorting is done on `Pointers(I) % Key % Mark` instead of `Student(I) % Mark`. This means that at the end of the sort, `Pointers(I) % Key` will point to the student record with the highest mark, because of the alias relationship. Note also that the ordinary assignments involving `Temp` and `X` actually involve pointer assignments of their `Key` components, again because of the alias set up.

If you are confused by this (and who wouldn't be?) convince yourself that a list of two records will be correctly ordered by drawing some diagrams of the aliases.

Note that this approach uses more memory than a key file, since the student records must be in the array `Student` to maintain the aliases.

13.2 Linked Lists

One of the classical and most powerful applications of pointers is in setting up and manipulating *linked lists*. It is also one of the most difficult to understand—I usually have to resort to drawing a lot of diagrams before I can follow what is going on. A thorough study of linked lists and related topics such as binary trees is beyond the scope of this book, and not in keeping with its ethos, so only relatively simple examples will be given here.

The basic idea is to represent a list of values with a chain of dynamic variables, all linked together (as an alternative, say, to an array). Each of these variables should hold a value, and also *point to the next variable* in the chain. Such a variable is called a *node*. It could have two components: a value, and a pointer to another node. Fortran 90 allows the following rather curious type definition:

```
TYPE NODE
  INTEGER Value
    TYPE (NODE), POINTER :: Next
END TYPE NODE
```

A variable of this type is usually represented as follows, the top box being for the value, and the bottom one for the pointer to the next node:

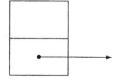

We will declare two variables of this type:

```
TYPE (NODE), POINTER :: Current, L
```

Current is the name of a general node, while L marks the end of the list. The two most important things about a linked list are where it starts and where it ends. We could have a separate pointer to mark the beginning of the list, but this can also be done with a null pointer (since this can be tested for). Initially, the list will be empty, so L should point to both the beginning and the end. This is effected by initially nullifying L:

```
NULLIFY( L )
```

The null pointer is usually represented by the symbol for earthing an electrical conductor:

Let's now set up a list with one node, containing the integer value Num. Firstly, dynamic storage must be allocated for Current:

```
ALLOCATE( Current )
```

Next, give it a value (that's easy):

```
Current % Value = Num
```

Finally, and this is the only really tricky part, we must arrange for L to point to the end of the list. Where is that? Well, the last (and only node) added is Current, so L must point to (be an alias of) Current:

```
L => Current
```

If the value of Num is 1, the situation now looks like this:

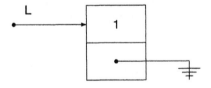

This process can be repeated as long as you like. The following piece of code will set up a linked list by reading numbers from the keyboard until a zero is entered:

```
DO WHILE (Num /= 0)
  READ*, Num
  IF (Num /= 0) THEN
     ALLOCATE( Current )             ! new node
     Current % Value = Num
     Current % Next => L             ! point it to previous node
     L => Current                    ! update end of list
```

```
    END IF
    END DO
```

If, for example, the values 1, 2, 3 are entered in that order, the list looks as shown in Figure 13.1.

Having set up the list, the next thing is to *traverse* it and print all the values. This is psychologically satisfying, because it's sometimes hard to believe the list is really there in memory, since none of the nodes have names. This is where it is important to know where the end of the list is—L points to it. So we start by making our general node Current an alias of L:

```
    Current => L
```

Then we print the value in that node, and make Current an alias of the *next* node, which is pointed to by Current % Next:

```
    PRINT*, Current % Value
    Current => Current % Next
```

How do we detect the beginning of the list? Remember that the pointer in the first node (at the beginning of the list) is null—this can be tested for, so the above two statements can be enclosed in a DO WHILE loop:

```
    DO WHILE (ASSOCIATED(Current))
      PRINT *, Current % Value
      Current => Current % Next ! now make Current alias of next node
    END DO
```

Current is only null after the last execution of the loop, when it is made an alias of the pointer in the first node. This process demonstrates how important it is to have the pointer L pointing to the end of the list—otherwise you could never find it.

One of the advantages of using a linked list is that it can be disposed of when no longer needed, releasing valuable memory. This may be done as we traverse the list from the end, although now a little more "housekeeping" is required.

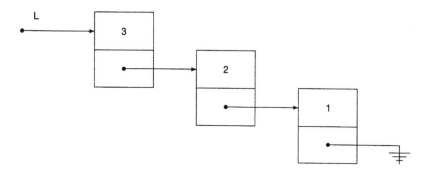

Fig. 13.1 A linked list

Once again, make `Current` an alias of the end of the list:

```
Current => L
```

You might be tempted to deallocate `Current` straight away. However, if you look at Figure 13.1 you will see that this is a prescription for disaster. With the last node removed, the link to the second last one is broken, and it consequently can never be found. So *before* deallocating `Current`, the end marker L should be made to point to the second last node:

```
L => Current % Next
```

Now `Current` may be safely deallocated, and the general node `Current` made an alias for the new end of the list:

```
Current => L
```

This process must be carried out as long as the end marker L is not null:

```
PRINT*, 'Deleting ...'
Current => L                   ! make Current alias of last node again
DO WHILE (ASSOCIATED(L))
  L => Current % Next ! disconnect L from last node, and make it ..
                      ! ... point to next one instead
  PRINT*, Current % Value, ' is about to go'  ! just to make sure
  DEALLOCATE( Current )
  Current => L                 ! alias of last remaining node
END DO
```

If you don't understand this, perhaps you should also resort to drawing some diagrams.

Before you go any further, you should put these pieces together in a working program to create a linked list, print it, and dispose of it.

13.3 Hidden Implementations of Abstract Data Types

One of the advantages of modules is that the details of the implementation of an *abstract data type* may be hidden from the user of a module. All the user is supplied with is the name of the data type and subprograms for manipulating it. This way, the details of the implementation in the module may be changed without affecting any code that uses the module.

To illustrate this most important principle, two modules are given in this section. One implements a list of integers as a linked list; the other implements the list as a dynamic array. The only change required in the driving main program is the name of the module used.

The linked list implementation is in the module ModLink. It is very similar to the example in Section 13.2, but has some important differences, which are discussed below:

```
MODULE ModLink
   ! Implementation of abstract data type as a linked list
```

```
    IMPLICIT NONE

    PRIVATE NODE

    TYPE NODE
      INTEGER Value
      TYPE (NODE), POINTER :: Next
    END TYPE NODE

    TYPE LIST
      PRIVATE
      TYPE (NODE), POINTER :: End
    END TYPE LIST

CONTAINS

SUBROUTINE Dispose( L )
  TYPE (NODE), POINTER :: Current
  TYPE (LIST) L
    Current => L % End             ! start at the end
    DO WHILE (ASSOCIATED(L % End))
      L % End => Current % Next     ! update the end before disposing
      PRINT*, Current % Value, ' is about to go'
      DEALLOCATE( Current )
      Current => L % End            ! alias of last node again
    END DO
END SUBROUTINE Dispose

SUBROUTINE Insert( L, Num )
  TYPE (NODE), POINTER :: Current
  TYPE (LIST) L
  INTEGER Num
  ALLOCATE( Current )             ! new node
  Current % Value = Num
  Current % Next => L % End       ! point it to previous node
  L % End => Current              ! update the end of the list
END SUBROUTINE Insert

SUBROUTINE PrintList( L )
  TYPE (NODE), POINTER :: Current
  TYPE (LIST) L
  ! Start at the end now
  PRINT*, 'From the end:'
  Current => L % End              ! alias of last node

  DO WHILE (ASSOCIATED(Current))
    PRINT *, Current % Value
    Current => Current % Next      ! alias of next node
  END DO
```

```
END SUBROUTINE PrintList

SUBROUTINE SetUp( L )
   TYPE (LIST) L
   NULLIFY( L % End )               ! list is empty at first
END SUBROUTINE SetUp

END MODULE ModLink
```

The most important difference is that our pointer L of Section 13.2, which marked the end of the linked list, is now specified with a derived type LIST. This is to enable a user of the module to declare a variable of this type to name his list, without needing to know precisely how the type is defined. All occurrences of L in the coding in Section 13.2 must therefore be replaced by L % End.

The PRIVATE specifications mean that the type NODE is inaccessible outside the module, and that the user will not have access to the internal structure of type LIST.

W.S. Brainerd, C.H. Goldberg and J.C. Adams, *Programmers' Guide to Fortran 90* (McGraw-Hill, 1990) suggest that the subroutine SetUp be written as a function, to return a null pointer to head the list,

```
FUNCTION SetUp()
   TYPE (LIST) SetUp
   NULLIFY (SetUp % End)
END FUNCTION SetUp
```

which is invoked in the accessing program as follows:

```
L = SetUp()
```

where L is of type LIST. This, however, is not allowed under the FTN90 compiler (it will not return a null pointer).

To use this implementation of a list, all that is needed is a main program like the following:

```
PROGRAM TestList
USE ModLink                 ! linked list implementation
IMPLICIT NONE
TYPE (LIST) L
INTEGER   :: Num = 1

CALL SetUp( L )

DO WHILE (Num /= 0)
   READ*, Num
   IF (Num /= 0) THEN
      CALL Insert( L, Num )
   END IF
END DO

CALL PrintList( L )
```

```
    CALL Dispose( L )                        ! always tidy up afterwards!

    END PROGRAM TestList
```

By contrast, the module ModArray implements the list as a dynamic array:

```
MODULE ModArray
   ! Implementation of abstract data type LIST as a dynamic array
   IMPLICIT NONE

   TYPE LIST
     PRIVATE
     INTEGER, DIMENSION(:), POINTER :: Elements   ! dynamic storage
   END TYPE LIST

CONTAINS

SUBROUTINE Dispose( L )
   TYPE (LIST) :: L
   DEALLOCATE( L % Elements )
END SUBROUTINE Dispose

SUBROUTINE Insert( L, Num )
   TYPE (LIST) :: L
   INTEGER, DIMENSION( SIZE( L % Elements ) ) :: OldL
   INTEGER N, Num
   OldL = L % Elements
   DEALLOCATE ( L % Elements )
   N = SIZE(OldL)
   N = N + 1
   ALLOCATE( L % Elements(N) )
   L % Elements = OldL
   L % Elements(N) = Num
END SUBROUTINE Insert

SUBROUTINE PrintList( L )
   TYPE (LIST), TARGET :: L                  ! note TARGET attribute
   INTEGER, DIMENSION(:), POINTER :: P
   INTEGER I
   P => L % Elements                         ! convenient alias
   PRINT*, 'From the end:'
   PRINT*, (P(I), I = SIZE(P), 1, -1 )
END SUBROUTINE PrintList

SUBROUTINE SetUp( L )
   TYPE (LIST) :: L
   ALLOCATE( L % Elements(0) )               ! size zero at first
END SUBROUTINE SetUp
```

```
END MODULE ModArray
```

The type LIST now has a component which is a pointer to a dynamic array (also inaccessible to the user).

Insert uses the technique of Chapter 9 to increase the size of a dynamic array by one element each time a new value is added.

PrintList uses an alias P to refer to the dynamic array purely for convenience. Note that the TARGET attribute of the derived type L is conferred on its component.

To use this implementation, all you have to do is to change the second line of the main program TestList to

```
USE ModArray    ! dynamic array implementation
```

We have seen in this section that modules with derived types can hide implementation details from the user. Type definitions and coding in the module procedures may be changed without affecting any code which uses the modules.

Summary

- A pointer variable has the POINTER attribute, and may point to (be an alias of) a variable of the same type, which has the TARGET attribute.
- An alias is simply another name for an object.
- Pointer assignment (=>) sets up or changes an alias.
- Ordinary assignment of pointer variables operates on their aliases.
- A pointer may be in one of three states: undefined, null, or associated.
- The NULLIFY statement puts a pointer into the null state. This may be tested for with the ASSOCIATED intrinsic function.
- The ASSOCIATED intrinsic function ascertains whether a pointer is an alias of some object or whether it is null. It can also determine whether a pointer is an alias of a particular target.
- An ordinary variable is allocated static storage at compile time.
- A dynamic variable is allocated dynamic storage at run time.
- A dynamic variable is created with the ALLOCATE statement and referenced with a pointer.
- Dynamic memory is released with DEALLOCATE.
- A dynamic array can have either the ALLOCATABLE or POINTER attribute. Its rank must be specified, but its bounds must be left undefined until an ALLOCATE statement has been executed for it.
- Arrays of pointers may not be declared directly in Fortran 90. However, a derived type may be defined with a pointer component, and an array of such a type can be declared.
- Implementation details of abstract data types may be hidden in modules.

Exercises

13.1 Write some lines of code which set up two pointers P1 and P2 as aliases of the integers I and J respectively.

Now write some additional code which effectively makes P1 an alias of J and P2 an alias of I, without referring to I and J explicitly.

13.2 Set up an array of structure variables with a single pointer component, and arrange for it to point to an array of integer values, suitably initialized.

Referring only to the "array" of pointers, use a Bubble Sort to sort the integer values into ascending order, and print the sorted list.

13.3 Set up an upper-triangular matrix of N rows and columns, with each row represented by a dynamic array of pointers.

13.4 Write a program to set up a linked list of integer values, read from the keyboard, print the list, and dispose of it.

14

Simulation

An extremely powerful application of modern computers is in *simulation*. A simulation is a *computer experiment* which mirrors some aspect of the real world that appears to be based on random processes, or is too complicated to understand properly. (Whether events can be really random is actually a philosophical or theological question.) Some examples are: radio-active decay, bacteria division and traffic flow. The essence of a simulation program is that the programmer is unable to predict before-hand exactly what the outcome of the program will be, which is true to the event being simulated. For example, when you spin a coin, you do not know exactly what the result will be.

14.1   Random Number Generation

The intrinsic subroutine RANDOM_NUMBER(R) may be used to simulate random events. It generates a uniformly distributed *pseudo-random number* in the range $0 \leq R < 1$. (A computer cannot generate truly random numbers, but they can be practically unpredictable.) R may be a scalar or an array, but it must be real. E.g.

```
REAL, DIMENSION(10) :: R
CALL RANDOM_NUMBER( R )
PRINT '(E14.7)', R
```

Output:

```
0.1077691E-01
0.1275343E00
0.4685287E00
0.5612317E00
0.6204859E00
0.5067996E00
0.7804365E00
0.7967151E00
0.3911508E00
0.7211771E-01
```

Of course if you re-use this piece of code again, you will get exactly the same sequence of "random" numbers, which is rather disappointing (and not true to life, as every gambler knows). To produce a different sequence each time, the generator can be *seeded* in a number of ways. Here's one way:

```
INTEGER Count
REAL, DIMENSION(10) :: R
INTEGER, DIMENSION(1)  :: Seed

CALL SYSTEM_CLOCK( Count )
Seed = Count

CALL RANDOM_SEED( PUT = Seed )
CALL RANDOM_NUMBER( R )
PRINT '(E14.7)', R
```

The intrinsic subroutine SYSTEM_CLOCK returns in its first (integer) argument the current value of the *system clock*. A second optional argument returns the number of clock counts per second.

RANDOM_SEED has an optional dummy argument PUT. This is a rank-one integer array which is used to reset the seed (Seed) for random number generation. It may be supplied directly by the user with a READ statement, or it may be generated itself from the system clock, as in this example. As long as the system clock keeps on ticking, you will get different results every time you run this code.

14.2 Spinning Coins

When a fair (unbiased) coin is spun, the probability of getting heads or tails in 0.5 (50%). Since a value returned by RANDOM_NUMBER is equally likely to anywhere in the interval [0, 1) we can represent heads, say, with a value less than 0.5; otherwise it will be tails.

Suppose an experiment calls for a coin to be spun 50 times, and the results recorded. In real life you are likely to want to repeat such an experiment a number of times; this is where computer simulation is handy. The following program simulates spinning a coin 50 times, and repeats the simulation five times:

```
INTEGER Count, I
REAL, DIMENSION(50) :: R
CHARACTER(1), DIMENSION(50) :: COINS
INTEGER, DIMENSION(1)  :: Seed

CALL SYSTEM_CLOCK( Count )
Seed = Count

DO I = 1, 5
  CALL RANDOM_SEED( PUT = Seed )
  PRINT*, Seed
  CALL RANDOM_NUMBER( R )
  WHERE (R < 0.5)
    COINS = 'H'
  ELSEWHERE
    COINS = 'T'
  END WHERE
  PRINT '(50A1)', COINS
  CALL RANDOM_SEED( GET  = Seed )
END DO

END
```

Output:

```
HHTTTHTTHHHHTTHHHTTTTTTHTTHTHTHTTHTTTHHTHTTHHHTTTHHT
HTHTTTHTTHHTHTTTTHTHHTHHHTTTHTTTTTTTTTTHTHTTHTTTTHHT
TTTHTTHHHTTHTTTHHHTTHHHTTTTHTHHHTTHTHTTHHTTHHHHHTT
HTHTHHTHHHHHTTHTHTTTHHHHHTTHHTTTHTTTTTHHHHTHHTTTTHH
HTHHTHHHTHTHHTHHTHTTHHHTHTTHTTTTTHHHTHHTHTTTTTTTHTH
```

The initial seed is once again generated by the system clock, and RANDOM_SEED is used to seed each simulation. At the end of each simulation, another optional argument GET is used to set Seed to the current value of the seed (each time a random number is generated the seed is reset internally). This means that an unbroken sequence of random seeds is used for the entire set of simulations (theoretically, this is preferable to reseeding the process with the system clock for each simulation).

Note the use of the WHERE construct to generate the array of results COINS from the array of random numbers R.

Note also that it should be impossible in principle to tell from the output alone whether the experiment was simulated or real (if the random number generator is sufficiently random).

14.3 Rolling Dice

When a fair die (plural "dice") is rolled, the number uppermost is equally likely to be any integer from 1 to 6. The following program segment simulates 20 rolls of a die. The output from two successive runs is shown.

```
INTEGER Count
REAL, DIMENSION(20) :: R
INTEGER, DIMENSION(20) :: Num
INTEGER, DIMENSION(1)  :: Seed

CALL SYSTEM_CLOCK( Count )
Seed = Count
CALL RANDOM_SEED( PUT  = Seed )
CALL RANDOM_NUMBER( R )
Num = INT( 6 * R + 1 )             ! applies to every element
PRINT '(20I3)', Num
```

Output:

```
2  1  4  2  5  4  3  4  3  4  3  4  6  4  4  6  2  3  6  2
3  6  4  5  3  4  2  1  3  4  4  1  5  5  2  2  6  5  3  4
```

If R is a real value in the range [0, 1), 6 * R will be in the range [0, 6), and 6 * R + 1 will be in the range [1, 7), i.e. between 1.000000 and 6.999999. Discarding the decimal part of this with INT will give an integer in the required range.

Note that the array R can be transformed into the array Num in a single statement. Once again, initializing the seed ensures that the two runs are different.

We can do statistics on our simulated experiment, just as if it were a real one. For example, we could estimate the mean of the number on the uppermost face when the die is rolled 100 times, say, and also the probability of getting a 6 (note that R is a scalar now, not an array):

```
INTEGER, PARAMETER :: Throws = 100
INTEGER Count, I, Num
REAL :: Num6, Mean, R
INTEGER, DIMENSION(1)  :: Seed

CALL SYSTEM_CLOCK( Count )
Seed = Count
CALL RANDOM_SEED( PUT  = Seed )
Mean = 0

DO I = 1, 20
  CALL RANDOM_NUMBER( R )
  Num = INT( 6 * R + 1 )
  Mean = Mean + Num
  IF (Num == 6) Num6 = Num6 + 1
END DO
```

```
    PRINT '("Mean:              ", F6.2)', Mean / Throws
    PRINT '("Chances of a 6:  ", F6.2)', Num6 / Throws
END
```

Output from two successive runs:

```
Mean:              3.32
Chances of a 6:    0.17

Mean:              3.62
Chances of a 6:    0.18
```

Run the program a number of times, increasing the value of Throws each time, and observe what happens to the mean and the chances of getting a 6.

14.4 Bacteria Division

If a fair coin is spun, or a fair die is rolled, the different events (e.g. getting "heads", or a 6) happen with equal likelihood. Suppose, however, that a certain type of bacteria divides (into two) in a given time interval with a probability of 0.75 (75%), and that if it does not divide, it dies. Since a value generated by RANDOM_NUMBER is equally likely to be anywhere between 0 and 1, the chances of it being less than 0.75 are 75%. We can therefore simulate this situation as follows:

```
CALL RANDOM_NUMBER( R )
IF (R < 0.75) THEN
  PRINT*, Count, R, "I am now we"
ELSE
  PRINT*, Count, R, "I am no more"
END IF
```

The basic principle of simulation is that one random number should be generated for each event being simulated. The single event here is whether or not the bacterium divides.

14.5 A Random Walk

A drunken sailor has to negotiate a jetty toward his ship. The jetty is 50 paces long and 20 wide. A mate places him in the middle of the jetty at the quay-end, and points him toward the ship. Suppose at every step he has a 60% chance of lurching toward the ship, but a 20% chance of lurching to the left or right (he manages always to be facing the ship). If he reaches the ship-end of the jetty, he is hauled aboard by waiting mates.

The problem is to simulate his progress along the jetty, and to estimate his chances of getting to the ship without falling into the sea. To do this correctly, we must simulate one *random walk* along the jetty, find out whether or not he reaches the ship, and then repeat this simulation 100 times, say. The proportion of simulations that end with the sailor safely in the ship will be an estimate of his chances of making it to the ship. For a given walk we assume that if he has not either reached the ship or fallen into the sea after, say, 10000 steps, he dies of thirst on the jetty.

To represent the jetty, we set up co-ordinates so that the x-axis runs along the middle of the jetty with the origin at the quay-end. x and y are measured in steps. The sailor starts his walk at the origin each time. The structure plan, program and output from two successive runs are as follows:

1. Initialize variables
2. Repeat 100 simulated walks down the jetty
   Start at the quay-end of the jetty
   While still on the jetty and still alive repeat:
      Get a random number R for the next step
      If R < 0.6 then
         Move forward (to the ship)
      Otherwise if R < 0.8 then
         Move port (left)
      Otherwise
         Move starboard
   If he got to the ship then
      Count that walk as a success
3. Compute and print estimated probability of reaching the ship

```
PROGRAM DrunkenSailor
IMPLICIT NONE
INTEGER   ::  Count                 ! system clock (to seed
                                    ! random number)
INTEGER :: NSafe = 0                ! number of times he makes it
INTEGER, DIMENSION(1) :: Seed ! seed for  random number generator
INTEGER :: Sims = 1000             ! number of simulations
INTEGER :: Steps = 0               ! number of steps taken on
                                    ! a given walk
INTEGER :: Walks                    ! counter
INTEGER :: X, Y                     ! position on jetty
REAL    :: PShip                    ! probability of reaching ship
REAL    :: R                        ! random number

CALL SYSTEM_CLOCK( Count )
Seed = Count
CALL RANDOM_SEED( PUT = Seed )     ! seed from system clock

DO Walks = 1, Sims
   Steps = 0; X = 0; Y = 0         ! each new walk starts
                                    ! at the origin
   DO WHILE (X <= 50 .AND. ABS(Y) <= 10 .AND. Steps < 10000)
      Steps = Steps + 1            ! that's another step
      CALL RANDOM_NUMBER( R )      ! random number for that step
      IF (R < 0.6) THEN            ! which way did he go?
```

```
      X = X + 1                        ! maybe forward
   ELSE IF (R < 0.8) THEN
      Y = Y + 1                        ! maybe to port
   ELSE
      Y = Y - 1                        ! maybe to starboard
   END IF

 END DO
 IF (X > 50) NSafe = NSafe + 1   ! he actually made it
END DO

PShip = NSafe * 100.0 / Sims       ! avoid integer division
PRINT '("Probability of reaching ship: ", F6.1, "%")', PShip
END PROGRAM DrunkenSailor
```

Ouput:

```
Probability of reaching ship:   89.1%
Probability of reaching ship:   87.8%
```

14.6 Dealing a Bridge Hand

Simulation is the basis of most computer games. The program in this section simulates a deal of 13 playing cards from a pack of 52.

The names of the four suits are assigned to elements 0 to 3 of the character array Suit, and the 13 face values are assigned to components 0 to 12 of the character array Value. Note that if a character array is initialized with a constructor, the character constants in the constructor must be blank-filled from the right to make them all the same length.

To deal a card, a random integer in the range 0 to 51 is generated, i.e. the 52 cards are represented uniquely by the numbers 0 to 51. The main problem is that a given card may only be dealt once. To ensure this, an integer array Check is set up. All its elements are initially zero (meaning no cards have been dealt yet). The function RanInt generates a random integer and assigns it to Num. Check(Num) is checked. If it is still zero, that card has not yet been dealt, so Num is put into the next element of Hand, and Check(Num) is set to 1. This indicates that card Num has now been dealt. If Check(Num) already has the value 1 when Num comes up, it means that card Num has already been dealt, so another random integer is generated. This process is repeated 13 times, until the array Hand contains 13 unique numbers in the range 0 to 51. This part of the problem may be structure planned as follows:

Repeat 13 times:
    Get a random number
    Convert it to an integer Num in the range 0 to 51
    While Check(Num) ≠ 0 repeat:
        Get another random integer Num
    Set Check(Num) to 1
    Assign Num to the next element of Hand.

To print the hand of cards, each element of Hand is subjected to integer division by 13. The quotient NS will be in the range 0 to 3 and gives the suit. The remainder NV will be in the range 0 to 12, and gives the face value. E.g. the number 43 on division by 13 gives a quotient of 4 (Clubs) and a remainder of 3 (Six), as shown in the first line of output after the program, which is as follows:

```
PROGRAM BridgeHand
IMPLICIT NONE
CHARACTER(8), DIMENSION(0:3) :: Suit = (/ "Spades  ", "Hearts  ", &
                                         "Diamonds", "Clubs   " /)
CHARACTER(5), DIMENSION(0:12) :: Value = (/ "Two  ", "Three", &
        "Four ", "Five ", "Six  ", "Seven", "Eight", "Nine ", &
        "Ten  ", "Jack ", "Queen", "King ", "Ace  " /)

INTEGER, DIMENSION(0:51) :: Check = 0
INTEGER                  :: Card, Count, Num, NS, NV
INTEGER, DIMENSION(13) :: Hand
INTEGER, DIMENSION(1)  :: Seed

CALL SYSTEM_CLOCK( Count )
Seed(1) = Count
CALL RANDOM_SEED( Put = Seed )

DO Card = 1, 13                         ! deal 13 cards
  Num = RanInt()
  DO WHILE (Check(Num) /= 0)            ! already dealt ...
    Num = RanInt()                      ! ... so try again
  END DO
  Check(Num) = 1                        ! tick it off
  Hand(Card) = Num
  NS = Hand(Card) / 13
  NV = MOD( Hand(Card), 13 )
  PRINT '(3A, T20, 3I5)', Value(NV), " of ", Suit(NS), &
                    Hand(Card), NS, NV
END DO

CONTAINS

FUNCTION RanInt()
  REAL R
  INTEGER RanInt
  CALL RANDOM_NUMBER( R )
  RanInt = INT( 52 * R )
END FUNCTION RanInt
END
```

A different hand will be dealt every time the program is run. Here is a sample hand (headings have been inserted into the text for clarity):

		Hand	NS	NV
Six	of Clubs	43	3	4
Jack	of Spades	9	0	9
Queen	of Clubs	49	3	10
Nine	of Diamonds	33	2	7
Three	of Diamonds	27	2	1
Two	of Clubs	39	3	0
Five	of Clubs	42	3	3
Three	of Clubs	40	3	1
Ace	of Clubs	51	3	12
Eight	of Diamonds	32	2	6
Six	of Hearts	17	1	4
Ten	of Hearts	21	1	8
Six	of Spades	4	0	4

You may feel that the method of "shuffling" the cards with the DO WHILE loop is very inefficient, because as more cards are dealt, so the number of calls to RANDOM_NUMBER goes up. The following code segment shuffles all 52 cards, by starting with a sorted pack (by initializing Hand), and swopping them at random, rather like a Bubble Sort.

```
INTEGER, DIMENSION(52) :: Hand = (/ (I, I = 0, 51) /)
...

DO Card = 1, 52
  CALL RANDOM_NUMBER( R )
  Num = INT( 52 * R ) + 1
  Temp = Hand(Num)
  Hand(Num) = Hand(Card)
  Hand(Card) = Temp
END DO
```

Note that Num is now in the range 1–52 since it represents the *position* of a card rather than the card itself. The only other change required is that Hand must have 52 elements. With a few amendments, a deal of all four hands can now be printed (you can also think about sorting each hand before it is printed, rather like players sort their cards after a deal).

You could test which of the two shuffling methods is more efficient by incrementing a counter each time RANDOM_NUMBER is called. A number of sample runs would then be needed to get an estimate of the average number of calls.

14.7 Traffic Flow

A major application of simulation is in modelling the traffic flow in large cities, in order to try out different traffic light patterns on the computer before inflicting them on the real traffic (this has been done on a large scale in Leeds in the United Kingdom, for example). In this example we look at a very small part of the problem: how to simulate the flow of a single line of traffic through one set of traffic lights.

We make the following assumptions (you can make additional or different ones if like):

(1) Traffic travels straight, without turning.
(2) The probability of a car arriving at the lights in any one second is independent of what happened during the previous second. This is called a *Poisson process*. This probability (call it *p*) may be estimated by watching cars at the intersection and monitoring their arrival pattern. In this simulation we take $p = 0.3$.
(3) When the lights are green, assume the cars move through at a steady rate of, say, eight every ten seconds.
(4) In the simulation, we will take the basic time interval to be ten seconds, so we want a display showing the length of the queue of traffic (if any) at the lights every ten seconds.
(5) We will set the lights red or green for variable multiples of ten seconds.

For the sample run below the lights are red for 40 seconds (Red = 4), green for 20 seconds (Green = 2). The simulation runs for 480 seconds (T = 48).

```
PROGRAM Traffic
IMPLICIT NONE
INTEGER   :: Cars       ! number of cars in queue
INTEGER   :: Count      ! system count
INTEGER   :: Green, Red ! period lights are green/red
INTEGER   :: GreenTimer ! counter for green lights
INTEGER   :: Sec, Sim   ! counters
INTEGER   :: RedTimer   ! counter for red lights
INTEGER   :: T          ! period of simulation
INTEGER, DIMENSION(1) :: Seed

REAL      :: P = 0.3    ! probability a car arrives in any second
REAL      :: R          ! random number

CHARACTER(1) :: Lights = "R"   ! lights are red at first
T = 48; Red = 4; Green = 2     ! parameters set
CALL SYSTEM_CLOCK( Count )
Seed = Count
RedTimer = 0                   ! cumulative counters initialized
GreenTimer = 0
Cars = 0

DO Sim = 1, T                          ! run for T 10-sec intervals
  DO Sec = 1, 10
    CALL RANDOM_NUMBER( R )
    IF (R < P) Cars = Cars + 1    ! another car arrives
  END DO
  IF (Lights == "G") THEN
    CALL Go
  ELSE
    CALL Stop
```

```
    END IF
END DO

CONTAINS

SUBROUTINE Go
! Lights are green here
  GreenTimer = GreenTimer + 1      ! advance green timer
  Cars = Cars - 8                  ! let 8 cars through
  IF (Cars < 0) Cars = 0           ! may have been less than 8!
  CALL PrintQ                      ! display traffic queue
  IF (GreenTimer == Green) THEN
    Lights = "R"                   ! change lights ...
    GreenTimer = 0                 ! ... and reset timer
  END IF
END SUBROUTINE Go

SUBROUTINE PrintQ
! print the queue of cars
  INTEGER I
  PRINT '(I3, 2X, A1, 2X, 70A1)', Sim, Lights, ('*', I = 1, Cars)
END SUBROUTINE PrintQ

SUBROUTINE Stop
! Lights are red here
  RedTimer = RedTimer + 1          ! advance red timer
  CALL PrintQ                      ! display traffic queue
  IF (RedTimer == Red) THEN
    Lights = "G"                   ! change lights ...
    RedTimer = 0                   ! ... and reset timer
  END IF
END SUBROUTINE Stop
END
```

Output:

```
 1  R  ***
 2  R  ********
 3  R  **********
 4  R  *************
 5  G  **********
 6  G  ****
 7  R  ******
 8  R  ******
 9  R  ********
10  R  ********
...
45  R  ************************
46  R  **************************
```

```
47  G   ********************
48  G   *************
```

From this particular run it seems that a traffic jam is building up, although more and longer runs are needed to see if this is really so. In that case, one can experiment with different periods for red and green lights in order to get an acceptable traffic pattern before setting the real lights to that cycle (try it). This is the great value of this sort of simulation. Of course, we can get closer to reality by considering two-way traffic, and allowing cars to turn in both directions, and occasionally to break down, but this program gives the basic ideas.

Summary

- A simulation is a computer program written to mimic a real-life situation which is apparently based on chance.
- The pseudo-random number generator RANDOM_NUMBER returns a uniformly distributed random number in the range [0, 1), and is the basis of the simulations discussed in this chapter.
- RANDOM_SEED enables the random number generator to be seeded by the user. The seed may be obtained from SYSTEM_CLOCK, which returns the system clock time.
- Every independent event being simulated requires a separate random number.

Exercises

14.1 In a game of Bingo the numbers 1 to 99 are drawn at random from a bag. Write a program to simulate the draw of the numbers (each number can be drawn only once), printing them ten to a line.

14.2 *One-dimensional random walk*: A gas molecule is constrained to move along the x-axis. It starts at the origin. It moves randomly a large number of times, to the left or right (with equal probability), one unit at a time. Let the frequency $F(X)$ be the number of times it is at position X. Write a program to compute these frequencies, and to print a bar chart representing them. Assume that the molecule never moves outside the range $-Xmax$ to $Xmax$.

14.3 RANDOM_NUMBER can be used to estimate π as follows   (such a method is called a Monte Carlo method). Write a program which generates random points in a square of length 2, say, and which counts what proportion of these points falls inside the circle of unit radius that fits exactly into the square. This proportion will be the ratio of the area of the circle to that of the square. Hence estimate π. (This is not a very efficient method, as you will see from the number of points required to get even a rough approximation.)

14.4 The aim of this exercise is to simulate bacteria growth.
    Suppose that a certain type of bacteria divides or dies according to the following assumptions:

1. during a fixed time interval, called a *generation*, a single bacterium divides into two identical replicas with probability p;
2. if it does not divide during that interval, it dies (i.e. ceases to be, "shuffles off this mortal coil");
3. the offspring (called daughters) will divide or die during the next generation, independently of the past history (there may well be no offspring, in which case the colony becomes extinct).

Start with a single individual and write a program which simulates a number of generations. Take $p = 0.75$. The number of generations which you can simulate will depend on your computer system. Carry out a large number (e.g. 100) of such simulations. The probability of ultimate extinction, $p(E)$, may be estimated as the proportion of simulations that end in extinction. You can also estimate the mean size of the nth generation from a large number of simulations. Compare your estimate with the theoretical mean of $(2p)^n$.

Statistical theory shows that the expected value of the extinction probability $p(E)$ is the smaller of 1, and $(1 - p)/p$. So for $p = 0.75$, $p(E)$ is expected to be $1/3$. But for $p \le 0.5$, $p(E)$ is expected to be 1, which means that extinction is certain (a rather unexpected result). You can use your program to test this theory by running it for different values of p, and estimating $p(E)$ in each case.

14.5 Dribblefire Jets Inc. make two types of aeroplane, the two-engined DFII, and the four-engined DFIV. The engines are terrible and fail with probability 0.5 on a standard flight (the engines fail independently of each other). The manufacturers claim that the planes can fly if at least half of their engines are working, i.e. the DFII will crash only if both its engines fail, while the DFIV will crash if all four, or if any three engines fail.

You have been commissioned by the Civil Aviation Board to ascertain which of the two models is less likely to crash. Since parachutes are expensive, the cheapest (and safest!) way to do this is to simulate a large number of flights of each model. For example, two calls of RANDOM_NUMBER could represent one standard DFII flight: if both random numbers are less than 0.5, that flight crashes, otherwise it doesn't. Write a program which simulates a large number of flights of both models, and estimates the probability of a crash in each case. If you can run enough simulations, you may get a surprising result. (Incidentally, the probability of n engines failing on a given flight is given by the binomial distribution, but you do not need to use this fact in the simulation.)

14.6 Two players, A and B, play a game called *Eights*. They take it in turns to choose a number 1, 2 or 3, which may not be the same as the last number chosen (so if A starts with 2, B may only choose 1 or 3 at the next move). A starts, and may choose any of the three numbers for the first move. After each move, the number chosen is added to a common running total. If the total reaches 8 exactly, the player whose turn it was wins the game. If a player causes the total to go over 8, the other player wins. For example, suppose A starts with 1 (total 1), B chooses 2 (total 3), A chooses 1 (total 4) and B chooses 2 (total 6). A would like to play 2 now, to win, but he can't because B cunningly played it on the last move, so A chooses 1 (total

7). This is even smarter, because *B* is forced to play 2 or 3, making the total go over 8 and thereby losing.

Write a program to simulate each player's chances of winning, if they always play at random.

15

Matrices and Their Applications

In this chapter we look at how to write programs to solve problems involving matrices, with examples from such areas as linear algebra, networks, population dynamics, and Markov processes.

The applications introduced here follow on from Chapter 9, where one-dimensional (rank-one) arrays were discussed (such arrays are also called *vectors*). In this chapter we deal with arrays having more than one subscript, or *multi-dimensional* arrays. Although up to seven dimensions are allowed in Fortran, we will discuss only two-dimensional arrays here, since these are the most common. An array with two subscripts can represent a *table* of numbers, since one subscript (usually the first) can label the *rows* in the table, while the second subscript labels the *columns*. This is also the convention adopted for matrices. Tables and matrices look exactly the same, but since matrices are used in mathematical applications, we will deal with them separately.

	D1	*D2*	*D3*
S1	3	12	10
S2	17	18	35
S3	7	10	24

Fig. 15.1 Cost table

15.1 Tables: a Concrete Example

A ready-mix concrete company has three factories (S1, S2 and S3) which must
supply three building sites (D1, D2 and D3). The costs, in some suitable currency,
of transporting a load of concrete from any factory to any site are given by the cost
table in Figure 15.1.

The factories can supply 4, 12 and 8 loads per day respectively, and the sites
require 10, 9 and 5 loads per day respectively. The real problem is to find the
cheapest way to satisfy the demands at the sites, but we are not considering that
here.

Suppose the factory manager proposes the following transportation scheme (each
entry represents the number of loads of concrete to be transported along that
particular route):

	D1	*D2*	*D3*
S1	4	0	0
S2	6	6	0
S3	0	3	5

This sort of scheme is called a *solution* to the transportation problem. The cost table
(and the solution) can then be represented by tables **C** and **X**, say, where c_{ij} is the
entry in row i and column j of the cost table, with a similar convention for **X**.

To compute the cost of the above solution, each entry in the solution table must
be multiplied by the corresponding entry in the cost table. This operation is not
to be confused with matrix multiplication, which is discussed below. We therefore
want to calculate

$$3 \times 4 + 12 \times 0 + \ldots + 24 \times 5.$$

The following program will do what is required:

```
INTEGER, DIMENSION(3,3) :: C, X
DATA ((C(I, J), J = 1,3), I = 1,3) &
                    / 3, 12, 10, 17, 18, 35, 7, 10, 24 /
DATA ((X(I, J), J = 1,3), I = 1,3) / 4, 0, 0, 6, 6, 0, 0, 3, 5 /
TotCost = 0

DO I = 1, 3
  DO J = 1, 3
```

```
      TotCost = TotCost + C(I,J) * X(I,J)
    END DO
  END DO

  PRINT*, "Total cost:", TotCost
  END
```

There are a number of important points to note.

- In Fortran 90 terms, the arrays C and X have two dimensions (rank two). Each dimension has an extent of 3, and the shape of the arrays is (3, 3).
- You might be wondering why the DATA statements need implied DO loops. Wouldn't it be much simpler to say

```
  DATA C / 3, 12, 10, 17, 18, 35, 7, 10, 24 /
```

This raises an extremely important point, which has caused many a programmer to come to grief. Certain Fortran statements, such as DATA, READ and PRINT treat the elements of multi-dimensional arrays in a particular order when the array is referenced by its name only. This order is called the *array element order*, and is obtained by changing the *left-most* subscript most rapidly. This is the reverse of *odometer* order, where the right-most subscript changes most rapidly, and which is used in many other languages.

As a result, the briefer form of the DATA statement used in this note is equivalent to the following assignments:

```
  C(1,1) = 3
  C(2,1) = 12
  C(3,1) = 10
  C(1,2) = 17
  C(2,2) = 18
  C(3,2) = 35
  C(1,3) = 7
  C(2,3) = 10
  C(3,3) = 24
```

Although it makes no difference to the answer here, the table is not represented by the conventional row-column order depicted in Figure 15.1. **It is therefore always necessary to use implied DO loops when initializing or reading multi-dimensional arrays if the data is presented by rows.**

- As an alternative to the DATA statement, the arrays could have been read from the keyboard, or a file, e.g.

```
  READ*, ((C(I, J), J = 1,3), I = 1,3)
```

assuming the data to be in row order.

- An array constructor may only be used to initialize a one-dimensional array. However, the intrinsic function RESHAPE may be used to initialize a multi-dimensional array from an array constructor, as shown in Chapter 9.

- Fortran 90 provides a neater way of calculating the total cost of the transport scheme above. Since the intrinsic operators, when applied to arrays, operate on all elements of the array, the operation C * X will return the (3, 3) array with elements $c_{ij}x_{ij}$. The intrinsic function SUM returns the (scalar) sum of all the elements of its array argument. Therefore the single statement

```
SUM( C * X )
```

will calculate the total cost. Try it out.

15.2   Graphs without Graphics

Standard Fortran 90 does not provide output to graphics devices, such as a PC graphics screen. The module GraphMod described in this section enables you to draw a rough graph of any function on the standard output device (e.g. the PC text screen or printer).

As an example, suppose you want to draw the graph of the function

$$y(t) = e^{-0.05t} \sin t,$$

over the range $0 \leq t \leq 4\pi$, in steps of $\pi/20$. There are two subroutines in the module which you need to call. The first is SetWindow(Xmin, Xmax, Ymin, Ymax), which sets up the *world co-ordinates* of your problem, i.e. the rectangular region of your co-ordinate system which will be plotted. So if you want a vertical range between -1 and 1, call SetWindow with the following arguments:

```
CALL SetWindow( 0.0, 4 * Pi, -1.0, 1.0 )
```

Note that the arguments must be real (integer constants will cause an error).

You then need to set up two one-dimensional arrays X and Y, say, in general, where X(I) and Y(I) are the x and y co-ordinates of the ith point to be plotted. (In this example the x co-ordinate will be t.) Finally, you need to supply the plotting symbol, and a title. E.g.

```
CALL Grapher( X, Y, "#", "Damped Oscillations" )
```

where # is the plotting symbol, and "Damped Oscillations" is the title.

The complete main program to draw this graph is then:

```
PROGRAM DrawGraph
USE GraphMod

IMPLICIT NONE
INTEGER, PARAMETER :: NPts = 80
INTEGER I
REAL, PARAMETER    :: Pi   = 3.1415927
REAL dt, T
REAL X(NPts), Y(NPts)

T = 0
dt = Pi / 20.0
```

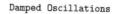

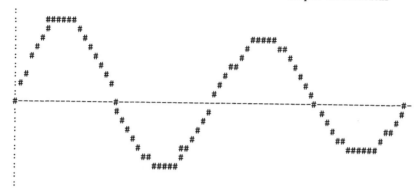

Fig. 15.2 Output generated by Grapher

```
DO I = 1, NPts
  Y(I) = EXP(-0.05 * T) * SIN(T)
  X(I) = T
  T = T + dt
END DO

CALL SetWindow( 0.0, 4 * Pi, -1.0, 1.0 )          ! real arguments
CALL Grapher( X, Y, "#", "Damped Oscillations" )

END PROGRAM DrawGraph
```

The output is shown in Figure 15.2. Note that the *x*- and *y*-axes are also drawn.

We need now to discuss the module, beginning with the mathematics required to transform the general point *y(x)* into a position on the screen or printer.

The plotting is done essentially by printing a two-dimensional character array Point (in Grapher), where the *y* co-ordinate is transformed to row *R*, and the *x* co-ordinate is transformed to column *C*. A plotting symbol is then stored in Point(R, C). Note that the *y* co-ordinate is represented by the *first* subscript, in keeping with the usual row-column notation.

To be more precise, the element Y(I) (y_i) of the array Y must be transformed to *R*. Since we want a linear transformation we must have

$$R = ay_i + b, \tag{15.1}$$

where the constants *a* and *b* must be determined. Let's call the highest point on the graph y_U. This is set by the argument Ymax of SetWindow, and must be transformed into row 1 (the top of the graph), so

$$1 = ay_U + b. \tag{15.2}$$

The lowest point on the graph, y_D (set by Ymin) must be transformed into the maximum row R_m (set in GraphMod by the constant MaxRow), so

$$R_m = ay_D + b. \tag{15.3}$$

Subtracting Equation 15.2 from Equation 15.3 immediately gives

$$a = (R_m - 1)/(y_D - y_U)$$

and substituting back into Equation 15.2 gives

$$b = 1 - y_U(R_m - 1)/(y_D - y_U).$$

These values for a and b may be used in Equation 15.1 to give

$$R = \frac{(y_i - y_U)(R_m - 1)}{y_D - y_U} + 1.$$

A similar transformation is used to scale the element X(I) (x_i) into a column C:

$$C = \frac{(x_i - x_L)(C_m - 1)}{x_R - x_L} + 1,$$

where x_L and x_R are the left-most and right-most points on the graph (set by Xmin and Xmax respectively), and C_m is the maximum column (set in GraphMod by MaxCol).

The transformations for R and C are coded in GraphMod as two functions YScale and XScale (i.e. YScale(Y(I)) returns R), so that they can be generally available, e.g. to draw the x- and y-axes.

The complete coding for GraphMod is as follows:

```
MODULE GraphMod
IMPLICIT NONE
INTEGER, PRIVATE, PARAMETER :: MaxRow = 20
INTEGER, PRIVATE, PARAMETER :: MaxCol = 75
REAL, PRIVATE :: XL, XR, YD, YU    ! first, last, down, up: global

CONTAINS

SUBROUTINE Grapher( X, Y, Symbol, Title )
! General graphing routine: arguments described in text
  INTEGER I, J
  REAL, INTENT(IN):: X(:), Y(:)
  CHARACTER(*), INTENT(IN) :: Symbol, Title      ! assumed length
  CHARACTER(1) Point( MaxRow, MaxCol )
  CHARACTER(10) MyFormat

  WRITE( MyFormat, '("("I2, "A1)")' ) MaxCol        ! internal file
  Point = " "                               ! all blanks initially
  ! really should check whether axes lie in range
  Point( 1:MaxRow, XScale(0.0) ) = ":"       ! y-axis
  Point( YScale(0.0), 1:MaxCol ) = "-"       ! x-axis

  DO I = 1, SIZE( X )
     Point( YScale(Y(I)), XScale(X(I)) ) = Symbol      ! Y is "row"
```

```
    END DO

    PRINT '(A80 /)', Title
    PRINT MyFormat, ((Point(I,J), J = 1, MaxCol), &
                                  I = 1, MaxRow) ! by rows
 END SUBROUTINE Grapher

 SUBROUTINE SetWindow( Xmin, Xmax, Ymin, Ymax )
 ! Imports grapher limits to be available as globals
    REAL Xmin, Xmax, Ymin, Ymax
       XL = Xmin
       XR = Xmax
       YU = Ymax
       YD = Ymin
 END SUBROUTINE SetWindow

 FUNCTION XScale( X )
 ! Scales x-coordinate to a column on the screen
    INTEGER XScale
    REAL X
       XScale = NINT( (X - XL) * (MaxCol - 1) / (XR - XL) + 1 )
 END FUNCTION XScale

 FUNCTION YScale( Y )
 ! Scales y-coordinate to a row on the screen
    INTEGER YScale
    REAL Y
       YScale = NINT( (Y - YU) * (MaxRow - 1) / (YD - YU) + 1 )
 END FUNCTION YScale
 END MODULE GraphMod
```

Once again, the use of a module with private variables means that it can be changed without reference to any code that uses it.

The variables XL, XR etc. (set by SetWindow) are global to the module, so that they can be used by all its subprograms.

The use of an internal file (the character variable MyFormat) enables the format specification for the main PRINT statement to be set at runtime according to the value of MaxCol. In this example, the value of MyFormat is "75A1".

The axes may not lie in the region being plotted—this should strictly be checked before attempting to draw them.

15.3   Matrices

A *matrix* is a two-dimensional array which may be used in a wide variety of representations. For example, a distance array representing the lengths of direct connections in a network is a matrix. We will deal mainly with *square* matrices in this chapter (i.e. matrices having the same number of rows as columns), although in principle a matrix can have any number of rows or columns. A matrix with only one column is also called a *vector*.

A matrix is usually denoted by a bold capital letter, e.g. **A**. Each entry, or element, of the matrix is denoted by the small letter of the same name followed by two subscripts, the first indicating the row of the element, and the second indicating the column. So a general element of the matrix **A** is called a_{ij}, meaning it may be found in row i and column j. If **A** has three rows and columns—(3 × 3) for short—it will look like this in general:

$$\begin{bmatrix} a_{11} & a_{12} & a_{13} \\ a_{21} & a_{22} & a_{23} \\ a_{31} & a_{32} & a_{33} \end{bmatrix}.$$

A special matrix which we will come across later is the *identity* matrix. This has ones on the *main diagonal*, and zeros everywhere else. E.g. the (3 × 3) identity matrix is

$$\begin{bmatrix} 1 & 0 & 0 \\ 0 & 1 & 0 \\ 0 & 0 & 1 \end{bmatrix}.$$

Various mathematical operations are defined on matrices. Addition and subtraction are obvious, and may be done with the intrinsic operators in Fortran 90. So the matrix addition

$$\mathbf{A} = \mathbf{B} + \mathbf{C}$$

translates directly into

```
A = B + C
```

where the arrays must clearly all have the same *shape*, i.e. the same extent along corresponding dimensions.

Matrix multiplication   Probably the most important matrix operation is matrix *multiplication*. It is used widely in such areas as network theory, solution of linear systems of equations, transformation of co-ordinate systems, and population modelling, for examples. The rules for multiplying matrices look a little weird if you've never seen them before, but will be justified by the applications that follow.

When two matrices **A** and **B** are multiplied together, their product is a third matrix **C**. The operation is written as

$$\mathbf{C} = \mathbf{AB},$$

and the general element c_{ij} of **C** is formed by taking the *scalar product* of the ith row of **A** with the jth column of **B**. (The scalar product of two *vectors* **x** and **y** is $x_1 y_1 + x_2 y_2 + \ldots$, where x_i and y_i are the components of the vectors.)

It follows that **A** and **B** can only be successfully multiplied (in that order) if the number of columns in **A** is the same as the number of rows in **B**.

The general definition of matrix multiplication is as follows: If **A** is a $(n \times m)$ matrix and **B** is a $(m \times p)$ matrix, their product **C** will be a $(n \times p)$ matrix such that the general element c_{ij} of **C** is given by

$$c_{ij} = \sum_{k=1}^{m} a_{ik} b_{kj}.$$

Note that in general **AB** is not equal to **BA** (matrix multiplication is not *commutative*).
    Example:

$$\begin{bmatrix} 1 & 2 \\ 3 & 4 \end{bmatrix} \times \begin{bmatrix} 5 & 6 \\ 0 & -1 \end{bmatrix} = \begin{bmatrix} 5 & 4 \\ 15 & 14 \end{bmatrix}$$

The Fortran 90 intrinsic operator * will not perform matrix multiplication. The intrinsic operation A * B, where A and B are arrays representing matrices, returns an array with each element the simple product of the two corresponding elements of A and B. We will discuss below how to redefine the intrinsic operator to perform matrix multiplication. But before we do this, it is instructive to write a subroutine to multiply two matrices directly:

```
SUBROUTINE MyMatMul( A, B, C )
 ! multiplies A (n x m) by B (m x p)
 ! and returns product in C (n x p)
 ! performs no checks on shapes of A and B
   REAL, DIMENSION(:,:) :: A, B, C
   INTEGER I, J, M, N, P
   N = SIZE( A, 1)      ! number of rows
   M = SIZE( A, 2)      ! number of columns
   P = SIZE( B, 2)
   DO I = 1, N
     DO J = 1, P
       C(I,J) = SUM( A(I,1:M) * B(1:M,J) )   ! scalar product
     END DO
   END DO
END SUBROUTINE MyMatMul
```

Note that the intrinsic function SIZE has an optional second argument specifying the dimension of which the size is required.
    The statement which computes C(I,J) illustrates the use of Fortran 90 array sections. A(I,1:M) is the Ith row of A and B(1:M,J) is the Jth column of B. Both these sections are one-dimensional. The sum of their intrinsic product returns the scalar product of the two sections. This could be done explicitly with

```
DO K = 1, M
  C(I,J) = C(I,J) + A(I,K) * B(K,J)
END DO
```

as long as C is first initialized to zero.
    Strictly, checks should be performed on the shapes of A and B to ensure that they are consistent.
    The main program below uses this subroutine to multiply matrices of any size:

```
IMPLICIT NONE
INTEGER I, J, N, M, P
REAL, DIMENSION(:,:), ALLOCATABLE :: A, B, C
PRINT*, "n, m, p:"
READ*, N, M, P
```

```
ALLOCATE( A(N,M) )
ALLOCATE( B(M,P) )
ALLOCATE( C(N,P) )
PRINT*, "matrix A:"
READ*, ((A(I,J), J = 1, M), I = 1, N)
PRINT*, "matrix B:"
READ*, ((B(I,J), J = 1, P), I = 1, N)
CALL MyMatMul( A, B, C )
PRINT*, ((C(I,J), J = 1, P), I = 1, N)
END
```

If you do this sort of thing often it will be worth your while to write subroutines to read and print matrices, in order to make sure that the data is read by rows.

At this stage I can confess that Fortran 90 has two intrinsic functions, which return a dot (scalar) product and a matrix product: DOT_PRODUCT(X, Y) and MATMUL(A, B). However, if you are serious about scientific programming it is part of your education to be able to code a matrix multiplication directly.

Defined operations for matrix handling   Matrix multiplication occurs so frequently in scientific programming that it would be convenient to define an operator for it. Consider the module MatMult:

```
MODULE MatMult

INTERFACE OPERATOR(.x.)
   MODULE PROCEDURE MatTimesMat, MatTimesVector
END INTERFACE

CONTAINS

FUNCTION MatTimesMat( A, B )
  REAL, DIMENSION(:,:) :: A, B
  REAL, DIMENSION( SIZE(A,1), SIZE(B,2) ) :: MatTimesMat
  MatTimesMat = MATMUL( A, B )
END FUNCTION MatTimesMat

FUNCTION MatTimesVector( A, X )
  REAL, DIMENSION(:,:) :: A
  REAL, DIMENSION(:)    :: X
  REAL, DIMENSION( SIZE(A,1) ) :: MatTimesVector
  MatTimesVector = MATMUL( A, X )
END FUNCTION MatTimesVector

END MODULE MatMult
```

The function MatTimesMat returns the matrix resulting from the multiplication of its two matrix arguments, using the intrinsic function MATMUL. Note that since MatTimesMat cannot return an assumed-shape array (unless it has the POINTER attribute), it must be declared with the dimensions of its arguments, which are obtained at runtime. We should strictly check that A and B have the right number of rows and columns for multiplication.

MatTimesVector is similar, except that it handles multiplication of a matrix by a *vector*. (Note, however, that the intrinsic function MATMUL can handle both these situations.) Since a vector is simply a one-dimensional matrix, the definition of matrix multiplication given above also applies in this case, e.g.

$$\begin{bmatrix} 1 & 2 \\ 3 & 4 \end{bmatrix} \times \begin{bmatrix} 2 \\ 3 \end{bmatrix} = \begin{bmatrix} 8 \\ 18 \end{bmatrix}.$$

A multiplication operator (.x.) is defined in the interface block. The following code uses this module to test the two forms of matrix multiplication:

```
USE MatMult

REAL :: A(2,3) = RESHAPE( (/1,3,2,4, 1, 2/), (/2,3/) )
REAL :: B(3,2) = RESHAPE( (/1, 2, 1, 0, 2, 3/), (/3,2/) )
REAL :: D(2,2) = RESHAPE( (/1,3,2,4/), (/2,2/) )
REAL :: X(2) = (/ 2,3 /)
REAL C(2,2)

C = A .x. B                              ! matrix times matrix
PRINT "(2F3.0)", ((C(I,J), J=1,2),I=1,2)
X = D .x. X                              ! matrix times vector
PRINT "(2F3.0)", X
```

It would be more elegant to redefine the intrinsic operator *, so that one could write statements like C = A * B. There is a complication here, though, because intrinsic multiplication is defined for arrays, as we have seen, and an intrinsic *operation* may not be redefined. The solution is to define a new type to represent matrices, and then to overload the * operator.

If a type

```
TYPE MATRIX
   REAL :: Elt
END TYPE MATRIX
```

is defined, matrices can be declared with

```
TYPE (MATRIX), DIMENSION (2,2) :: M1, M2, M3
```

A function which explicitly multiplies two matrices defined in this way can then be written:

```
FUNCTION MatTimesMat( A, B )
   TYPE (MATRIX), DIMENSION(:,:) :: A, B
   TYPE (MATRIX), DIMENSION( SIZE(A,1), SIZE(B,2) ) :: MatTimesMat
   INTEGER I, J, EM
   EM = SIZE(A,2)            ! columns of A must equal rows of B
   DO I = 1, SIZE(A,1)       ! rows of A
      DO J = 1, SIZE(B,2)    ! columns of B
```

```
                MatTimesMat(I,J) % Elt = SUM( A(I,1:EM) % Elt &
                                * B(1:EM,J) % Elt ) ! scalar product
            END DO
          END DO
        END FUNCTION MatTimes( A, B )
```

The * operator can then be overloaded with an interface block, as above.
  Multiplication of a scalar by a matrix can be defined by a similar function, say,

```
    FUNCTION ScalarTimesMat( X, B )
      REAL X
      TYPE (MATRIX), DIMENSION(:,:) B
      TYPE (MATRIX), DIMENSION( SIZE(B,1), &
        SIZE(B,2) ) :: ScalarTimesMat
      ...
```

to handle expressions like 2 * B, where the operands are represented by the arguments, in that order. If you also want to be able to write B * 2 you would need a
third function, say,

```
    FUNCTION MatTimesScalar( A, X )
      REAL X
      TYPE (MATRIX), DIMENSION(:,:) A
      TYPE (MATRIX), DIMENSION( SIZE(A,1), &
        SIZE(A,2) ) :: MatTimesScalar
      ...
```

The interface block would then look like this (the functions must all be in the same
module):

```
    INTERFACE OPERATOR(*)
      MODULE PROCEDURE MatTimesMat, ScalarTimesMat, MatTimesScalar
    END INTERFACE
```

It might also be convenient to redefine the assignment operator, to allow statements
like A = 0. This must be done with a *subroutine*, where the two arguments represent
the left- and right-hand sides of the assignment, e.g.

```
    SUBROUTINE MatFromScalar( Mat, X )
      REAL X
      TYPE (MATRIX), DIMENSION(:,:) :: Mat
      Mat % Elt = X
    END SUBROUTINE MatFromScalar
```

The following interface block is then needed:

```
    INTERFACE ASSIGNMENT(=)
      MODULE PROCEDURE MatFromScalar
    END INTERFACE
```

It would be a nice project to build these facilities into a working module. Unfortunately, FTN90 version 1.2 would not compile it.

If you do a lot of heavy number crunching you might need to use double precision real kind.

15.4 Array Handling Features

Array expressions It is worth recalling that when the intrinsic operators are applied to matrices, they are applied to each element of the matrix. The expression 1 / A will not therefore return the matrix inverse of **A**, but rather a conformable array with every element the reciprocal of the corresponding element of **A**.

Array sections Consider the array C representing the cost table in Figure 15.1. The statement

    A = C(1:2,1:2) + C(1:2,2:3)

where A has shape (2, 2) adds two sections of C. The first consists of the first two rows and columns, and the second consists of the first two rows and the second and third columns. The statement is therefore equivalent to the matrix addition

$$\begin{bmatrix} 3 & 12 \\ 17 & 18 \end{bmatrix} + \begin{bmatrix} 12 & 10 \\ 18 & 35 \end{bmatrix} = \begin{bmatrix} 15 & 22 \\ 35 & 53 \end{bmatrix}.$$

Note that the addition is performed on corresponding positions along a dimension, not on corresponding subscripts.

As another example, suppose **A** is a (3×3) matrix. In order to find its inverse by Gauss reduction, a (3×6) *augmented* matrix **B** is formed, with **A** occupying its first three columns, and the identity matrix occupying its last three columns. E.g. if **A** is given by

$$\begin{bmatrix} 2 & -1 & 1 \\ 1 & 1 & 1 \\ 3 & -1 & -1 \end{bmatrix},$$

B will be

$$\begin{bmatrix} 2 & -1 & 1 & 1 & 0 & 0 \\ 1 & 1 & 1 & 0 & 1 & 0 \\ 3 & -1 & -1 & 0 & 0 & 1 \end{bmatrix}.$$

If Idn represents the identity matrix, **B** can be set up in two lines:

    B(1:3, 1:3) = A
    B(1:3, 4:6) = Idn

Some more intrinsic functions It is generally more efficient to use the intrinsic functions to handle arrays, rather than to operate directly on their elements. E.g. add up the elements of an array with SUM, rather than in a DO loop.

MAXVAL(A) and MINVAL(A) return the maximum and minimum elements of the array A respectively.

MERGE(A, B, MASK) is an elemental function, meaning it operates on each element of its arguments, returning a corresponding element. It returns A if the logical array MASK is true, and B otherwise. E.g. if the arguments represent matrices

```
C = MERGE( A, B, A > B )
```

returns a matrix **C** such that c_{ij} is the larger of a_{ij} and b_{ij}.

RESHAPE(SOURCE, SHAPE) reshapes the array SOURCE into the shape given by the elements of the array SHAPE (which must be constant), i.e. the first element of SHAPE gives the extent (size) of the first dimension of the result. The reshaping is done by *array element order*, i.e. SOURCE is first strung out in array element order, and then reshaped.

The following code

```
INTEGER A(2,3), B(3,2)
A(1,1:3) = (/ 1, 2, 3 /)
A(2,1:3) = (/ 4, 5, 6 /)
B = RESHAPE( A, SHAPE = (/ 3, 2 /) )
```

reshapes the array A from

```
1 2 3
4 5 6
```

into the array B:

```
1 5
4 3
2 6
```

Get it?

Since an array constructor can only be used to construct a one-dimensional array, RESHAPE may be used to reshape such a constructor into a two-dimensional array. The following code sets up a (3×3) identity matrix:

```
INTEGER, DIMENSION(3,3) :: Idn
Idn = RESHAPE( SOURCE = (/ 1, 0, 0, 0, 1, 0, 0, 0, 1 /), &
               SHAPE = (/ 3, 3 /) )
```

Note that intrinsic functions may be called with keyword actual argument, using the dummy argument names as keywords. Dummy argument names are given in Appendix C.

SHAPE(A) returns a one-dimensional array holding the shape of A.

SIZE(A [,DIM]) returns the size of the array A if DIM is absent, or the extent along dimension DIM if it is present.

SPREAD(SOURCE, DIM, NCOPIES) makes NCOPIES duplicates of SOURCE by increasing its rank. The argument DIM specifies the dimension of the result along which the duplication takes place. This is best understood by examples, which may be generated by the following program:

```
INTEGER, PARAMETER :: M = 3
INTEGER DIM, NCOPIES, I, J, R, C
INTEGER :: A(M) = (/ (I, I = 1, M) /)
INTEGER, ALLOCATABLE :: B(:,:)
PRINT*, "DIM, NCOPIES"
READ*, DIM, NCOPIES
IF (DIM == 1) THEN
  R = NCOPIES                ! rows
  C = M                      ! columns
ELSE IF (DIM == 2) THEN
  R = M                      ! rows
  C = NCOPIES                ! columns
END IF
ALLOCATE( B(R,C) )
B = SPREAD( A, DIM, NCOPIES )
DO I = 1, R
  PRINT*, (B(I,J), J = 1, C)
END DO
END
```

The one-dimensional array A, with elements 1, 2, and 3 in this example, is to be duplicated. If DIM is 1 and NCOPIES is 4, B is returned as

```
1 2 3
1 2 3
1 2 3
1 2 3
```

i.e. 4 copies are made along the first dimension of B. If DIM is 2 and NCOPIES is 2, the result is

```
1 1
2 2
3 3
```

i.e. 2 copies are made along the second dimension. The source A may also be an array section.

TRANSPOSE(A) returns the *transpose* of matrix **A** (rows and columns interchanged).

UNPACK(VECTOR, MASK, FIELD) returns an array with the same shape as the logical array MASK. The elements of the result corresponding to true elements of MASK are assembled in array element order from the one-dimensional array VECTOR. All other elements of the result are equal to FIELD if it is a scalar. E.g. the following code replaces all positive elements of A by the integers 1, 2, 3, ..., and all negative elements by zero:

```
INTEGER A(4,4), V(16), F
V = (/ (I, I = 1, 16) /)
F = 0
... assign values to A
```

```
A = UNPACK( V, A > 0, F )
```

PACK performs the reverse operation.
Further array handling intrinsic functions are described in Appendix C.

15.5 Networks

In our first application of matrix multiplication we consider a problem which at first glance seems to have nothing to do with it.

A spy ring Suppose five spies in an espionage ring have the code names Alex, Boris, Cyril, Denisov and Eric (whom we can label A, B, C, D and E respectively). The hallmark of a good spy network is that no agent is able to contact all the others. The arrangement for this particular group is:

- Alex can contact only Cyril;
- Boris can contact only Alex or Eric;
- Denisov can contact only Cyril;
- Eric can contact only Cyril or Denisov.

(Cyril can't contact anyone in the ring: he takes information out of the ring to the spymaster. Similarly, Boris brings information in from the spymaster: no-one in the ring can contact him.) The need for good spies to know a bit of matrix theory becomes apparent when we spot that the possible paths of communication between the spies can be represented by a (5 × 5) matrix, with the rows and columns representing the transmitting and receiving agents respectively, thus:

	A	B	C	D	E
A	0	0	1	0	0
B	1	0	0	0	1
C	0	0	0	0	0
D	0	0	1	0	0
E	0	0	1	1	0

We will call this matrix **A**. It represents a *directed network* with the spies at the *nodes*, and with *arcs* all of length 1, where a network is a collection of points called nodes. The nodes are joined by lines called arcs. In a directed network, movement (e.g. of information) is only possible along the arcs in one direction (see Figure 15.3).
    The matrix **A** is known as an *adjacency* matrix, with a 1 in row i and column j if there is an arc from node i to node j, or a 0 in that position if there is no arc between those two nodes. The diagonal elements of **A** (i.e. a_{11}, a_{22}, etc.) are all zero because good spies do not talk to themselves (since they might then talk in their sleep and give themselves away). Each 1 in **A** therefore represents a single path of length 1 arc in the network.

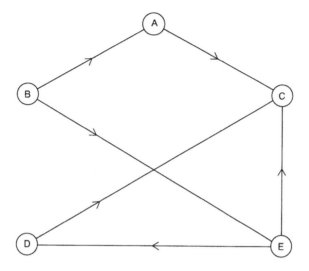

Fig. 15.3 The network represented by the matrix **A**

Now let's multiply the adjacency matrix **A** by itself, to get what is called $\mathbf{A}^2$:

$$\begin{bmatrix} 0 & 0 & 1 & 0 & 0 \\ 1 & 0 & 0 & 0 & 1 \\ 0 & 0 & 0 & 0 & 0 \\ 0 & 0 & 1 & 0 & 0 \\ 0 & 0 & 1 & 1 & 0 \end{bmatrix} \times \begin{bmatrix} 0 & 0 & 1 & 0 & 0 \\ 1 & 0 & 0 & 0 & 1 \\ 0 & 0 & 0 & 0 & 0 \\ 0 & 0 & 1 & 0 & 0 \\ 0 & 0 & 1 & 1 & 0 \end{bmatrix} = \begin{bmatrix} 0 & 0 & 0 & 0 & 0 \\ 0 & 0 & 2 & 1 & 0 \\ 0 & 0 & 0 & 0 & 0 \\ 0 & 0 & 0 & 0 & 0 \\ 0 & 0 & 1 & 0 & 0 \end{bmatrix}.$$

Row 2 and column 3 have been emboldened in the two versions of **A** above to help interpret $\mathbf{A}^2$. The element 2 in $\mathbf{A}^2$ (row 2, column 3) results when row 2 of **A** is multiplied term by term with column 3, and the products added. This gives us the scalar product

$$1 \times 1 + 0 \times 0 + 0 \times 0 + 0 \times 1 + 1 \times 1 = 2.$$

The first non-zero term arises because there is a path from node 2 to node 1, which we will denote by (2–1), followed by a path (1–3), giving a composite path (2–1–3) of length 2, i.e. from Boris to Cyril via Alex. The second non-zero term arises because there is a path (2–5) followed by a path (5–3), giving a second composite path (2–5–3) of length 2, i.e. from Boris to Cyril again, but via Eric this time. It is clear that the entries in $\mathbf{A}^2$ represent the number of paths of length 2 between the various nodes in the network (on the strict understanding that all arcs are of length 1). There are therefore only four paths of length 2: two from Boris to Cyril, as we have seen, one from Boris to Denisov, and one from Eric to Cyril.

If we now multiply the matrix $\mathbf{A}^2$ by $\mathbf{A}$ again, to form the third power of $\mathbf{A}$, we get the rather dull matrix

$$\mathbf{A}^3 = \begin{bmatrix} 0 & 0 & 0 & 0 & 0 \\ 0 & 0 & 1 & 0 & 0 \\ 0 & 0 & 0 & 0 & 0 \\ 0 & 0 & 0 & 0 & 0 \\ 0 & 0 & 0 & 0 & 0 \end{bmatrix}.$$

The single 1 in $\mathbf{A}^3$ tells us that there is only one path of length 3 in the network (i.e. with two intermediaries) and that it is from Boris to Cyril. Drawing the network, or alternatively examining the appropriate row and column in $\mathbf{A}^2$ and $\mathbf{A}$ that give rise to this single entry in $\mathbf{A}^3$, reveals that the actual route is Boris-Eric-Denisov-Cyril.

If we now compute $\mathbf{A}^4$, we will find that every element is zero (such a matrix is called the null matrix), signifying that there are no paths of length 4 in the network, which can be verified by inspection. All higher powers of $\mathbf{A}$ will also obviously be null, since if there are no paths of length 4, there can hardly be any that are longer!

In general, then, the element in row i and column j of the kth power of an adjacency matrix is equal to the number of paths consisting of k arcs linking nodes i and j.

Coming back to our spy network, since the elements of $\mathbf{A}$ are the number of paths of length 1, and the elements of $\mathbf{A}^2$ are the number of paths of length 2, etc., then clearly the sum of all these powers of $\mathbf{A}$ will tell us how many paths of any length there are altogether between the various nodes. We can therefore define a *reachability* matrix $\mathbf{R}$ for this (5 × 5) network:

$$\mathbf{R} = \mathbf{A} + \mathbf{A}^2 + \mathbf{A}^3 + \mathbf{A}^4.$$

$\mathbf{R}$ is also a (5 × 5) matrix, and its elements give the total number of paths of communication between the agents. Doing the calculation gives us

$$\mathbf{R} = \begin{bmatrix} 0 & 0 & 1 & 0 & 0 \\ 1 & 0 & 3 & 1 & 1 \\ 0 & 0 & 0 & 0 & 0 \\ 0 & 0 & 1 & 0 & 0 \\ 0 & 0 & 2 & 1 & 0 \end{bmatrix}.$$

So we can read off from the reachability matrix $\mathbf{R}$ the fact that there are, for example, three different paths between Boris and Cyril, but only two between Eric and Cyril (the actual lengths of these paths will have been calculated in finding the powers of $\mathbf{A}$). The name "reachability" is used because the non-zero elements of $\mathbf{R}$ indicate who may contact whom, directly or indirectly, or for a general distance network, which nodes can be reached from each node.

The reachability matrix   In general, the reachability matrix $\mathbf{R}$ of a $(n \times n)$ network may be defined as the sum of the first $(n-1)$ powers of its associated adjacency matrix $\mathbf{A}$. You may be wondering why we can stop at the $(n-1)$th power of $\mathbf{A}$. The elements of $\mathbf{A}^{(n-1)}$ will be the number of paths that have $(n-1)$ arcs, i.e. that connect n nodes (since each arc connects two nodes). Since there are no further nodes that can be reached, it is not necessary to raise $\mathbf{A}$ to the nth power.

The subroutine Reachable in the program below computes the reachability matrix

R for any network given the adjacency matrix **A**, i.e. it computes

$$R = A + A^2 + A^3 + \ldots + A^{(n-1)},$$

where **A** is $(n \times n)$. It uses the array B to store the intermediate powers of the array A, adding them to R each time.

The complete program to compute a reachability matrix follows. It uses the module MatMult defined in Section 15.3:

```
PROGRAM Reach
USE MatMult

IMPLICIT NONE
REAL, DIMENSION(:,:), ALLOCATABLE :: A, R   ! use dynamic arrays
INTEGER I, J, N

PRINT*, "Number of nodes in network:"
READ*, N
ALLOCATE( A(N,N), R(N,N) )
PRINT*, "Enter Adjacency matrix by rows:"
READ*, ((A(I,J), J=1,N), I = 1,N)

CALL Reachable( A, R )

PRINT*, "Reachability matrix:"
PRINT*

DO I = 1, N
  PRINT "(20F3.0)", (R(I,J), J = 1, N)
END DO

CONTAINS

SUBROUTINE Reachable( A, R )
  REAL, DIMENSION(:,:) :: A, R
  REAL, DIMENSION( SIZE(A,1), SIZE(A,2) ) :: B  ! automatic object
  B = A
  R = A
  N = SIZE(A,1)
  DO I = 1, N-2
    B = B .x. A
    R = R + B
  END DO
END SUBROUTINE Reachable

END PROGRAM Reach
```

It may help to go through Reachable by hand for $n = 5$ to see how it works. Keep track of the contents of B and R in terms of the adjacency matrix A.

15.6   Leslie Matrices: Population Growth

Another very interesting and useful application of matrices is in population dynamics.

The rabbit population model of Chapter 10 can be made a lot more realistic if we allow some rabbits to die from time to time. The approach we are going to take requires that we divide the rabbit population up into a number of age classes, where the members of each age class are one time unit older than the members of the previous class, the time unit being whatever is convenient for the population being studied (days, months, etc.).

If X_i is the size of the ith age class, we define a *survival factor* P_i as the proportion of the ith class that survive to the $(i + 1)$th age class, i.e. the proportion that "graduate". F_i is defined as the *mean fertility* of the ith class. This is the mean number of newborn individuals expected to be produced during one time interval by each member of the ith class at the beginning of the interval (only females count in biological modelling, since there are always enough males to go round!).

Suppose for our modified rabbit model we have three age classes, with X_1, X_2 and X_3 members respectively. We will call them young, middle-aged and old-aged for convenience. We will take our time unit as one month, so X_1 are the number that were born during the current month, and which will be considered as youngsters at the end of the month. X_2 are the number of middle-aged rabbits at the end of the month, and X_3 the number of oldsters. Suppose the youngsters cannot reproduce, so that $F_1 = 0$. Suppose the fertility rate for middle-aged rabbits is 9, so $F_2 = 9$, while for oldsters $F_3 = 12$. The probability of survival from youth to middle-age is one third, so $P_1 = 1/3$, while no less than half the middle-aged rabbits live to become oldsters, so $P_2 = 0.5$ (we are assuming for the sake of illustration that all old-aged rabbits die at the end of the month—this can be corrected easily). With this information we can quite easily compute the changing population structure month by month, as long as we have the population breakdown to start with.

If we now denote the current month by t, and next month by $(t + 1)$, we can refer to this month's youngsters as $X_1(t)$, and to next month's as $X_1(t + 1)$, with similar notation for the other two age classes. We can then write a scheme for updating the population from month t to month $(t + 1)$ as follows:

$$
\begin{aligned}
X_1(t + 1) &= F_2 X_2(t) + F_3 X_3(t), \\
X_2(t + 1) &= P_1 X_1(t), \\
X_3(t + 1) &= P_2 X_2(t).
\end{aligned}
$$

We now define a population vector $\mathbf{X}(t)$, with three components, $X_1(t)$, $X_2(t)$, and $X_3(t)$, representing the three age classes of the rabbit population in month t. The above three equations can then be rewritten as

$$
\begin{bmatrix} X_1 \\ X_2 \\ X_3 \end{bmatrix}_{(t+1)} = \begin{bmatrix} 0 & F_2 & F_3 \\ P_1 & 0 & 0 \\ 0 & P_2 & 0 \end{bmatrix} \times \begin{bmatrix} X_1 \\ X_2 \\ X_3 \end{bmatrix}_t
$$

where the subscript at the bottom of the vectors indicates the month. We can write this even more concisely as the matrix equation

$$
\mathbf{X}(t + 1) = \mathbf{L}\,\mathbf{X}(t), \tag{15.4}
$$

where **L** is the matrix

$$
\begin{bmatrix}
0 & 9 & 12 \\
1/3 & 0 & 0 \\
0 & 1/2 & 0
\end{bmatrix}
$$

in this particular case. **L** is called a *Leslie matrix*. A population model can always be written in the form of Equation 15.4 if the concepts of age classes, fertility, and survival factors, as outlined above, are used.

Now that we have established a matrix representation for our model, we can easily write a program using matrix multiplication and repeated application of Equation 15.4:

$$
\begin{aligned}
\mathbf{X}(t+2) &= \mathbf{L}\,\mathbf{X}(t+1), \\
\mathbf{X}(t+3) &= \mathbf{L}\,\mathbf{X}(t+2), \text{ etc.}
\end{aligned}
$$

However, we only need a single one-dimensional array X in the program, because repeated matrix multiplication by the two-dimensional array L will continually update it:

```
X = L .x. X
```

(using the .x. matrix multiplication operator defined in module MatMult). We will assume to start with, that we have one old (female) rabbit, and no others, so $X_1 = X_2 = 0$, and $X_3 = 1$.

The program is then simply:

```
PROGRAM Leslie
USE MatMult
IMPLICIT NONE

REAL, DIMENSION(3,3) :: L  ! Leslie matrix
REAL, DIMENSION(3)   :: X  ! Population vector
INTEGER T

L = 0
L(1,2) = 9
L(1,3) = 12
L(2,1) = 1.0 / 3
L(3,2) = 0.5
X = (/ 0, 0, 1 /)
PRINT "(A5, 4A14)", "Month", "Young", "Middle", "Old", "Total"
PRINT*

DO T = 1, 24
  X = L .x. X
  PRINT "(I5, 4F14.1)", T, X, SUM( X )
END DO

END PROGRAM Leslie
```

The output, over a period of 24 months, is:

Month	Young	Middle	Old	Total
1	12.0	0.0	0.0	12.0
2	0.0	4.0	0.0	4.0
3	36.0	0.0	2.0	38.0
4	24.0	12.0	0.0	36.0
5	108.0	8.0	6.0	122.0
6	144.0	36.0	4.0	184.0
. . .				
22	11184720.0	1864164.0	466020.0	13514904.0
23	22369716.0	3728240.0	932082.0	27030038.0
24	44739144.0	7456572.0	1864120.0	54059836.0

Note how A format may be used to get headings in the right place.

It so happens that there are no "fractional" rabbits in this example. If there are any, they should be kept, and not rounded (and certainly not truncated). They occur because the fertility rates and survival probabilities are averages.

If you look carefully at the output you may spot that after some months the total population doubles every month. This factor is called the *growth factor*, and is a property of the particular Leslie matrix being used (for those who know about such things, it's the *dominant eigenvalue* of the matrix). The growth factor is 2 in this example, but if the values in the Leslie matrix are changed, the long-term growth factor changes too (try it and see).

You probably didn't spot that the numbers in the three age classes tend to a limiting ratio of 24:4:1. This can be demonstrated very clearly if you run the model with an initial population structure having this limiting ratio. This limiting ratio is called the *stable age distribution* of the population, and again it is a property of the Leslie matrix (in fact, it is the *eigenvector* belonging to the dominant eigenvalue of the matrix). Different population matrices lead to different stable age distributions.

The interesting point about this is that a given Leslie matrix always eventually gets a population into the *same* stable age distribution, which increases eventually by the *same* growth factor each month, *no matter what the initial population breakdown is*. For example, if you run the above model with any other initial population, it will always eventually get into a stable age distribution of 24:4:1 with a growth factor of 2 (try it and see).

15.7   Markov Chains

Often a process that we wish to model may be represented by a number of possible *discrete* (i.e. discontinuous) states that describe the outcome of the process. For example, if we are spinning a coin, then the outcome is adequately represented by the two states "heads" and "tails" (and nothing in between). If the process is random, as it is with spinning coins, there is a certain probability of being in any of the states at a given moment, and also a probability of changing from one state to another. If the probability of moving from one state to another depends on the present state only, and not on any previous state, the process is called a *Markov chain*. The progress of the drunk sailor in Chapter 14 is an example of such a process. Markov chains are used widely in such diverse fields as biology and business decision making, to name just two areas.

A random walk This example is a variation on the random walk problem of Chapter 14. A street has six intersections. A drunk man wanders down the street. His home is at intersection 1, and his favourite bar at intersection 6. At each intersection other than his home or the bar he moves in the direction of the bar with probability 2/3, and in the direction of his home with probability 1/3. He never wanders down a side street. If he reaches his home or the bar, he disappears into them, never to re-appear (when he disappears we say in Markov jargon that he has been *absorbed*).

We would like to know: what are the chances of him ending up at home or in the bar, if he starts at a given corner (other than home or the bar, obviously)? He can clearly be in one of six states, with respect to his random walk, which can be labelled by the intersection number, where state 1 means *Home* and state 6 means *Bar*. We can represent the probabilities of being in these states by a six-component *state vector* $\mathbf{X}(t)$, where $X_i(t)$ is the probability of him being at intersection i at moment t. The components of $\mathbf{X}(t)$ must sum to 1, since he has to be in one of these states.

We can express this Markov process by the following *transition probability matrix*, **P**, where the rows represent the next state (i.e. corner), and the columns represent the present state:

	Home	2	3	4	5	Bar
Home	1	1/3	0	0	0	0
2	0	0	1/3	0	0	0
3	0	2/3	0	1/3	0	0
4	0	0	2/3	0	1/3	0
5	0	0	0	2/3	0	0
Bar	0	0	0	0	2/3	1

The entries for *Home-Home* and *Bar-Bar* are both 1 because he stays put there with certainty.

Using the probability matrix **P** we can work out his chances of being, say, at intersection 3 at moment $(t + 1)$ as

$$X_3(t + 1) = 2/3 X_2(t) + 1/3 X_4(t).$$

To get to 3, he must have been at either 2 or 4, and his chances of moving from there are 2/3 and 1/3 respectively.

Mathematically, this is identical to the Leslie matrix problem. We can therefore form the new state vector from the old one each time with a matrix equation:

$$\mathbf{X}(t + 1) = \mathbf{P}\,\mathbf{X}(t).$$

If we suppose the man starts at intersection 2, the initial probabilities will be (0; 1; 0; 0; 0; 0). The Leslie matrix program may be adapted with very few changes to generate future states:

```
PROGRAM Drunk
USE MatMult
IMPLICIT NONE

REAL, DIMENSION(6,6) :: P       ! probability transition matrix
REAL, DIMENSION(6)   :: X       ! state vector
INTEGER I, T

P = 0                           ! construct probability matrix
DO I = 3,6
  P(I,I-1) = 2./3
  P(I-2,I-1) = 1./3
END DO
P(1,1) = 1
P(6,6) = 1
X = (/ 0, 1, 0, 0, 0, 0 /)      ! initialize state vector

PRINT "(A4, 6A9)", "Time", "Home", "2", "3", "4", "5", "Bar"
PRINT*

DO T = 1, 50
  X = P .x. X
  PRINT "(I4, 6F9.4)", T, X
END DO

END PROGRAM Drunk
```

Output:

Time	Home	2	3	4	5	Bar
1	0.3333	0.0000	0.6666	0.0000	0.0000	0.0000
2	0.3333	0.2222	0.0000	0.4444	0.0000	0.0000
3	0.4074	0.0000	0.2962	0.0000	0.2962	0.0000
4	0.4074	0.0987	0.0000	0.2962	0.0000	0.1975
5	0.4403	0.0000	0.1646	0.0000	0.1975	0.1975
6	0.4403	0.0548	0.0000	0.1755	0.0000	0.3292
7	0.4586	0.0000	0.0951	0.0000	0.1170	0.3292
8	0.4586	0.0317	0.0000	0.1024	0.0000	0.4072
9	0.4691	0.0000	0.0552	0.0000	0.0682	0.4072
10	0.4691	0.0184	0.0000	0.0596	0.0000	0.4527
...						
40	0.4838	0.0000	0.0000	0.0000	0.0000	0.5161
...						
50	0.4838	0.0000	0.0000	0.0000	0.0000	0.5161

By running the program for long enough, we soon find the limiting probabilities: he ends up at home about 48% of the time, and at the bar about 52% of the time. Perhaps this is a little surprising; from the transition probabilities, we might have expected him to get to the bar rather more easily. It just goes to show that you should never trust your intuition when it comes to statistics!

Note that the Markov chain approach is *not* a simulation: one gets the *theoretical* probabilities each time (this can all be done mathematically, without a computer). But it is interesting to confirm the limiting probabilities by *simulating* the drunk's progress, using a random number generator (see Exercise 15.3 at the end of the chapter).

15.8 Solution of Linear Equations

A problem that often arises in scientific applications is the solution of a system of linear equations, e.g.

$$2x - y + z = 4 \tag{15.5}$$
$$x + y + z = 3 \tag{15.6}$$
$$3x - y - z = 1. \tag{15.7}$$

One method of solution is by *Gauss reduction*, which we discuss now.

Gauss reduction   Write the coefficients of the left-hand side as a matrix, with the right-hand side constants as a vector to the right of the matrix, separated by a vertical line, thus:

$$\begin{bmatrix} 2 & -1 & 1 & | & 4 \\ 1 & 1 & 1 & | & 3 \\ 3 & -1 & -1 & | & 1 \end{bmatrix}.$$

This is simply shorthand for the original set, and is sometimes called the *augmented matrix* of the system. As long as we perform only *row* operations on the numbers, we can omit the symbols x, y, and z each time. We will refer to the augmented matrix as **A**.

We start with the first row (R_1), and call it the *pivot row*. We call the element $a_{11} (= 2)$ the *pivot element*. Divide the whole pivot row by the pivot element, so the augmented array now looks like this:

$$\begin{bmatrix} 1 & -1/2 & 1/2 & | & 2 \\ 1 & 1 & 1 & | & 3 \\ 3 & -1 & -1 & | & 1 \end{bmatrix}.$$

Rows R_2 and R_3 are now called *target rows*. The object is to get zeros in all the target rows below (and above, if necessary) the pivot element. Take the target row R_2. Replace each element in the row by itself minus the corresponding element in the pivot row. The array now looks like this:

$$\begin{bmatrix} 1 & -1/2 & 1/2 & | & 2 \\ 0 & 3/2 & 1/2 & | & 1 \\ 3 & -1 & -1 & | & 1 \end{bmatrix}.$$

Now take the target row R_3. To reduce a_{31} to zero with an operation involving the pivot row requires replacing the target row by itself minus the pivot row multiplied by a_{31} (bearing in mind for the subsequent computer solution that this operation can change the value of a_{31} itself!):

$$\begin{bmatrix} 1 & -1/2 & 1/2 & 2 \\ 0 & 3/2 & 1/2 & 1 \\ 0 & 1/2 & -5/2 & -5 \end{bmatrix}.$$

We now designate R_2 as the pivot row, and the new a_{22} as the pivot element. The whole procedure is repeated, except that the target rows are now R_1 and R_3, and the object is to get zeros in these two rows above and below the pivot element. The result is:

$$\begin{bmatrix} 1 & 0 & 2/3 & 7/3 \\ 0 & 1 & 1/3 & 2/3 \\ 0 & 0 & -8/3 & -16/3 \end{bmatrix}.$$

Now take R_3 as the pivot row, with the new a_{33} as the pivot element, and R_1 and R_2 as target rows. After repeating similar operations on them, the array finally looks like this:

$$\begin{bmatrix} 1 & 0 & 0 & 1 \\ 0 & 1 & 0 & 0 \\ 0 & 0 & 1 & 2 \end{bmatrix}.$$

Since we have retained the mathematical integrity of the system of equations by performing operations on the rows only, this is equivalent to

$$x + 0y + 0z = 1$$
$$0x + y + 0z = 0$$
$$0x + 0y + z = 2.$$

The solution may therefore be read off as $x = 1$, $y = 0$, $z = 2$.

The subroutine Gauss in the program below performs a Gauss reduction on a system of any size. The augmented array A is passed as an argument. On entry, its rightmost column should contain the right-hand side constants of the equations. On return, the rightmost column will contain the solution.

```
PROGRAM GaussTest
IMPLICIT NONE

REAL, DIMENSION(:,:), ALLOCATABLE :: A      ! augmented matrix
INTEGER I, J, N

PRINT*, "How many equations?"
READ*, N
ALLOCATE( A(N, N+1) )                        ! extra column for RHS
PRINT*, "Enter augmented matrix by rows:"
READ*, ((A(I,J), J = 1,N+1), I = 1,N)
CALL Gauss( A )
PRINT*
PRINT*, "Solution is in last column:"
DO I = 1, N
   PRINT "(10F7.2)", (A(I,J), J = 1, N+1)
END DO
```

```
CONTAINS

SUBROUTINE Gauss( A )
  REAL, DIMENSION(:,:) :: A
  REAL PivElt, TarElt
  INTEGER :: N                        ! number of equations
  INTEGER PivRow, TarRow

  N = SIZE( A, 1 )
  DO PivRow = 1, N                    ! process every row
    PivElt = A( PivRow, PivRow )      ! choose pivot element
    A( PivRow, 1:N+1 ) = A( PivRow, 1:N+1 ) / PivElt ! divide
                                      ! whole row
    ! now replace all other rows by target row minus pivot row ...
    ! ... times element in target row and pivot column:

    DO TarRow = 1, N
      IF (TarRow /= PivRow) THEN
        TarElt = A( TarRow, PivRow )
        A( TarRow, 1:N+1 ) = A( TarRow, 1:N+1 )      &
                           - A( PivRow, 1:N+1 ) * TarElt
      END IF
    END DO
  END DO
END SUBROUTINE Gauss
END PROGRAM GaussTest
```

Note that the two statements

```
A( PivRow, 1:N+1 ) = A( PivRow, 1:N+1 ) / PivElt ! divide
                                      ! whole row
A( TarRow, 1:N+1 ) = A( TarRow, 1:N+1 )      &
                   - A( PivRow, 1:N+1 ) * TarElt
```

process entire rows. If you do a lot of numerical analysis you will appreciate the power of such Fortran 90 array expressions.

Unfortunately, things can go wrong with our subroutine:

(1) The pivot element could be zero. This happens quite easily when the coefficients are all integers. However, rows of the array can be interchanged (see below) without changing the system of equations. So a non-zero pivot element can often be found in this way (but see the next two cases).

(2) A row of zeros could appear right across the array, in which case a non-zero pivot element cannot be found. In this case the system of equations is indeterminate and the solution can only be determined down to as many arbitrary constants as there are rows of zeros.

(3) A row of the array could be filled with zeros, except for the extreme right-hand

element. In this case the equations are inconsistent, which means there are no solutions.

It is a nice programming project to extend the subroutine Gauss to deal with these three cases.

Matrix inversion by Gauss reduction   Consider the system of equations:

$$2x + 2y + 2z \ = \ 0$$
$$3x + 2y + 2z \ = \ 1$$
$$3x + 2y + 3z \ = \ 1.$$

If we define the matrix **A** as

$$\mathbf{A} = \begin{bmatrix} 2 & 2 & 2 \\ 3 & 2 & 2 \\ 3 & 2 & 3 \end{bmatrix},$$

and the vectors **x** and **b** as

$$\mathbf{x} = \begin{bmatrix} x \\ y \\ z \end{bmatrix}, \qquad \mathbf{b} = \begin{bmatrix} 0 \\ 1 \\ 1 \end{bmatrix},$$

we can write the above system of three equations in matrix form as

$$\begin{bmatrix} 2 & 2 & 2 \\ 3 & 2 & 2 \\ 3 & 2 & 3 \end{bmatrix} \begin{bmatrix} x \\ y \\ z \end{bmatrix} = \begin{bmatrix} 0 \\ 1 \\ 1 \end{bmatrix},$$

or even more concisely as the single matrix equation

$$\mathbf{Ax} = \mathbf{b}.$$

The solution may then be written as

$$\mathbf{x} = \mathbf{A}^{-1}\mathbf{b}, \tag{15.8}$$

where $\mathbf{A}^{-1}$ is the matrix inverse of **A** (i.e. the matrix which when multiplied by **A** gives the identity matrix).

   This provides a slightly route to the solution. Gauss reduction can also be used to invert a matrix. To invert the matrix **A**, construct the augmented matrix **A | I**, where **I** is the identity matrix:

$$\begin{bmatrix} 2 & 2 & 2 & | & 1 & 0 & 0 \\ 3 & 2 & 2 & | & 0 & 1 & 0 \\ 3 & 2 & 3 & | & 0 & 0 & 1 \end{bmatrix}.$$

Now perform a Gauss reduction until the identity matrix has appeared to the left of the vertical line, so that the augmented array finally looks as follows:

$$\begin{bmatrix} 1 & 0 & 0 & | & -1 & 1 & 0 \\ 0 & 1 & 0 & | & 3/2 & 0 & -1 \\ 0 & 0 & 1 & | & 0 & -1 & 1 \end{bmatrix}.$$

The matrix to the right of the line is the inverse of **A**. If **A** is not invertible, the process breaks down and a row of zeros appears. The solution may then be found directly from Equation 15.8: $x = 1$, $y = -1$, $z = 0$.

Our subroutine Gauss can be adapted quite easily to find the matrix inverse. It is rewritten below as a function Inv, which returns the inverse of its argument. Inv can be included in the module MatMult of Section 15.3 and overloaded with a defined operator .INV. for matrix inversion:

```
MODULE MatMult
...
INTERFACE OPERATOR(.INV.)
  MODULE PROCEDURE Inv
END INTERFACE

CONTAINS
...
FUNCTION Inv( Mat )
  REAL, DIMENSION(:,:) :: Mat
  REAL, DIMENSION( SIZE(Mat,1), SIZE(Mat,1) ) :: Inv    ! must be
                                                        ! square
  REAL, DIMENSION( SIZE(Mat,1), 2 * SIZE(Mat,1) ) :: A ! augmented
  REAL, DIMENSION(:), ALLOCATABLE :: TempRow            ! spare row
  REAL PivElt, TarElt
  INTEGER :: N                         ! number of equations
  INTEGER PivRow, TarRow

  N = SIZE( Mat, 1 )
  A = 0                                ! initialize
  A( 1:N, 1:N ) = Mat                  ! first N columns
  DO I = 1, N                          ! identity in cols N+1 to 2N
    A( I, N+I ) = 1
  END DO

  DO PivRow = 1, N                     ! process every row
    PivElt = A( PivRow, PivRow )       ! choose pivot element
    IF (PivElt == 0) THEN              ! check for zero pivot
      K = PivRow + 1      ! run down rows to find a non-zero pivot
      DO WHILE (PivElt == 0 .AND. K <= N)
        PivElt = A( K, PivRow )        ! try next row
        K = K + 1                      ! K will be 1 too big
      END DO
      IF (PivElt == 0) THEN            ! it's still zero
        PRINT*, "Couldn't find a non-zero pivot: solution rubbish"
        RETURN
      ELSE
        ! non-zero pivot in row K, so swop rows PivRow and K:
        ALLOCATE( TempRow(2*N) )       ! dynamic store
        TempRow = A( PivRow, 1:2*N )
        K = K - 1                      ! adjust for overcount
        A( PivRow, 1:2*N ) = A( K, 1:2*N )
```

```
            A( K, 1:2*N ) = TempRow
            DEALLOCATE( TempRow )          ! throw away
        END IF
    END IF
    A( PivRow, 1:2*N ) = A( PivRow, 1:2*N ) / PivElt ! divide
                                              ! whole row
        ! now replace all other rows by target row minus pivot row ...
    ! ... times element in target row and pivot column:

    DO TarRow = 1, N
      IF (TarRow /= PivRow) THEN
        TarElt = A( TarRow, PivRow )
        A( TarRow, 1:2*N ) = A( TarRow, 1:2*N )      &
                           - A( PivRow, 1:2*N ) * TarElt

      END IF
    END DO
  END DO

  ! finally extract the inverse from columns N+1 to 2N:
  Inv = A( 1:N, N+1:2*N )
END FUNCTION Inv
END MODULE MatMult
```

Note the following features:

- The argument Mat is the matrix to be inverted. A is the augmented matrix: it must have twice as many columns as A. Mat is assigned to the first N columns of A; the identity matrix is assigned to the rightmost N columns.
- The number of columns, N+1, in Gauss must be replaced by 2*N.
- Inv handles a zero pivot element, by looking down the column under the pivot, until it finds a non-zero element. If it cannot find a non-zero pivot, it returns with a message. If it finds a non-zero pivot in row K, it swops row K with the pivot row, PivRow. Note how easily this is done with array sections. A temporary row, TempRow, is allocated from dynamic storage and deallocated after the swop.
- Finally, the rightmost N columns of A are assigned to Inv and returned.

Using the amended version of MatMult we can find the solution of Equation 15.8 in one statement:

```
X = .INV. A .x. B
```

Below is a main program to solve any linear system of equations in this way:

```
PROGRAM TestInv
USE MatMult
IMPLICIT NONE

REAL, DIMENSION(:,:), ALLOCATABLE :: A, AInv, X(:), B(:)
INTEGER I, J, N
```

```
PRINT*, "Number of equations:"
READ*, N
ALLOCATE( A(N, N), AInv(N, N), X(N), B(N) )
PRINT*, "Enter coefficient matrix A by rows:"
READ*, ((A(I,J), J = 1,N), I = 1,N)
PRINT*, "Enter RHS vector B:"
READ*, B

X = .INV. A .x. B
PRINT*
PRINT*, "Solution:"
PRINT "(10F7.2)", X

END PROGRAM TestInv
```

You can test it on Equations 15.5–15.7, if you like, with the coefficient of x in the first equation replaced by zero. This gives a non-zero pivot immediately. The solution is $x = 1$, $y = -1$, $z = 3$.

This method, which is fairly straightforward to code, and very elegant, is quite adequate for small systems (less than about 20 equations?). Larger systems will often have many zero elements, which makes the Gauss reduction inefficient, since most of the row operations will be on zeros. There are more efficient procedures for such systems.

Summary

- A table or matrix may be represented in Fortran 90 by a two-dimensional array.
- Statements such as DATA, READ and PRINT treat the elements of multi-dimensional array in array element order, by default, i.e. the leftmost subscript changes most rapidly. Implied DO loops may be used to treat elements by rows.
- Array constructors may only be used to initialize one-dimensional arrays. However, the intrinsic function RESHAPE can reshape a constructor into any shape.
- There are a number of useful intrinsic functions for matrix handling.
- The operators .x. and .INV. were defined for matrix multiplication and inversion respectively.
- The intrinsic operator * cannot be redefined to multiply arrays, since this is an existing intrinsic operation. Either a different token must be used, or a derived type must be defined.

Exercises

15.1 When I first learnt to program there were very few fancy functions to do all the work for you! Write your own subroutine TRANS(A) which replaces A by its transpose, *without* using any additional arrays.

15.2 Compute the limiting probabilities for the drunk in Section 15.7 when he starts at each of the remaining intersections in turn, and confirm that the closer he starts to the bar, the more likely he is to end up there.

15.3   Write a program to *simulate* the progress of the drunk in Section 15.7 down the street. Start him at a given intersection, and generate a random number to decide whether he moves toward the bar or home, according to the probabilities in the transition matrix. For each simulated random walk, record whether he ends up at home or in the bar. Repeat a large number of times. The proportion of walks that end up in either place should approach the limiting probabilities computed using the Markov model referred to in Exercise 15.2. **Hint**: if the random number is less than 2/3 he moves toward the bar (unless he is already at home or the bar, in which case that random walk ends), otherwise he moves toward home.

15.4   Write a few lines of code to interchange columns i and j of the matrix **A**.

15.5   The following system, suggested by T.S. Wilson, illustrates nicely the problem of ill-conditioning mentioned in Exercise 7.3:

$$
\begin{aligned}
10x + 7y + 8z + 7w &= 32 \\
7x + 5y + 6z + 5w &= 23 \\
8x + 6y + 10z + 9w &= 33 \\
7x + 5y + 9z + 10w &= 31
\end{aligned}
$$

Use the Gauss reduction program in this chapter to show that the solution is $x = y = z = w = 1$. Then change the right-hand side constants to 32.01, 22.99, 32.99 and 31.01 (a change of about 1 in 3000) and find the new solution. Finally, change the right-hand side constants to 32.1, 22.9, 32.9 and 31.1 and observe what effect this has on the "solution".

16

Introduction to Numerical Methods

A major scientific use of computers is in finding numerical solutions to mathematical problems which have no analytical solutions, i.e. solutions which may be written down in terms of polynomials and the known mathematical functions. In this chapter we look briefly at three areas where *numerical methods* have been highly developed: solving equations, evaluating integrals, and solving differential equations.

16.1 Equations

In this section we consider how to solve equations in one unknown numerically. The general way of expressing the problem is to say that we want to solve the equation

$f(x) = 0$, i.e. we want to find its *root* (or roots) x. There is no general method for finding roots analytically for any given $f(x)$.

Newton's method   This is perhaps the easiest numerical method to implement for solving equations, and was introduced earlier. It is an *iterative* method, meaning that it repeatedly attempts to improve an estimate of the root: if x_k is an approximation to the root, the next approximation x_{k+1} is given by

$$x_{k+1} = x_k - \frac{f(x_k)}{f'(x_k)}$$

where $f'(x)$ is $\mathrm{d}f/\mathrm{d}x$.

A structure plan to implement Newton's method is:

1. Read in starting value x_0 and required accuracy e
2. While $|f(x_k)| \geq e$ repeat up to $k = 20$, say:
    $x_{k+1} = x_k - f(x_k)/f'(x_k)$
    Print x_{k+1} and $f(x_{k+1})$
3. Stop.

It is necessary to limit step 2 since the process may not converge.

A program using Newton's method to solve the equation $x^3 + x - 3 = 0$, starting with $x_0 = 2$, is given in Chapter 8. If you run it you will see that the values of x converge rapidly to the root.

As an exercise, try running the program with different starting values of x_0 to see whether the algorithm always converges.

Also try finding a non-zero root of $2x = \tan(x)$, using Newton's method. You might have some trouble with this one. If you do, you will have demonstrated the one serious problem with Newton's method: it converges to a root only if the starting guess is "close enough". Since "close enough" depends on the nature of $f(x)$ and on the root, one can obviously get into difficulties here. The only remedy is some intelligent trial-and-error work on the initial guess—this is made considerably easier by sketching $f(x)$ carefully.

If the method fails to find a root, the Bisection method, discussed below, should be used.

Complex roots   Newton's method can also find complex roots, but only if the starting guess is complex. The following program finds a complex root of $x^2 + x + 1 = 0$:

```
PROGRAM ComplexNewton
COMPLEX :: X

READ*, X
PRINT "(2A10)", "Re(x)", "Im(x)"
PRINT*

N = 1
DO WHILE (ABS( F(X) ) >= 1E-6 .AND. N < 20)
   X = X - F(X) / DF(X)
   PRINT "(2F10.4)", X
```

```
    N = N + 1
  END DO

  CONTAINS
    FUNCTION F(X)
      COMPLEX X, F
      F = X ** 2 + X + 1
    END FUNCTION F

    FUNCTION DF(X)
      COMPLEX X, DF
      DF = 2 * X + 1
    END FUNCTION DF
  END PROGRAM ComplexNewton
```

If you start with (0, 2), i.e. $x = 2\sqrt{-1}$, x converges rapidly:

Re(x)	Im(x)
-0.2941	1.1765
-0.4511	0.8975
-0.4982	0.8653
-0.5000	0.8660
-0.5000	0.8660

Since complex roots occur in complex conjugate pairs, the other root is $(-0.5, -0.866)$.

Note that a complex constant must be enclosed in parentheses for list-directed input.

You can use this version to find real roots also, except you must then obviously give real starting values.

The Bisection method   Consider again the problem of solving the equation $f(x) = 0$, where

$$f(x) = x^3 + x - 3.$$

We attempt to find by inspection, or trial-and-error, two values of x, call them x_L and x_R, such that $f(x_L)$ and $f(x_R)$ have different signs, i.e. $f(x_L)f(x_R) < 0$. If we can find two such values, the root must lie somewhere in the interval between them, since $f(x)$ changes sign on this interval (see Figure 16.1). In this example, $x_L = 1$ and $x_R = 2$ will do, since $f(1) = -1$ and $f(2) = 7$. In the Bisection method, we estimate the root by x_M, where x_M is the midpoint of the interval $[x_L, x_R]$, i.e.

$$x_M = (x_L + x_R)/2. \tag{16.1}$$

Then if $f(x_M)$ has the same sign as $f(x_L)$, as drawn in the figure, the root clearly lies between x_M and x_R. We must then redefine the left-hand end of the interval as having the value of x_M, i.e. we let the new value of x_L be x_M. Otherwise, if $f(x_M)$ and $f(x_L)$ have *different* signs, we let the new value of x_R be x_M, since the root must lie between x_L and x_M in that case. Having redefined x_L or x_R, as the case may be,

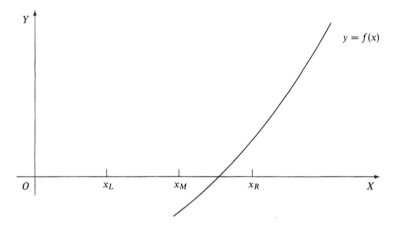

Fig. 16.1   The Bisection method

we bisect the new interval again according to Equation 16.1 and repeat the process until the distance between x_L and x_R is as small as we please.

The neat thing about this method is that we can calculate *before* starting how many bisections are needed to obtain a certain accuracy, given initial values of x_L and x_R. Suppose we start with $x_L = a$, and $x_R = b$. After the first bisection the worst possible error (E_1) in x_M is $E_1 = |a - b|/2$, since we are estimating the root as being at the midpoint of the interval $[a, b]$. The worst that can happen is that the root is actually at x_L or x_R, in which case the error is E_1. Carrying on like this, after n bisections the worst possible error E_n is given by $E_n = |a - b|/2^n$. If we want to be sure that this is less than some specified error E, we must see to it that n satisfies the inequality $|a - b|/2^n < E$, i.e.

$$n > \frac{\log(|a - b|/E)}{\log(2)} \tag{16.2}$$

Since n is the number of bisections, it must be an integer. The smallest integer n that *exceeds* the right-hand side of Inequality 16.2 will do as the maximum number of bisections required to guarantee the given accuracy E.

The following scheme may be used to program the Bisection method. It will work for any function $f(x)$ that changes sign (in either direction) between the two values a and b, which must be found beforehand by the user. The implementation follows below.

1. Read a, b and E
2. Initialize x_L and x_R
3. Compute maximum bisections n from Inequality 16.2
4. Repeat n times:
       Compute x_M according to Equation 16.1
       If $f(x_L)f(x_M) > 0$ then
          Let $x_L = x_M$
       otherwise
          Let $x_R = x_M$

5. Print root x_M

6. Stop.

We have assumed that the procedure will not find the root exactly; the chances of this happening with real variables are infinitesimal.

The main advantage of the Bisection method is that it is guaranteed to find a root if you can find two starting values for x_L and x_R between which the function changes sign. You can also compute in advance the number of bisections needed to attain a given accuracy. Compared to Newton's method it is inefficient. Successive bisections do not necessarily move closer to the root, as usually happens with Newton's method. In fact, it is interesting to compare the two methods on the same function to see how many more steps the Bisection method requires than Newton's method. For example, to solve the equation $x^3 + x - 3 = 0$, the Bisection method takes 21 steps to reach the same accuracy as Newton's in five steps.

Passing procedures as arguments   You may want to write a general purpose numerical methods module containing among other procedures a subroutine to carry out the Bisection method. In that case, it would be convenient to pass the function $f(x)$ as an argument. This can be done if the function is defined as an external or module function. An explicit interface is needed in this case.

The module NumUtils below contains a subroutine Bisect which accepts a function name Fung as a dummy argument:

```
MODULE NumUtils
IMPLICIT NONE

CONTAINS

  SUBROUTINE Bisect(A, B, E, N, XM, Fung)
  ! implements Bisection method
    REAL, INTENT(IN) :: A, B, E       ! limits and accuracy
    REAL, INTENT(OUT) :: XM           ! root
    INTEGER, INTENT(OUT) :: N         ! number of bisections
    REAL XL, XR
    INTEGER I
    INTERFACE                         ! recommended not required
      FUNCTION Fung(X)
        REAL Fung
        REAL, INTENT(IN) :: X
      END FUNCTION Fung
    END INTERFACE

    XL = A                            ! initialize
    XR = B
    N = LOG( ABS(A-B)/E ) / LOG(2.0) + 1 ! N must exceed
                                      ! formula value
    DO I = 1, N                       ! perform bisections
      XM = (XL + XR) / 2
      IF (Fung(XL) * Fung(XM) > 0) THEN
```

```
          XL = XM
       ELSE
          XR = XM
       END IF
     END DO
   END SUBROUTINE Bisect
 END MODULE NumUtils
```

Note:

- The dummy argument `Fung` is declared in an interface block inside `Bisect`.
- The subroutine returns the number of bisections `N` and the root `XM`.

The actual name of the function is `F`. It is defined as an external function:

```
FUNCTION F(X)
  REAL F
  REAL, INTENT(IN) :: X
  F = X ** 3 + X - 3
END FUNCTION F
```

A main program to put this all together is then:

```
PROGRAM TestBisect
USE NumUtils

IMPLICIT NONE
REAL A, B, E, X
INTEGER N
INTERFACE
  FUNCTION F(X)
    REAL F
    REAL, INTENT(IN) :: X
  END FUNCTION F
END INTERFACE

PRINT*, "Enter A, B and E:"
READ*, A, B, E

CALL Bisect( A, B, E, N, X, F )

PRINT*, "Number of bisections:", N
PRINT "('X and F(X):', F8.4, E12.4)", X, F(X)

END PROGRAM TestBisect
```

Note:

- The procedure to be passed as an argument must be an external or module procedure.

- An interface block gives the actual name of the function now, since that is what is passed to `Bisect`. Metcalf and Reid comment that interface blocks are not strictly necessary in this case, but are recommended. I could not, however, get this example to compile under FTN90 without the interface blocks.
- Since `Bisect` has a dummy function name, the only recompilation needed to change $f(x)$ is of the external function F defining it.

Here is some output from a sample run:

```
Enter A, B and E:
1 2 1e-6
Number of bisections: 20
X and F(X):   1.2134   0.3457E-05
```

16.2 Integration

Although most "respectable" mathematical functions can be differentiated analytically, the same cannot be said for integration. There are no general rules for integrating, as there are for differentiating. For example, the indefinite integral of a function as simple as e^{-x^2} cannot be found mathematically. We therefore need numerical methods for evaluating integrals.

This is actually quite easy to do, and depends on the well-known fact that the definite integral of a function $f(x)$ between the limits $x = a$ and $x = b$ is equal to the area under $f(x)$ bounded by the x-axis and the two vertical lines $x = a$ and $x = b$. So all numerical methods for integrating simply involve more or less ingenious ways of estimating the area under $f(x)$.

The Trapezoidal Rule The method we will use here is called the Trapezoidal (or Trapezium) Rule. The area under $f(x)$ is divided into vertical panels each of width h, called the *step-length*. If there are n such panels, then $nh = b - a$, i.e. $n = (b - a)/h$. If we join the points where successive panels cut $f(x)$, we can estimate the area under $f(x)$ as the sum of the area of the resulting trapezia. If we call this approximation to the integral S, then

$$S = \frac{h}{2}[f(a) + f(b) + 2 \sum_{i=1}^{n-1} f(x_i)], \qquad (16.3)$$

where $x_i = a + ih$. Equation 16.3 is the Trapezoidal Rule, and provides an estimate for the integral

$$\int_a^b f(x)\mathrm{d}x.$$

We can include a function `Trap` to evaluate an integral in this way in our module `NumUtils`:

```
FUNCTION Trap( A, B, H, Fung )
   INTERFACE
      FUNCTION Fung(X)
```

```
            REAL Fung
            REAL, INTENT(IN) :: X
         END FUNCTION Fung
      END INTERFACE
      REAL Trap
      REAL, INTENT(IN) :: A, B, H
      INTEGER I, N

      N = NINT( (B-A) / H )
      Trap = 0
      DO I = 1, N-1
      ! using notation defined in text
         Trap = Trap + Fung( A + I * H )
      END DO
      Trap = H / 2 * (Fung(A) + Fung(B) + 2 * Trap)
   END FUNCTION Trap
```

Its dummy argument Fung is again the function to be integrated, so there is an interface block for Fung.

It is assumed that the user will choose h in such a way that the number of steps n will be an integer—a check for this could be built in.

As an example, let's integrate $f(x) = x^3$ between the limits 0 and 4. We need to write an external function again:

```
FUNCTION F(X)
   REAL F
   REAL, INTENT(IN) :: X
   F = X ** 3
END FUNCTION F
```

A main program could look like this:

```
PROGRAM TestTrap
USE NumUtils
IMPLICIT NONE

REAL A, B, H
INTERFACE
   FUNCTION F(X)
      REAL F, X
   END FUNCTION F
END INTERFACE

PRINT*, "Enter A, B, H:"
READ*, A, B, H
PRINT "('Integral:', F8.4)", Trap( A, B, H, F )

END PROGRAM TestTrap
```

With $h = 0.01$, the estimate is 64.0004 (the exact integral is 64). You will find that as h gets smaller, the estimate gets more accurate.

This example assumes that $f(x)$ is a continuous function which may be evaluated at any x. In practice, the function could be defined at discrete points supplied as results of an experiment. For example, the speed of an object $v(t)$ might be measured every so many seconds, and one might want to estimate the distance travelled as the area under the speed-time graph. In this case, Trap would have to be changed by replacing Fung with an array Values(0:N), say. References to Fung(A), Fung(A+I*H) and Fung(B) would have to be changed to Values(0), Values(I) and Values(N) respectively.

Intrinsic functions as arguments Trap can be used to integrate an intrinsic function, which must then be declared in an INTRINSIC statement. E.g. to integrate sine insert the statement

```
INTRINSIC SIN
```

into TestTrap, and change the call to Trap:

```
PRINT "('Integral:', F8.4)", Trap( A, B, H, SIN )
```

Simpson's Rule Simpson's rule is a method of numerical integration which is a good deal more accurate than the Trapezoidal Rule, and should always be used before you try anything fancier. It also divides the area under the function to be integrated, $f(x)$, into vertical strips, but instead of joining the points $f(x_i)$ with straight lines, every set of three such successive points are fitted with a parabola. To ensure that there are always an even number of panels, the step-length n is usually chosen so that there are $2n$ panels, i.e. $n = (b - a)/(2h)$.

Using the same notation as above, Simpson's rule estimates the integral as

$$S = \frac{h}{3}[f(a) + f(b) + 2\sum_{i=1}^{n-1} f(x_{2i}) + 4\sum_{i=1}^{n} f(x_{2i-1})].$$

The coding for this formula, which can be included in the module NumUtils is:

```
FUNCTION Simp( A, B, H, Fung )
  REAL, INTENT(IN) :: A, B, H
  REAL Simp
  INTEGER I, N
  INTERFACE
    FUNCTION Fung(X)
      REAL Fung
      REAL, INTENT(IN) :: X
    END FUNCTION Fung
  END INTERFACE

  Simp = 0
  N = NINT( (B-A) / (2 * H) )          ! 2N panels now

  DO I = 1, N-1
  ! using notation defined in text
```

```
    Simp = Simp + 2 * Fung( A +  2 * I * H )
  END DO
  DO I = 1, N
    Simp = Simp + 4 * Fung( A +  (2 * I - 1) * H )
  END DO

  Simp = H / 3 * (Fung(A) + Fung(B) + Simp)

END FUNCTION Simp
```

Note that N is half its previous size.

If you try Simpson's Rule out on $f(x) = x^3$ between any limits, you will find rather surprisingly, that it gives the same result as the exact mathematical solution. This is a nice extra benefit of the rule: it integrates cubic polynomials exactly (which can be proved).

16.3   Numerical Differentiation

The *Newton quotient* for a function $f(x)$ is given by

$$\frac{f(x + h) - f(x)}{h}, \tag{16.4}$$

where h is "small". As h tends to zero, this quotient approaches the first derivative, df/dx. The Newton quotient may therefore be used to estimate a derivative numerically. It is a useful exercise to do this with a few functions for which you know the derivatives. This way you can see how small you can make h before rounding errors cause problems. These arise because Expression 16.4 involves subtracting two terms that eventually become equal when the limit of the computer's accuracy is reached.

As an example, the following program uses the Newton quotient to estimate $f'(x)$ for $f(x) = x^2$ at $x = 2$, for smaller and smaller values of h (the exact answer is 4).

```
REAL NQ, X, H
INTEGER I, N
X = 2
H = 1
PRINT*, "How many?"
READ*, N
PRINT "(A10, A12)", "H", "NQ"

DO I = 1, N
  NQ = (F(X + H) - F(X)) / H
  PRINT "(E10.4, F12.8)", H, NQ
  H = H / 10
END DO

CONTAINS
  FUNCTION F(X)
```

```
      REAL F, X
        F = X ** 2
      END FUNCTION F
    END
```

Output:

```
          H            NQ
    0.1000E+01   5.00000000
    0.1000E00    4.09999371
    0.1000E-01   4.01000977
    0.1000E-02   4.00066423
    0.1000E-03   3.99589586
    0.1000E-04   4.00543261
    0.1000E-05   3.81469774
```

The results show that the best h for this particular problem is about 10^{-3}. But for h much smaller than this the estimate becomes totally unreliable. Using double precision real kind improves the accuracy. Change REAL to REAL(2):

```
          H            NQ
    ...
    0.1000E-04   4.00001000
    0.1000E-05   4.00000100
    0.1000E-06   4.00000009
    0.1000E-07   3.99999998
    0.1000E-08   4.00000033
    0.1000E-09   4.00000033
    0.1000E-10   4.00000033
    0.1000E-11   4.00035560
```

The best value is now about 10^{-8}.

Generally, the best h for a given problem can only be found by trial and error. Finding it constitutes a major problem of numerical analysis. This problem does not arise with numerical integration, because numbers are added to find the area, not subtracted.

16.4 First-order Differential Equations

The most interesting situations in real life that we may want to model, or represent quantitatively, are usually those in which the variables change in time (e.g. biological, electrical or mechanical systems). If the changes are continuous, the system can often be represented with equations involving the derivatives of the dependent variables. Such equations are called *differential* equations. The main aim of a lot of modelling is to be able to write down a set of differential equations that describe the system being studied as accurately as possible. Very few differential equations can be solved analytically, so once again, numerical methods are required. We will consider the simplest method of numerical solution in this section: Euler's method (Euler rhymes with boiler). We will also consider briefly how to improve it.

Vertical motion under air resistance: Euler's method   To illustrate Euler's method, we will take an example from Newtonian dynamics, of motion under gravity against air resistance. Suppose a skydiver steps out of a hovering helicopter, but does not open his parachute for 24 seconds. We would like to find his velocity as a function of time during this period. Assuming air resistance cannot be neglected (ask any skydiver!), he falls subject to two opposing vertical forces: gravity acting downward, and air resistance acting upward. The air resistance force is assumed to be proportional to the square of his velocity (this is fairly accurate). Applying Newton's second law to the skydiver, we have

$$m\mathrm{d}v/\mathrm{d}t = mg - pv^2,$$

where m is his mass, g the acceleration due to gravity, v his velocity, and p is a constant of proportionality. Dividing by m, we can rewrite this as

$$\mathrm{d}v/\mathrm{d}t = g - kv^2, \tag{16.5}$$

where $k = p/m$. Equation 16.5 is the differential equation describing the motion of the skydiver under gravity. The constant k varies with shape and mass, and may be found experimentally from the *terminal velocity* of the falling object. This terminal velocity (v_T) is reached when the object stops accelerating, and may be found by equating the right-hand side of Equation 16.5 to zero. Thus

$$v_T = \sqrt{g/k}.$$

For a man wearing an unopened parachute, k is found to be about 0.004 in MKS units. Before we proceed with the numerical solution of Equation 16.5 we should note that this particular differential equation can be solved analytically, since it is of the type called variable separable:

$$v(t) = \frac{a(C - e^{-2akt})}{C + e^{-2akt}}, \tag{16.6}$$

where $a = v_T$ and $C = [a + v(0)]/[a - v(0)]$.

Euler's method for solving Equation 16.5 numerically consists of replacing the derivative on the left-hand side with its Newton quotient, and equating this to the right-hand side as it stands. After a slight rearrangment of terms, we get

$$v(t + h) = v(t) + h[g - kv^2(t)]. \tag{16.7}$$

If we divide up the time period t into n intervals of h, then $t = nh$. If we define v_n as $v(t)$, then $v_{n+1} = v(t + h)$. We can therefore replace Equation 16.7 with the iterative scheme

$$v_{n+1} = v_n + h(g - kv_n^2). \tag{16.8}$$

Since we are given the initial condition $v_0 = 0$, Equation 16.8 provides a numerical scheme for finding the Euler approximation v_n to $v(t)$ in general.

It is very easy to program Euler's method. We can also test its accuracy by trying different values of h and comparing the results with the exact solution. The following program uses Euler's method as implemented in Equation 16.8 to estimate v for the first 24 seconds of the skydiver's motion. It also computes the exact solution for comparison.

```
PROGRAM Para
IMPLICIT NONE
REAL, PARAMETER :: g = 9.8
REAL K, H, T, T0, Tend, V, V0, X
INTEGER I, N

PRINT*, "Enter K, H, T0, V(T0), Tend:"
READ*, K, H, T0, V0, Tend
X = (Tend - T0) / H
N = INT( X + SPACING(X)) + 1        ! trip count
T = T0
V = V0
PRINT "(3A10)", "Time", "Euler", "Exact"

DO I = 1, N
  PRINT "(3F10.2)", T, V, Vexact(T, V0, G, K)
  V = V + H * (g - K * V * V)
  T = T + H
END DO

CONTAINS
  FUNCTION Vexact(T, V0, G, K)
    REAL Vexact
    REAL, INTENT(IN) :: g, K, T, V0
    REAL A, C
    A = SQRT( g / K )
    C = (A + V0) / (A - V0)
    Vexact = A * (C - EXP(-2*A*K*T))/(C + EXP(-2*A*K*T))
  END FUNCTION Vexact
END PROGRAM Para
```

Taking $h = 2$ and $k = 0.004$ we get:

Time	Euler	Exact
0.00	0.00	0.00
2.00	19.60	18.64
4.00	36.13	32.64
6.00	45.29	41.08
8.00	48.48	45.50
10.00	49.28	47.65
12.00	49.45	48.65
14.00	49.49	49.11
16.00	49.50	49.32
18.00	49.50	49.42
20.00	49.50	49.46
22.00	49.50	49.48
24.00	49.50	49.49

Euler's method gets more accurate if you reduce h, e.g. with $h = 0.5$ the worst error is only about 3%. Note that the errors get smaller as terminal velocity approaches.

In a real problem, we don't usually know the exact answer, or we wouldn't be using a numerical method in the first place. The only check is to use smaller and smaller values of h until it doesn't seem to make much difference, e.g. continue halving h until the results for a fixed t only change by an acceptably small amount.

Now let's see what happens when the skydiver opens his parachute. The air resistance term will be different now. For an open parachute, $k = 0.3$ is quite realistic. We can use the same program as before, although we need to supply a new starting value of 49.49 for v. Since $h = 0.5$ worked well before, we try the same value now. The results are rather surprising (t is the time elapsed since the parachute opened):

Time	Euler	Exact
0.00	49.49	49.49
0.50	-313.00	7.62
1.00	-15003.36	6.02
1.50	**********	5.77
2.00	**********	5.73

Not only does Euler's solution show that the man flies upward, he does so with tremendous speed, and soon exceeds the speed of light! The results make nonsense physically. Fortunately, in this example our intuition tells us that something is wrong. The only remedy is to reduce h. Some experimenting will reveal that the results for $h = 0.01$ are much better:

Time	Euler	Exact
0.00	49.49	49.49
0.01	42.24	43.18
0.02	36.99	38.31
0.03	32.98	34.45
0.04	29.81	31.31
0.05	27.25	28.71
...		
0.10	19.30	20.43
...		
0.20	12.69	13.32
...		
1.00	5.98	6.02
...		
2.00	5.72	5.73

Finally, note that Euler's method will be just as easy to compute if the air resistance term is not kv^2, but $kv^{1.8}$ (which is more realistic), although now an analytic solution cannot be found.

Euler's method in general   In general we want to solve a first-order differential equation of the form

$$dy/dx = f(x, y), \quad y(0) \text{ given.}$$

Table 16.1 Bacteria growth

Time	Euler	Predictor-Corrector	Exact
0.0	1000	1000	1000
0.5	1400	1480	1492
1.0	1960	2190	2226
1.5	2744	3242	3320
2.0	3842	4798	4953
...			
5.0	28925	50422	54598
...			
8.0	217795	529892	601845
...			
10.0	836683	2542344	2980958

Euler's method replaces dy/dx by its Newton quotient, so the differential equation becomes

$$\frac{y(x+h) - y(x)}{h} = f(x, y).$$

Rearranging, we get

$$y_{n+1} = y_n + hf(x_n, y_n), \qquad (16.9)$$

defining y_n as $y(x_n)$, where $x_n = x = nh$, and where $y_0 = y(0)$.

Bacteria growth: Euler's method Euler's method performs quite adequately in the skydiver problem once we have got the right value of the step-length h. In case you think that the numerical solution of all differential equations is just as easy, we will now consider an example where Euler's method doesn't do too well.

Suppose a colony of 1000 bacteria are multiplying at the rate of $r = 0.8$ per hour per individual (i.e. an individual produces an average of 0.8 offspring every hour). How many bacteria are there after 10 hours? Assuming that the colony grows continuously and without restriction, we can model this growth with the differential equation

$$dN/dt = rN, \quad N(0) = 1000, \qquad (16.10)$$

where $N(t)$ is the population size at time t. This process is called *exponential growth*. Equation 16.10 may be solved analytically to give the well-known formula for exponential growth:

$$N(t) = N(0)e^{rt}.$$

To solve Equation 16.10 numerically, we apply Euler's algorithm to it to get

$$N_{k+1} = N_k + rhN_k, \qquad (16.11)$$

where $N_k = N(t)$, and $N_0 = 1000$. Taking $h = 0.5$ gives the results shown in Table 16.1, where the exact solution is also given.

This time the numerical solution (in the column headed *Euler*) is not too good. In fact, the error gets worse at each step, and after 10 hours of bacteria time it is about 72%. Of course, the numerical solution will improve if we take h smaller, but there will still always be some value of t where the error exceeds some acceptable limit.

We may ask why Euler's method works so well with the skydiver, but so badly with the bacteria. By using the Newton quotient each time in Euler's method, we are actually assuming that the derivative changes very little over the small interval h, i.e. that the *second* derivative is very small. Now in the case of the skydiver, by differentiating Equation 16.5 again with respect to time, we see that

$$d^2v/dt^2 = -(2kv)dv/dt,$$

which approaches zero as the falling object reaches its terminal velocity. In the bacteria case, the second derivative of $N(t)$ is found by differentiating Equation 16.10:

$$d^2N/dt^2 = rdN/dt = r^2N(t).$$

This is far from zero at $t = 10$. In fact, it is approaching three million! The Newton quotient approximation gets worse at each step in this case.

There are better numerical methods for overcoming these sorts of problems. Two of them are discussed below. More sophisticated methods may be found in most textbooks on numerical analysis. However, Euler's method may always be used as a first approximation as long as you realize where and why errors may arise.

A predictor-corrector method   One improvement on the solution of

$$dy/dx = f(x, y), \quad y(0) \text{ given}$$

is as follows. The Euler approximation, which we are going to denote by an asterisk, is given by

$$y_{k+1}^* = y_k + hf(x_k, y_k) \tag{16.12}$$

But this formula favours the old value of y in computing $f(x_k, y_k)$ on the right-hand side. Surely it would be better to say

$$y_{k+1}^* = y_k + h[f(x_{k+1}, y_{k+1}^*) + f(x_k, y_k)]/2, \tag{16.13}$$

where $x_{k+1} = x + h$, since this also involves the new value y_{k+1}^* in computing f on the right-hand side? The problem of course is that y_{k+1}^* is as yet unknown, so we can't use it on the right-hand side of Equation 16.13. But we could use Euler to estimate (predict) y_{k+1}^* from Equation 16.12 and then use Equation 16.13 to correct the prediction by computing a *better* version of y_{k+1}^*, which we will call y_{k+1}. So the full procedure is:

Repeat as many times as required:
Use Euler to predict: $y_{k+1}^* = y_k + hf(x_k, y_k)$
Then correct y_{k+1}^* to: $y_{k+1} = y_k + h[f(x_{k+1}, y_{k+1}^*) + f(x_k, y_k)]/2.$

This is called a *predictor-corrector* method. The program Para above can easily be adapted to this problem. The relevant lines of code, which will generate all the entries in Table 16.1 at once, are:

```
DO I = 1, N
  PRINT "(F5.1, 3F12.0)", T, NE, NC, NO * EXP( R * T )
  NE = NE + R * H * NE            ! straight Euler
  NP = NC + R * H * NC            ! Predictor
  NC  = NC + R * H * (NP + NC) / 2  ! Corrector
  T = T + H
END DO
```

NE stands for the "straight" (uncorrected) Euler solution, NP is the Euler predictor, and NC is the corrector. The worst error is now only 15%. This is much better than the uncorrected Euler solution, although there is still room for improvement.

16.5 Runge-Kutta Methods

There are a variety of algorithms, under the general name of Runge-Kutta, which can be used to integrate systems of ordinary differential equations. The *fourth-order* formula is given below, for reference. A derivation of this and the other Runge-Kutta formulae can be found in most books on numerical analysis.

Runge-Kutta fourth-order formulae   The general first-order differential equation is

$$dy/dx = f(x, y), \quad y(0) \text{ given.} \tag{16.14}$$

The fourth-order Runge-Kutta estimate y^* at $x + h$ is given by

$$y^* = y + (k_1 + 2k_2 + 2k_3 + k_4)/6,$$

where

$$
\begin{aligned}
k_1 &= hf(x, y) \\
k_2 &= hf(x + 0.5h, y + 0.5k_1) \\
k_3 &= hf(x + 0.5h, y + 0.5k_2) \\
k_4 &= hf(x + h, y + k_3).
\end{aligned}
$$

Systems of differential equations: a predator-prey model   The Runge-Kutta formulae may be adapted to integrate *systems* of first-order differential equations. Here we adapt the fourth-order formulae to integrate the well-known Lotka-Volterra *predator-prey* model:

$$
\begin{aligned}
dx/dt &= px - qxy \tag{16.15} \\
dy/dt &= rxy - sy, \tag{16.16}
\end{aligned}
$$

where $x(t)$ and $y(t)$ are the prey and predator population sizes at time t, and p, q, r and s are biologically determined parameters. We define $f(x, y)$ and $g(x, y)$ as the right-hand sides of Equations 16.15 and 16.16 respectively. In this case, the Runge-Kutta estimates x^* and y^* at time $(t + h)$ may be found from x and y at time t with the formulae

$$
\begin{aligned}
x^* &= x + (k_1 + 2k_2 + 2k_3 + k_4)/6 \\
y^* &= y + (m_1 + 2m_2 + 2m_3 + m_4)/6,
\end{aligned}
$$

where

$$
\begin{aligned}
k_1 &= hf(x, y) \\
m_1 &= hg(x, y) \\
k_2 &= hf(x + 0.5k_1, y + 0.5m_1) \\
m_2 &= hg(x + 0.5k_1, y + 0.5m_1) \\
k_3 &= hf(x + 0.5k_2, y + 0.5m_2) \\
m_3 &= hg(x + 0.5k_2, y + 0.5m_2) \\
k_4 &= hf(x + k_3, y + m_3) \\
m_4 &= hg(x + k_3, y + m_3)
\end{aligned}
$$

It should be noted that in this example x and y are the dependent variables, and t (which does *not* appear explicitly in the equations) is the independent variable. In Equation 16.14 y is the dependent variable, and x is the independent variable.

16.6   A Differential Equation Modelling Package

This section implements a skeleton *interactive modelling* program, Driver. Its basis is a fourth-order Runge-Kutta procedure to integrate a time-based system (of any size) of first-order differential equations. It consists of four program units (which can be compiled separately), only one of which needs to be recompiled by users:

- a module DrGlobal with global declarations of derived types and variables;
- an external subroutine DEqs which defines the model differential equations—in principle, this is the only program unit which needs to be recompiled when the user sets up or changes a model;
- a module DrUtils with some basic utility subroutines, including a Runge-Kutta subroutine;
- a main program Driver to run the package.

Each of these program units will be described in turn. To illustrate the package, it is set up here to run the predator-prey model of Section 16.5, with $x(0) = 105$, $y(0) = 8$, $p = 0.4$, $q = 0.04$, $r = 0.02$, and $s = 2$.

DrGlobal contains declarations to be used by DEqs and DrUtils:

```
MODULE DrGlobal
! Global declarations for Driver

TYPE VarType               ! type for model variables
   Character(4) Name       ! name
   REAL InVal              ! initial value
   REAL Val                ! current value
END TYPE VarType

TYPE ParType               ! type for model parameters
   Character(4) Name       ! name
```

```
     REAL Val                      ! value
   END TYPE ParType

   TYPE (ParType), ALLOCATABLE, TARGET :: Params(:)      ! parameters
   TYPE (VarType), ALLOCATABLE :: Vars (:)               ! variables
   REAL, ALLOCATABLE, TARGET :: X(:)     ! current values of variables
   REAL T, dt                    ! model time and step-length
                                 ! for Runge-Kutta
   INTEGER Itime, RunTime        ! counter, number of integrations
   INTEGER NumVars, NumParams    ! number of model variables, parameters
   Character(1) Opt              ! response to main menu

 END MODULE DrGlobal
```

Each element of the array Vars (of derived type VarType) represents properties of
a model variable: name, initial value and current value. The current value is kept so
that the user may run the model either from the initial values, or the current values.
The array Params represents the model parameters.

It is convenient to have a separate array X to hold the current values of the model
variables. It has the TARGET attribute to allow aliasing in DEqs. The other variables
are described in comments.

The user defines the model differential equations in the external subroutine DEqs:

```
SUBROUTINE DEqs( F )
! evaluates RHS of DEs
  USE DrGlobal
  IMPLICIT NONE
  REAL, INTENT(OUT) :: F(:)
  REAL, POINTER :: Prey, Pred, p, q, r, s
  ! model equations are:
  ! dx/dt = F1 = px - qxy
  ! dy/dt = F2 = rxy - sy
  Prey => X(1)                    ! symbolic aliases ...
  Pred => X(2)                    ! ... reduce likelihood of errors
  p => Params(1) % Val
  q => Params(2) % Val
  r => Params(3) % Val
  s => Params(4) % Val
  F(1) = p * Prey - q * Prey * Pred
  F(2) = r * Prey * Pred - s * Pred
END SUBROUTINE DEqs
```

DEqs evaluates and returns the right-hand side of the *i*th differential equation in
the *i*th element of the array F. To allow the user to use more meaningful symbolic
names for parameters and variables, aliases are set up between the symbolic names
and the system variables declared in DrGlobal. This is why DEqs must access the
module DrGlobal, and why the current values of the model variables must be held
in the array X. The use of aliases makes it much easier to code large models.

The module DrUtils must access DrGlobal, and looks as follows:

```
MODULE DrUtils
! Driver utility subroutines

USE DrGlobal
IMPLICIT NONE

INTERFACE
  SUBROUTINE DEqs( F )               ! defines model DEs
    REAL F(:)
  END SUBROUTINE DEqs
END INTERFACE

CONTAINS

SUBROUTINE Headings                  ! generates output headings
  INTEGER I
  PRINT "(3A11)", "Time", (Vars(I) % Name, I = 1, NumVars)
  PRINT*
  PRINT "(3F11.2)", T, X
END SUBROUTINE Headings

SUBROUTINE Initialize
! All this info could be read from a disk file
  NumVars = 2
  NumParams = 4
  ALLOCATE( Vars(NumVars), Params(NumParams), X(NumVars) )
  Vars(1) % Name = "Prey"
  Vars(1) % InVal = 105
  Vars(2) % Name = "Pred"
  Vars(2) % InVal = 8
  Params(1) % Val = 0.4
  Params(2) % Val = 0.04
  Params(3) % Val = 0.02
  Params(4) % Val = 2.0
  Vars % Val = 0              ! set current values to zero for safety
  dt = 1
  T = 0
  RunTime = 10
END SUBROUTINE Initialize

     SUBROUTINE Run                        ! run the model
CALL Headings
DO Itime = 1, RunTime
  T = T + dt
  CALL Runge
  PRINT "(3F11.2)", T, X
END DO
Vars % Val = X                     ! current values
     END SUBROUTINE Run
```

```
SUBROUTINE Runge
! 4th order Runge-Kutta
  REAL :: F(NumVars)
  REAL, DIMENSION( NumVars ) :: A, B, C, D, V  ! working space
  REAL h
  A = 0; B = 0; C = 0; D = 0  ! initialize
  V = X                       ! initialize for Runge-Kutta

  CALL DEqs( F )
  A = dt * F
  X = V + A / 2               ! V has original X, update X
  CALL DEqs( F )
  B = dt * F
  X = V + B / 2
  CALL DEqs( F )
  C = dt * F
  X = V + C
  CALL DEqs( F )
  D = dt * F
  X = V + (A + 2 * B + 2 * C + D) / 6 ! finally update X for return
END SUBROUTINE Runge

SUBROUTINE TidyUp
! close files, throw away dynamic storage, etc.
  DEALLOCATE( Vars, Params, X )
END SUBROUTINE

END MODULE DrUtils
```

It has an (optional) interface block for the external subroutine DEqs.

Headings generates headings for the output from a run, including the initial values for that run.

Initialize allocates dynamic storage, sets up model variable and parameter names and values, and also initializes other global variables. Note that all this information could be read from a disk file (which itself could be set up by another subroutine).

The subroutine Run actually runs the model. It generates headings, integrates the differential equations RunTime times by calling Runge, and finally sets the final values of the variables from X. Note that Vars % Val is a valid array section: the array X can therefore be assigned to it.

Runge integrates the differential equations over one step-length dt, calling DEqs to supply their right-hand sides.

TidyUp deallocates dynamic storage, and would be the place to close files, etc.

Finally, the package is driven by the main program Driver:

```
PROGRAM Driver
! Runs differential equations models
! Model DE must be defined in external subroutine DEqs
```

```
USE DrGlobal              ! global declarations
USE DrUtils               ! Driver subroutines
IMPLICIT NONE

CALL Initialize
Opt = ""
PRINT*, "Driver Sample Model"
PRINT*
DO WHILE (Opt /= "Q" .AND. Opt /= "q")
  PRINT*, "C: Carry on"
  PRINT*, "I: Initial run"
  PRINT*, "Q: Quit"
  PRINT*
  READ*, Opt
  PRINT*
  SELECT CASE (Opt)
  CASE ("C", "c")
    X = Vars % Val
    CALL Run
  CASE ("I", "i")
    X = Vars % InVal
    T = 0
    CALL Run
  END SELECT
END DO
CALL TidyUp

END PROGRAM Driver
```

Driver uses both modules, and allows two basic options at the moment: to run the model from its initial values (I), or to run from the current values (C).

If an initial run is selected, X is assigned initial values, and T is set to zero, before Run is called. If a carry on is selected, X is assigned current values, and T is left unchanged.

A sample run using the data in this example is as follows:

```
Driver Sample Model

C: Carry on
I: Initial run
Q: Quit

Enter your option:
I
        Time      Prey      Pred

        0.00     105.00      8.00
        1.00     110.88      9.47
        2.00     108.32     11.65
```

3.00	98.83	12.57
4.00	91.12	11.26
5.00	90.30	9.24
6.00	95.81	7.98
7.00	104.30	7.99
8.00	110.45	9.34
9.00	108.61	11.48
10.00	99.58	12.52

. . .

Depending on your enthusiasm, you could extend this skeleton a great deal. You could even write a procedure for setting up a new model, which asks the user for symbolic names of variables and parameters, and which *generates the aliasing code* for subsequent inclusion into DEqs. This is very useful for large models.

16.7   Partial Differential Equations: a Tridiagonal System

The numerical solution of partial differential equations (PDEs) is a vast subject. Space only permits one example, which serves two important purposes. It demonstrates a powerful method of solving a class of PDEs called *parabolic*. It also illustrates a method of solving tridiagonal systems of linear equations.

Heat conduction   The conduction of heat along a thin uniform rod may be modelled by the partial differential equation

$$\frac{\partial U}{\partial t} = \frac{\partial^2 U}{\partial x^2},$$ (16.17)

where $U(x,t)$ is the temperature distribution a distance x from one end of the rod at time t. It is assumed that no heat is lost from the rod along its length.

Half the battle in solving PDEs is mastering the notation. We set up a rectangular grid, with step-lengths of h and k in the x and t directions respectively. A general point on the grid has co-ordinates $x_i = ih$, $y_j = jk$. A concise notation for $U(x,t)$ at x_i, y_j is then simply $U_{i,j}$.

Now $U_{i,j}$ is of course the exact solution of the PDE. Exact solutions can only be found in a few special cases; we want a general method for finding approximate solutions. This is done by using truncated Taylor series to replace the PDE by a *finite difference scheme*. We define $u_{i,j}$ as the solution of the finite difference scheme at the grid point x_i, y_j. We now attempt to find numerical solutions for $u_{i,j}$, which will therefore be our approximation to the exact solution $U_{i,j}$.

The left-hand side of Equation 16.17 is usually approximated by a *forward difference*:

$$\frac{\partial U}{\partial t} = \frac{u_{i,j+1} - u_{i,j}}{k}.$$

One way of approximating the right-hand side of Equation 16.17 is as follows:

$$\frac{\partial^2 U}{\partial x^2} = \frac{u_{i+1,j} - 2u_{i,j} + u_{i-1,j}}{h^2}.$$ (16.18)

This leads to a scheme, which although easy to compute, is only conditionally stable.

If however we replace the right-hand side of the scheme in Equation 16.18 by the mean of the finite difference approximation on the jth and $(j + 1)$th time rows, we get the following scheme for Equation 16.17:

$$- ru_{i-1,j+1} + (2 + 2r)u_{i,j+1} - ru_{i+1,j+1} = ru_{i-1,j} + (2 - 2r)u_{i,j} + ru_{i+1,j}, \qquad (16.19)$$

where $r = k/h^2$. This is known as the Crank-Nicolson *implicit* method, since it involves the solution of a system of simultaneous equations, as we shall see.

To illustrate the method numerically, let's suppose that the rod has a length of 1 unit, and that its ends are in contact with blocks of ice, i.e. the *boundary conditions* are $U(0,t) = U(1,t) = 0$. Suppose also that the initial temperature is given by the *initial condition*

$$U(x,0) = \begin{cases} 2x, & 0 \le x \le 1/2, \\ 2(1 - x), & 1/2 \le x \le 1. \end{cases}$$

This situation could come about by heating the centre of the rod for a long time, with the ends kept in contact with the ice, removing the heat source at time $t = 0$. This particular problem has symmetry about the line $x = 1/2$; we exploit this fact in finding the solution.

If we take $h = 0.1$ and $k = 0.01$, we will have $r = 1$, and Equation 16.19 becomes

$$-u_{i-1,j+1} + 4u_{i,j+1} - u_{i+1,j+1} = u_{i-1,j} + u_{i+1,j}.$$

Putting $j = 0$ then generates the following set of equations for the unknowns $u_{i,1}$ up to the midpoint of the rod, represented by $i = 5$, i.e. $x = ih = 0.5$. Exact and approximate solutions coincide on the boundaries and at time $t = 0$. The subscript $j = 1$ has been dropped for clarity:

$$
\begin{aligned}
0 + 4u_1 - u_2 &= 0 + 0.4 \\
-u_1 + 4u_2 - u_3 &= 0.2 + 0.6 \\
-u_2 + 4u_3 - u_4 &= 0.4 + 0.8 \\
-u_3 + 4u_4 - u_5 &= 0.6 + 1.0 \\
-u_4 + 4u_5 - u_6 &= 0.8 + 0.8.
\end{aligned}
$$

Symmetry then allows us to replace u_6 in the last equation by u_4. This system can be written in matrix form as

$$
\begin{bmatrix}
4 & -1 & 0 & 0 & 0 \\
-1 & 4 & -1 & 0 & 0 \\
0 & -1 & 4 & -1 & 0 \\
0 & 0 & -1 & 4 & -1 \\
0 & 0 & 0 & -2 & 4
\end{bmatrix}
\begin{bmatrix}
u_1 \\ u_2 \\ u_3 \\ u_4 \\ u_5
\end{bmatrix}
=
\begin{bmatrix}
0.4 \\ 0.8 \\ 1.2 \\ 1.6 \\ 1.6
\end{bmatrix}. \qquad (16.20)
$$

The matrix (**A**) on the left of Equation 16.20 is known as a *tridiagonal* matrix. Such a matrix can be represented by three one-dimensional arrays: one for each diagonal. The system can then be solved very efficiently by Gauss *elimination*. This will not be explained here, but simply presented in a working program.

Care needs to be taken with the matrix representation. The following form is often chosen:

$$
\mathbf{A} =
\begin{bmatrix}
b_1 & c_1 & & & & & \\
a_2 & b_2 & c_2 & & & & \\
 & a_3 & b_3 & c_3 & & & \\
 & & & \ddots & & & \\
 & & & & a_{n-1} & b_{n-1} & c_{n-1} \\
 & & & & & a_n & b_n
\end{bmatrix}.
$$

Noting how the subscripts run, we will have to dimension as follows: A(2:N), B(N), C(1:N-1).

The following program implements the Crank-Nicolson method to solve this particular problem over 10 time steps of $k = 0.01$. The step-length h is specified by N: $h = 1/(2N)$ because of the symmetry. r is therefore not restricted to the value 1, although it takes this value in the program.

```
PROGRAM CrankNicolson
IMPLICIT NONE
INTEGER, PARAMETER :: N = 5
REAL A(2:N), B(N), C(1:N-1), U(0:N+1), G(N), UX(N)
INTEGER I, J
REAL H, K, R, T

K = 0.01
H = 1.0 / (2 * N)        ! symmetry assumed
R = K / H ** 2
! set up A, B, C
A = -R
A(N) = - 2 * R           ! symmetry
B = 2 + 2 * R
C = -R

DO I = 0, N              ! initial conditions
   U(I) = 2 * I * H
END DO
U(N+1) = U(N-1)          ! symmetry

T = 0
PRINT "(A6, 10F8.4)", "X =", (I * H, I = 1, N)
PRINT*, " T"
PRINT "(F6.2, 10F8.4)", T, U(1:N)

DO J = 1, 10
   T = T + 0.01
   G = R * (U(0:N-1) + U(2:N+1)) + (2 - 2 * R) * U(1:N) ! general R
   CALL TriDiag( A, B, C, UX, G )
   PRINT "(F6.2, 10F8.4)", T, UX
   U(1:N) = UX
   U(N+1) = U(N-1)                     ! symmetry
END DO
```

```fortran
CONTAINS

SUBROUTINE TriDiag( A, B, C, X, G )
! Solves the tridiagonal system Ax = g by Gauss elimination
  IMPLICIT NONE
  REAL B(:)                     ! main diagonal
  REAL A(2:)                    ! lower diagonal
  REAL C(:)                     ! upper diagonal
  REAL, INTENT(OUT) :: X(:)     ! unknown
  REAL G(:)                     ! RHS
  REAL W( SIZE(B) )             ! working space
  REAL T
  INTEGER I, J, N

  N = SIZE(B)
  W = B
  DO I = 2, N
    T = A(I) / W(I-1)
    W(I) = W(I) - C(I-1) * T
    G(I) = G(I) - G(I-1) * T
  END DO
  ! back substitution
  X(N) = G(N) / W(N)
  DO I = 1, N-1
    J = N-I
    X(J) = (G(J) - C(J) * X(J+1)) / W(J)
  END DO
END SUBROUTINE TriDiag

END PROGRAM CrankNicolson
```

Output:

```
   X =  0.1000  0.2000  0.3000  0.4000  0.5000
   T
   0.00  0.2000  0.4000  0.6000  0.8000  1.0000
   0.01  0.1988  0.3955  0.5834  0.7381  0.7690
   0.02  0.1936  0.3789  0.5396  0.6460  0.6920
   ...
   0.10  0.0948  0.1803  0.2482  0.2918  0.3068
```

Note the use of array sections in the main program.

Note also that the subroutine TriDiag can be used to solve any tridiagonal system, and could be made part of a general utility module.

Summary

- A numerical method is an approximate computer method for solving a mathematical problem which often has no analytical solution.
- A numerical method is subject to two distinct types of error: rounding error in the computer solution, and *truncation error*, where an infinite mathematical process, like taking a limit, is approximated by a finite process.
- An external or module procedure may be passed as an argument of a procedure. An interface block is recommended.

Exercises

16.1   Use Newton's method in a program to solve some of the following (you may have to experiment a bit with the starting value):

(a) $x^4 - x = 10$ (two real and two complex roots)
(b) $e^{-x} = \sin x$ (infinitely many roots)
(c) $x^3 - 8x^2 + 17x - 10 = 0$ (three real roots)
(d) $\log x = \cos x$
(e) $x^4 - 5x^3 - 12x^2 + 76x - 79 = 0$ (two real roots near 2; find the complex roots as well).

16.2   Use the Bisection method to find the square root of 2, taking 1 and 2 as initial values of x_L and x_R. Continue bisecting until the maximum error is less than 0.05. Use Inequality 16.2 to determine how many bisections are needed.

16.3   Use the Trapezoidal to evaluate $\int_0^4 x^2 dx$, using a step-length of $h = 1$.

16.4   A human population of 1000 at time $t = 0$ grows at a rate given by

$$dN/dt = aN,$$

where $a = 0.025$ per person per year. Use Euler's method to project the population over the next 30 years, working in steps of (a) $h = 2$ years, (b) $h = 1$ year and (c) $h = 0.5$ years. Compare your answers with the exact mathematical solution.

16.5   The basic equation for modelling radio-active decay is

$$dx/dt = -rx,$$

where x is the amount of the radio-active substance at time t, and r is the decay rate.

   Some radio-active substances decay into other radio-active substances, which in turn also decay. For example, Strontium 92 ($r_1 = 0.256$ per hr) decays into Yttrium 92 ($r_2 = 0.127$ per hr), which in turn decays into Zirconium. Write down a pair of differential equations for Strontium and Yttrium to describe what is happening.

   Starting at $t = 0$ with 5×10^{26} atoms of Strontium 92 and none of Yttrium, use the Runge-Kutta formulae to solve the equations up to $t = 8$ hours in steps of $1/3$ hours. Also use Euler's method for the same problem, and compare your results.

16.6   The impala population $x(t)$ in the Kruger National Park in South Africa may be modelled by the equation

$$dx/dt = (r - bx \sin at)x,$$

where r, b, and a are constants. Write a program which

- reads values for r, b, a and the step-length h (in months);
- reads the initial value of x;
- uses Euler's method to compute the impala population;
- prints the population at *monthly* intervals over a period of two years.

16.7   The luminous efficiency (ratio of the energy in the visible spectrum to the total energy) of a black body radiator may be expressed as a percentage by the formula

$$E = 64.77T^{-4} \int_{4\times10^{-5}}^{7\times10^{-5}} x^{-5}(e^{1.432/Tx} - 1)^{-1}dx,$$

where T is the absolute temperature in degrees Kelvin, x is the wavelength in cm, and the range of integration is over the visible spectrum. Taking $T = 3500°K$, use Simpson's rule to compute E, firstly with 10 intervals ($n = 5$), and then with 20 intervals ($n = 10$), and compare your results.

16.8   Van der Pol's equation is a second-order non-linear differential equation which may be expressed as two first-order equations as follows:

$$dx_1/dt = x_2$$
$$dx_2/dt = \epsilon(1 - x_1^2)x_2 - b^2x_1.$$

The solution of this equation has a stable limit cycle, which means that if you plot the phase trajectory of the solution (the plot of x_1 against x_2) starting at any point in the positive x_1-x_2 plane, it always moves continuously into the same closed loop. Use the Runge-Kutta method to solve this system numerically, with $h = 0.1$, $x_1(0) = 0$, and $x_2(0) = 1$. If you have access to graphics facilities, draw the phase trajectory for $b = 1$ and ϵ ranging between 0.01 and 1.0.

Epilogue

Programming Style

Throughout this book the emphasis has been on writing clear, coherent programs to solve interesting problems. A program which is written any old how, although it may do what is required, is going to be difficult to understand when you go through it again after a month or two. Serious programmers therefore pay a fair amount of attention to what is called *programming style*, in order to make their programs clearer and more readable both to themselves, and to other potential users. You may find this irritating, if you are starting to program for the first time, because you will naturally be impatient to get on with the job. But a little extra attention to your program layout will pay enormous dividends in the long run, especially when it comes to debugging.

Some hints on how to improve your programming style are given below.

- You should make liberal use of comments, both at the beginning of a program unit or subprogram, to describe briefly what it does and any special methods that may have been used, and also throughout the coding to introduce different logical sections. Any restrictions on the size and type of data that may be used as input should be stated clearly in the comments (e.g. maximum sizes of arrays).
- The meaning of each variable should be described briefly in a comment at its declaration. You should declare variables systematically, e.g. in alphabetical order by type.
- Subprograms should be arranged in alphabetical order with at least one blank line between them.
- Blank lines should be freely used to separate sections of coding (e.g. before and after loop structures).
- Coding inside structures (loops, decisions, etc) should be indented a few columns to make them stand out.
- Blanks should be used in statements to make them more readable, e.g.

- on either side of operators and equal signs;
- after commas.

However, blanks may be omitted in places in complicated expressions, where this may make the structure clearer.
- FORMAT statements should be grouped together.
- The GOTO statement should **never be used**, under *any* circumstances.
- You should try to avoid breaking out of structures in the middle, e.g. with CYCLE or EXIT.
- Statements which generate an obsolescence warning should be avoided—they could well disappear during revision for the next standard.

A

Order of Statements in a Program Unit

The following table shows the order of statements in a Fortran 90 program unit. Statements may be moved across vertical lines, but not across horizontal lines.

PROGRAM, FUNCTION, SUBROUTINE, or MODULE statement		
USE statements		
FORMAT statements	IMPLICIT NONE statement	
	PARAMETER and DATA statements	derived-type definitions, interface blocks, type declaration statements, specification statements
	executable statements	
CONTAINS statement		
internal subprograms or module subprograms		
END statement		

B

Summary of Fortran 90 Statements

All the statements of Fortran 90 are summarized below, with examples of their most commonly used forms. Square brackets denote optional items. In many cases this is a "ready reference", with fuller descriptions in the main text. The summary here is more detailed where statements are not described fully in the main text.

The use of some statements is not recommended because they encourage sloppy programming. This is a personal view; not all programmers will agree on which statements should be proscribed. They are nevertheless listed for completeness and historical interest, since you may one day be faced with a piece of antediluvian Fortran to decipher. Other statements are *obsolescent* (on the way out), and should be avoided, since they may not be in the next standard.

Attributes that may appear in type declaration statements, or in separate type *specification* statements, are generally discussed under REAL, since this is the most common type.

ALLOCATABLE specifies the ALLOCATABLE attribute for an array. See REAL.

ALLOCATE allocates dynamic storage to a pointer variable at run-time, e.g.

```
REAL, POINTER :: P1, P2(:)
ALLOCATE( P1, P2(100) )
```

It may also be used to allocate memory to an allocatable array:

```
REAL, ALLOCATABLE :: X
READ*, N
ALLOCATE( X(N) )
```

In general:

```
ALLOCATE( list[, STAT = st] )
```

If the STAT specifier is present, st is given the value zero after a successful allocation, and a positive value otherwise (in which case execution continues). If STAT is absent, execution stops after an unsuccessful attempt to allocate.

ASSIGN (**obsolescent and not recommended**) is used in conjunction with the *assigned* GO TO. E.g.

```
ASSIGN 5 TO N
...
GOTO N [(4, 5, 6)]
```

will transfer control to statement 5 after the execution of the GOTO.

BACKSPACE positions a file before the preceding record, e.g.

```
BACKSPACE 2                ! file is connected to unit 2
BACKSPACE( [UNIT =] u[, IOSTAT = io] [, ERR = label] )
```

See READ for the meaning of the specifiers.

BLOCK DATA (**not recommended**) names a BLOCK DATA program unit for the initialization of objects in named COMMON blocks:

```
BLOCK DATA Rubbish
  COMMON / NAME / X, Y, X
  DATA X, Y, X / 1, 2, 3 /
END BLOCK DATA Rubbish
```

CALL invokes a subroutine:

```
CALL PLONK
CALL PLINK( A, B, C )
```

CASE allows a selection of various options:

```
SELECT CASE (Ch)
CASE ("a":"z")                  ! CASE (low:high)
  PRINT*, "lower case"
CASE ("A":"Z")
  PRINT*, "UPPER CASE"
CASE DEFAULT
  PRINT*, "not a char"
END SELECT
```

One of the bounds may be absent, e.g. CASE (:0) selects non-positive numbers. The full definition is in Chapter 6.

CHARACTER specifies character type. The declaration has a number of forms, e.g.

```
CHARACTER*4 Word              ! Word has length 4
CHARACTER (LEN = 8) Names(100) ! array of 100 names
                              ! each of length 8
CHARACTER (4) N, Line*80      ! N has length 4, Line has
                              ! length 80
CHARACTER (LEN = 20, KIND = 2) GreekWord
CHARACTER (*), INTENT(IN) :: Name   ! assumed length
                                    ! dummy argument
CHARACTER (*), PARAMETER &
  :: Message = "No such file" ! named constant
```

CHARACTER is the only one of the five intrinsic types to have two parameters: length and kind.

CLOSE disconnects a file from a unit, e.g.

```
CLOSE( 13 )
```

In general:

```
CLOSE( [UNIT =] u[, IOSTAT = io] [, ERR = label] &
    [, STATUS = st] )
```

See OPEN for the meanings of the first three specifiers.

st is a character expression which must have the value KEEP or DELETE. This specifies what happens to the file after disconnection. st defaults to KEEP, unless the file has status SCRATCH, in which case its only value is DELETE.

COMMON (**not recommended**) allocates memory in a COMMON block of storage, which may be blank or named. The blocks may be accessed from different program units, using the same or different variable names. E.g.

```
COMMON /JUNK/ A, B, X(5)
```

in one program unit, and

```
COMMON /JUNK/ X, Y(4), Z1, Z2
```

in another, means that A and X, B and Y(1), ..., X(5) and Z2 share the same storage locations. As you can imagine, this can be highly dangerous. If data must be shared between program units, it should be declared in a module accessed by any program units needing it.

Blank COMMON refers to the unnamed COMMON block, of which there is only one:

```
COMMON M, G
```

COMPLEX specifies complex type:

```
COMPLEX X
X = (0, 1)              ! sqrt(-1)
```

Complex constants in list-directed input with READ* must be in parentheses.

CONTAINS signals the presence of one or more internal or module subprograms.

CONTINUE is a dummy statement which does nothing. Its main usage was as a labelled statement at the end of a DO loop:

```
DO 10 I = 1, 100
   ...
   10  CONTINUE
```

This is **not recommended**; use DO with END DO instead.

CYCLE (**not recommended**) transfers control to the END DO statement of the current DO construct. The next iteration (if there is one) is initiated. If you want to leave out part of a loop sometimes you should rewrite it.

DATA initializes objects during compile time. This is particularly useful for arrays:

```
REAL A(10), X(5), B, C, D
DATA A / 10 * 1 /[,] (X(I), I = 2, 4) / 1, 2, 3 /
DATA B, C, D / 4, 5, 6 /
```

Note the optional comma separating a value list from a following object list.

DEALLOCATE releases dynamic storage:

```
DEALLOCATE( P1, P2 )
```

In general:

```
DEALLOCATE( list[, STAT = st] )
```

See ALLOCATE for the analogous meaning of STAT.

DIMENSION declares an array. It is not recommended as a separate statement. See REAL for its use as an attribute.

DO repeats a block of statements a specified number of times, e.g.

```
DO I = 1, 100        ! I incremented by 1 by default
   ...
END DO
```

and

```
DO K = 10, 1, -2     ! K decremented by 2
   ...
END DO
```

DO may also be used with a conditional EXIT, e.g.

```
DO
   IF (ABS( F(X) ) < 1E-6) EXIT
   ...
END DO
```

DO parameters should be integers. The use of real parameters is obsolescent and not recommended.

The full definition of DO is in Chapter 7.

DO WHILE repeats a block of statements conditionally:

```
DO WHILE (ABS( F(X) ) >= 1E-6)
  . . .
END DO
```

Metcalf and Reid warn that DO WHILE may be inefficient when execution time is a critical factor. Since most examples in this book do not fall in this category, I have used it in preference to DO with EXIT. It makes the logic much clearer.

DOUBLE PRECISION (**not recommended**) specifies a real variable with a precision higher than the default:

```
DOUBLE PRECISION X
```

It is the Fortran 77 user's cop out for not learning about kind type parameters, which are discussed fully in Chapter 3.

END is the final statement in a program unit or subprogram.

ENDFILE writes an endfile record to a sequential file. In general:

```
ENDFILE( [UNIT =] u[, IOSTAT = io][, ERR = label] )
```

The specifiers have the same meaning as in OPEN.

ENTRY (**not recommended**) allows a subprogram to be entered at points other than at the beginning, and therefore defeats the purpose of writing subprograms as logical units:

```
SUBROUTINE JUNK( dummy-arglist )
  . . .
  ENTRY SILLY( dummy-arglist )
  . . .
  ENTRY WORSE( dummy-arglist )
  . . .
END SUBROUTINE
```

You can then call JUNK, SILLY or even WORSE, depending on exactly where you would like to start!

EQUIVALENCE (**not recommended**) enables two or more objects in the same program unit to share the same storage area. E.g.

```
EQUIVALENCE (A, B), (X, Y)
```

allows A and B on the one hand, and X and Y on the other, to share the same storage area. Since array elements occupy consecutive storage locations, you can get some really weird results. E.g.

```
INTEGER A(2), B(3), X(2,2)
EQUIVALENCE (A(2), B(1), X(1,2))
```

implements the following arrangement (elements in the same column share storage):

	A(1)	A(2) B(1)	B(2)	B(3)
X(1,1)	X(2,1)	X(1,2)	X(2,2)	

If you want to use different names for the same object, set up an alias with a pointer.

EXIT (**conditionally recommended**) allows exit from a DO construct (see example under DO). You should exit from as close to the top or bottom of a DO as possible in order to make the exit condition easy to see. Multiple exits are definitely **not recommended**.

EXTERNAL specifies each name listed as the name of an external or dummy procedure. The interface remains implicit. If an explicit interface is needed, use an INTERFACE block; this is generally recommended. E.g.

```
EXTERNAL F
```

FORMAT provides an I/O format specification. It is described fully in Chapter 10. See PRINT for examples.

FUNCTION names a function subprogram:

```
FUNCTION Factorial( N )
  ...
END FUNCTION Factorial
```

In the case of a recursive function the form is, e.g.

```
RECURSIVE FUNCTION Factorial( N ) RESULT (Fact)
```

The type can be specified in the FUNCTION statement, as in

```
INTEGER FUNCTION Factorial( N )
```

GOTO (**not recommended**) transfers control unconditionally to a labelled statment:

```
GOTO 70
```

There are two other forms of GOTO: assigned GOTO (see ASSIGN) and computed GOTO. The computed GOTO looks like this:

```
GOTO ( 20, 50, 10, 40 ) N
```

Control passes to the statement with the Nth label in the list, e.g. to the statement labelled 10 if N evaluates to 3.

IF transfers control conditionally. There are three distinct forms.

- The "logical" IF *statement* is used when a single statement is to be executed under a certain condition:

    ```
    IF (A /= 0) X = B / (2 * A)
    ```

- The IF *construct* is used when blocks of statements are to be executed under certain conditions:

    ```
    IF (Num > 0) THEN
      PRINT*, "positive"
    ELSE IF (Num == 0) THEN
      PRINT*, "zero"
    ELSE
      PRINT*, "negative"
    END IF
    ```

- The "arithmetic" IF is a

    dangerous statement, since its use tends to be coupled with the occurrence of numerous GOTO statements—A. Balfour and D.H. Marwick, *Programming in Standard FORTRAN 77* (Heinemann, London, 1979, p. 291)

    It is **obsolescent and not recommended**. E.g.

    ```
    IF (B**2 - 4*A*C) 10, 20, 30
    ```

    Control passes to statements 10, 20, or 30 according as B**2 - 4*A*C is negative, zero, or positive.

IMPLICIT (**not recommended**) declares variables of a specified type according to their initial letter. E.g.

```
IMPLICIT INTEGER (A, X-Z)
```

specifies integer type for all variables starting with the letters A, X, Y and Z. It is better to specify the type of each variable separately in a type declaration statement.

IMPLICIT NONE suspends the implicit type rule, whereby all variables with the initial letter I to N inclusive are specified as integers, with all others real. This statement should appear in every program unit to force you to declare all objects specifically.

INCLUDE (**not recommended**) enables text from another file to be included in the source file during compilation. It is not technically a Fortran statement, and has the form

```
INCLUDE "filename"
```

INQUIRE ascertains the status and attributes of a file. It has three forms: inquire by I/O list, inquire by file and inquire by unit.

Inquire by I/O list returns the length of an unformatted output record by means of the IOLENGTH specifier, e.g.

```
INQUIRE( IOLENGTH = reclen ) Student
```

reclen can then be used to give the record length with the RECL specifier of an OPEN statement.

The other two forms are

```
INQUIRE( FILE = filename, spec-list )      ! by file
INQUIRE( [UNIT =] u, spec-list )           ! by unit
```

where `filename` and `u` are character and integer expressions respectively. `spec-list` is a list of optional specifiers. Their names, and values returned, are (char means character):

EXIST (logical): TRUE if it exists, FALSE otherwise.

OPENED (logical): TRUE if connected, FALSE otherwise.

NUMBER (integer): value of unit number connected, or −1 if no unit is connected.

NAMED (logical): TRUE if file has a name, FALSE otherwise.

NAME (char): returns name if file has a name.

ACCESS (char): SEQUENTIAL, DIRECT, or UNDEFINED (if there is no connection).

SEQUENTIAL and DIRECT (char): YES, NO or UNKNOWN, depending on allowed mode of access.

FORM (char): FORMATTED, UNFORMATTED, or UNDEFINED.

RECL (integer): maximum record length allowed.

NEXTREC (integer): number of most recent record read or written.

BLANK (char): NULL or ZERO depending on whether blanks in numeric fields are interpreted by default as null fields or zeros.

POSITION (char): REWIND, APPEND, ASIS or UNDEFINED—see OPEN.

ACTION (char): READ, WRITE, READWRITE or UNDEFINED.

READ, WRITE and READWRITE (char): YES, NO or UNKNOWN.

DELIM (char): APOSTROPHE, QUOTE, NONE or UNKNOWN—see OPEN.

PAD (char): YES or NO—see OPEN.

E.g.

```
LOGICAL connected
CHARACTER(10) acc
INTEGER nrec
INQUIRE( 1, OPENED = connected, ACCESS = acc, NEXTREC = nrec )
```

INTEGER declares objects with integer type, e.g.

```
INTEGER N, X
INTEGER List(0:100)
```

See REAL for attributes which may be specified.

INTENT specifies the intent attribute for a dummy argument. See REAL.

INTERFACE specifies an explicit interface for an external subprogram, e.g.

```
INTERFACE
  FUNCTION F(X)
    REAL F
    REAL, INTENT(IN) :: X
  END FUNCTION F
END INTERFACE
```

Interface blocks can also overload procedures with a generic name:

```
INTERFACE SuperFung
  MODULE PROCEDURE IntFung, RealFung    ! defined in module
END INTERFACE
```

Procedures may be overloaded with an operator, e.g.

```
INTERFACE OPERATOR(*)
  FUNCTION MyMult( A, B )               ! must be a function
    TYPE (MyType) MyMult
    TYPE (AnotherType), INTENT(IN) :: A, B
  END FUNCTION MyMult
END INTERFACE
```

and also with the assignment operator:

```
INTERFACE ASSIGNMENT(=)
  SUBROUTINE MyAss( Left, Right )
    TYPE (MyType), INTENT(IN) :: Left
    TYPE (AnotherType), INTENT(IN) :: Right
  END SUBROUTINE
END INTERFACE
```

INTRINSIC specifies that a name listed is that of an intrinsic procedure. The statement is normally optional, but makes it clear to the reader (who may be unfamiliar with the plethora of new intrinsic procedures available under Fortran 90) which procedures are intrinsic and which are not.

An intrinsic procedure which is passed as an argument *must* be specified in an INTRINSIC statement.

LOGICAL declares logical type:

```
LOGICAL Switch
LOGICAL TruthTable(4,4)        ! array of logical elements
```

See REAL for attributes which may be specified.

MODULE defines a module:

```
MODULE Clobber
   ...
END MODULE Clobber
```

NAMELIST is an obscure feature which enables you to specify in the input stream which items in a NAMELIST group are to be read. E.g.

```
INTEGER A, B, C
NAMELIST /MyLot/ A, B, C
READ( *, [NML =] MyLot )
```

Input stream:

```
&MyLot A = 3 C = 39/
```

(a value for B has been omitted). See Chapter 10 for another example.

NULLIFY gives a pointer variable disassociated status, which may be tested for by the ASSOCIATED intrinsic function, e.g.

```
NULLIFY( P1 )
```

OPEN connects an external file to a unit. The file can be created first if necessary. It can also change some properties of a connection. The general form is

```
OPEN( [UNIT =] u, spec-list )
```

where u is the unit number. The specifiers in spec-list are (char means character):

IOSTAT (integer): returns zero if the statement successfully executes, and a positive value otherwise.

ERR (integer constant): label of statement to which control passes if an error occurs.

FILE (char): provides file name; if this specifier is omitted, the STATUS specifier must be set to SCRATCH, and the file is deleted when the connection is closed.

STATUS (char): OLD (file must already exist), NEW (file must not exist, but is created), REPLACE (if file does not exist it is created, if it does exist it is deleted and a new one created), SCRATCH (file is created, and deleted when connection is closed), UNKNOWN.

ACCESS (char): SEQUENTIAL (default), DIRECT.

FORM (char): FORMATTED (default for sequential access), UNFORMATTED (default for direct access).

RECL (positive integer): record length for direct access (obligatory), maximum record length for sequential access (optional); for formatted files length is number of characters in record, for unformatted files length is system dependent but may be found with INQUIRE.

BLANK (char): NULL (default), ZERO; sets default for interpretation of blanks as nulls or zeros; formatted records only.

POSITION (char): ASIS (default—file is opened at previous position), REWIND (opened at initial position), APPEND (opened ahead of endfile record); sequential access only.

ACTION (char): READ (read only), WRITE (write only), READWRITE (both); default is system dependent.

DELIM (char): APOSTROPHE, QUOTE, NONE (default); indicates delimiter character used for character constants with list-directed or NAMELIST formatting.

PAD (char): YES (default—formatted input record regarded as padded with blanks if input list and associated format specify more data than appear in record), NO.

E.g.

```
OPEN (2, FILE = "Students", ACCESS = "DIRECT", &
      STATUS = "OLD", RECL = 40)
```

OPTIONAL specifies the OPTIONAL attribute for dummy arguments. See REAL.

PARAMETER specifies the PARAMETER attribute to name a constant. See REAL.

PAUSE (**obsolescent and not recommended**) suspends execution pending external intervention.

POINTER specifies the POINTER attribute, e.g.

```
REAL, POINTER :: P
REAL, TARGET :: R
. . .
P => R              ! P is an alias for its target R
```

It may also be used to allocate dynamic storage:

```
REAL, POINTER :: X(:)
. . .
ALLOCATE( X(N) )
```

PRINT sends output to the standard output unit. Output may be formatted or list-directed:

```
    PRINT*, "The answer is:", X + Y              ! list-directed
    PRINT "(A, F5.2)", "The answer is:", X
    PRINT 10, "The answer is:", X                ! labelled format
10  FORMAT( A, F5.2 )
    PRINT*, ((A(I,J), J = 1, N), I = 1, N)       ! implied DO
```

PRIVATE specifies the PRIVATE attribute for some or all of the entities in a module, and for components of derived types. See REAL and TYPE.

PROGRAM optionally names a program:

```
[PROGRAM MyOne]
  ...
END [PROGRAM [MyOne]]      ! name can't appear without PROGRAM
```

PUBLIC specifies the PUBLIC attribute for module entities. See REAL.

READ transfers data from an input device. It has a number of forms, e.g.

```
    READ*, A, B, C            ! list-directed from standard
                              ! input device
    READ (*, *) A, B, C       ! list-directed from standard
                              ! input device
    READ (5, *) A, B, C       ! list-directed from unit 5
    READ (1, 15) A, B, C      ! from unit 1, format labelled 15
15  FORMAT( 3F6.2 )
    READ( *, "(3F6.2)" ) A, B, C  ! from standard input device
    READ (1) A, B, C          ! from unit 1, unformatted
```

The general form is:

```
  READ ([UNIT =] u, [FMT =] fmt [,spec-list] ) [list]
```

The specifiers may be in any order, subject to the following conditions: if the UNIT keyword is omitted, u must be first; if the FMT keyword is omitted, fmt must be second, following u without its keyword.

The other specifiers are:

IOSTAT (integer): returns a negative value if end-of-record encountered during non-advancing input, a different negative value if end-of-file detected, a positive value if an error is detected, or zero otherwise.

END = n: control passes to statement labelled n when end-of-file detected.

ERR = n: control passes to statement labelled n when an error is detected; labels for END and ERR may be the same; if END and ERR labels are not specified and an exception occurs, the program will crash unless IOSTAT is specified.

REC (integer): specifies record number to be read during direct access.

NML (name): replaces the FMT specifier; name is the name specified in a NAMELIST group.

E.g.

```
  READ( 2, REC = 75, IOSTAT = IO ) Student
```

In addition, non-advancing input may be specified with ADVANCE = "NO" (default YES). In this case, two additional specifiers are available:

EOR = n: control passes to statement n when an end-of-*record* condition occurs.

SIZE (integer): returns the number of characters actually read.

The unit specifier can be an internal file, denoted by a character variable:

```
CHARACTER (4) BUFFER
READ (BUFFER, "(I4)" ) YEAR
```

REAL declares objects with real type. It has a number of forms, e.g.

```
REAL [::] A            ! colons optional
REAL :: B = 10         ! initialization; colons obligatory
REAL X(0:10)           ! array
```

The following attributes may be specified in a type declaration: ALLOCATABLE, DIMENSION, EXTERNAL, INTENT, INTRINSIC, OPTIONAL, PARAMETER, POINTER, PRIVATE, PUBLIC, SAVE, TARGET.

Most attributes may be specified with any of the intrinsic types (CHARACTER, COMPLEX, INTEGER, LOGICAL and REAL) or a derived type.

Attributes may specified in separate statements, e.g.

```
REAL P, Q, R, S
POINTER P, S
TARGET Q, R
```

A double colon must appear whenever there is an initialization expression, or an attribute is specified. If a constant is named with the PARAMETER attribute, there must be an initialization expression. Array bounds may be specified after a name, instead of with the DIMENSION attribute. E.g.

```
REAL, PARAMETER :: g = 9.8                   ! named constant
INTEGER, PARAMETER :: Max = 100
REAL, DIMENSION(Max) :: X
INTEGER :: N(Max) = (/ (I, I = 1, Max) /)  ! array constructor
INTEGER, ALLOCATABLE :: Network(:,:)
REAL, DIMENSION(10) :: A, B(5), C(4,4)  ! only A is rank 1
                                        ! size 10
REAL, OPTIONAL, INTENT(IN) :: Y     ! optional dummy argument
REAL, INTENT(INOUT) :: M            ! dummy only
```

Certain (fairly obvious) combinations of attributes are not allowed, e.g. POINTER on the one hand and TARGET, or INTENT on the other; TARGET and PARAMETER; POINTER and ALLOCATABLE.

A kind parameter may be specified for any type:

```
REAL ([KIND = ]2) X
```

RECURSIVE specifies a recursive procedure. See FUNCTION.

RETURN returns control from a subprogram at a point other than its END statement. This can lead to unstructured design, and should be avoided if possible. There is another form of RETURN called the "alternate" RETURN, which is **obsolescent and not recommended**, because it allows returns to alternate points in the calling program:

```
      . . .
      CALL GUNGE( A, B, C, *10, *30 )
      . . .
      CONTAINS
        SUBROUTINE GUNGE( X, Y, Z, *, * )
        . . .
        RETURN 1
        . . .
        RETURN 2
        . . .
        END SUBROUTINE GUNGE
      END
```

If the integer expression in the RETURN statement is less than 1 or greater than the number of asterisks in the dummy argument list, a "normal" return is executed (i.e. to the point of call). Otherwise, if it has the value *i*, control passes to the statement in the calling program whose label is the actual argument corresponding to the *i*th dummy asterisk. So RETURN 1 effects a return to statement 10, while RETURN 2 returns to statement 30.

REWIND repositions a sequential file at its initial point. The syntax is the same as for backspace, e.g.

```
      REWIND 3
      REWIND( 2, IOSTAT = IO )
```

SAVE specifies the SAVE attribute for local variables declared in subprograms, i.e. such variables retain their current values between calls. See REAL.

All variables which have been initialized acquire the SAVE attribute automatically.

SELECT CASE See CASE.

SEQUENCE (**not recommended**) specifies the SEQUENCE attribute for derived types. Two type definitions in different scoping units define the same data type if they have the same name and components, and if both have the SEQUENCE attribute (giving them what is called storage association). It is better to have a single definition in a module accessible to both scoping units.

STOP (**not recommended**) stops program execution. This is needed by people who want to stop their programs at places other than at the END.

SUBROUTINE names a subroutine:

```
      [RECURSIVE] SUBROUTINE NAME( A, B, C, \ldots )
      . . .
      END SUBROUTINE NAME
```

If there are no arguments, the name is written without parentheses:

```
      SUBROUTINE NONE
```

TARGET specifies the TARGET attribute for an object which is the target of a pointer:

```
REAL, TARGET :: R
REAL, POINTER :: P1
...
P1 => R
```

See also REAL.

TYPE defines a derived type, e.g.

```
TYPE Person
  [PRIVATE]                ! if no access allowed to components
  CHARACTER (20) Name
  ...
END TYPE Person
```

Objects of derived type may be declared, e.g.

```
TYPE (Person), DIMENSION(:), INTENT(IN) :: Town
TYPE (Person) Me
```

USE enables access to the entities in a module by use association:

```
USE MyModule            ! only one module per USE
USE YourModule
```

Other possibilities are:

```
USE YourMod, MyPlonk => YourPlonk    ! MyPlonk is an alias
                        ! ... for object YourPlonk in the module
USE USE YourMod, ONLY :: This, That ! access only to
                                    ! This and That
```

WHERE performs operations on selected array elements. There are two forms. The WHERE *statement* has the form

```
REAL A(20,20)
...
WHERE (A > 0) A = 1   ! all elements > 0 replaced by 1
```

The WHERE *construct* looks like this:

```
INTEGER A(20,20)
...
WHERE (A > 0)
  A = 1              ! all positive elements replaced by 1
```

```
    [ELSEWHERE
      A = 0]              ! all the rest replaced by 0
    END WHERE
```

WRITE sends output to an output unit. In general:

```
    WRITE ([UNIT =] u, [FMT =] fmt [,spec-list]) [list]
```

The specifiers are the same as for READ, except that there is obviously no END specifier. E.g.

```
    WRITE (2, "(10F5.3)") (X(I), I = 1, N)
    WRITE (1, * ) "List directed output on unit 1"
    WRITE (3, REC = 76) A     ! direct access write to record 76
```

Non-advancing WRITE is useful for writing prompts:

```
    WRITE (*, "(A)", ADVANCE = "NO") &
       "Enter a number: " ! not list-directed/
```

There are no EOR or SIZE specifiers for non-advancing output.

C

Intrinsic Procedures

It is helpful to categorize intrinsic procedures as follows, although the descriptions below are grouped somewhat differently, for convenience of reference:

- *Elemental procedures* may be applied to scalars or arrays. When applied to arrays, the operation is performed on each element of the array. Arguments may be real or complex, unless otherwise stated, or unless the context clearly requires otherwise. Arguments must generally be of the same type.
- *Inquiry functions* return properties of their arguments.

- *Transformational functions* usually have array arguments and an array result depending in some way on the elements of the arguments.
- *Non-elemental subroutines*.

Descriptions below are given with dummy arguments, so that optional arguments (indicated [thus]) may be passed using the dummy argument names as keywords.

Results are usually returned in the default kind, unless the KIND keyword is used (where appropriate).

Trigonometric functions assume arguments are in radians, and return radians.

Almost all of the procedures are functions. To highlight the few that are subroutines the keyword CALL has been included in the description.

C.1   Elemental Numeric Functions

Note that the arguments may be real or complex scalars or arrays, unless otherwise stated.

ABS(A): absolute value of integer, real or complex A.

ACOS(X): inverse cosine (arc cosine).

AIMAG(Z): imaginary part.

AINT(A [,KIND]): largest whole real number not exceeding its argument, e.g. AINT(3.9) returns 3.0.

ANINT(A [,KIND]): nearest whole real number, e.g. ANINT(3.0) returns 4.0.

ASIN(X): inverse sine (arc cosine).

ATAN(X): inverse tangent (arc tangent), in the range $-\pi/2$ to $\pi/2$.

ATAN2(Y, X): inverse tangent (arc tangent), as principal value of the argument of the complex number (X, Y), in the range $-\pi$ to π.

CEILING(A): smallest integer not less than A.

CMPLX(X [,Y] [,KIND]): converts X or (X, Y) to complex type.

CONJG(Z): conjugate of complex Z.

COS(X): cosine.

COSH(X): hyperbolic cosine.

DIM(X, Y): max(X-Y, 0).

EXP(X): exponential function.

FLOOR(A): largest integer not exceeding its argument, e.g. FLOOR(-3.9) returns -4.

INT(A [,KIND]): converts to integer type, truncating towards zero.

LOG(X): natural logarithm; for complex X result is the principal value.

LOG10(X): common (base 10) logarithm.

MAX(A1, A2 [,A3,...]): maximum of arguments.

MIN(A1, A2 [,A3,...]): minimum of arguments.

MOD(A, P): remainder of A modulo P, i.e. A-INT(A/P)*P. E.g. MOD(2.2, 2.0) returns 0.2.

MODULO(A, P): A modulo P for A and P both real or both integer, i.e. A-FLOOR(A/P)*P in the real case, and A-FLOOR(A÷P)*P in the integer case, where ÷ represents mathematical division. E.g. MODULO(-10, 3) returns 2, MODULO(-2.2, 2.0) returns 1.8.

NINT(A [,KIND]): integer nearest to A.

REAL(A [,KIND]): converts to real.

SIGN(A, B): absolute value of A times sign of B.
SIN(A): sine.
SINH(A): hyperbolic sine.
SQRT(A): square root.
TAN(A): tangent
TANH(A): hyperbolic tangent.

C.2 Elemental Character-handling Functions

Compilers must support the ASCII collating sequence, but may also support other collating sequences.

ACHAR(I): character with ASCII code I for I in the range 0–127 (see Appendix D).
ADJUSTL(STRING): string of same length by changing leading blanks into trailing blanks (left justify).
ADJUSTR(STRING): string of same length by changing trailing blanks into leading blanks (right justify).
CHAR(I [,KIND]): character in position I of the system collating sequence with given kind.
IACHAR(C): ASCII code of character C (see Appendix D).
ICHAR(C): position of character C in the system collating sequence.
INDEX(STRING, SUBSTRING [BACK]): starting position of SUBSTRING as a substring of STRING, or zero if it does not occur. The position of the first or last substring is returned according as BACK is absent/FALSE or TRUE.
LEN_TRIM(STRING): length of STRING without trailing blanks.
LGE(STRING_A, STRING_B): TRUE if STRING_A follows STRING_B in the ASCII sequence or is equal to it (i.e. is "lexically" greater than or equal to it), FALSE otherwise.
LGT(STRING_A, STRING_B): TRUE if STRING_A follows STRING_B in the ASCII sequence, FALSE otherwise.
LLE(STRING_A, STRING_B): TRUE if STRING_A precedes STRING_B in the ASCII sequence or is equal to it, FALSE otherwise.
LLT(STRING_A, STRING_B): TRUE if STRING_A precedes STRING_B in the ASCII sequence, FALSE otherwise.
SCAN(STRING, SET [,BACK]): position of a character of STRING that occurs in SET, or zero if no such character. The position of the left-most or right-most such character is returned according as BACK is absent/FALSE or TRUE.
VERIFY(STRING, SET [,BACK]): zero if each character of STRING appears in SET, or the position of a character of STRING that is not in SET. The position of the left-most or right-most such character is returned according as BACK is absent/FALSE or TRUE.

C.3 Non-elemental Character-handling Functions

LEN(STRING): (inquiry function) number of characters in STRING if scalar, or in an element of STRING if it is an array.
REPEAT(STRING, NCOPIES): concatenation of NCOPIES of STRING; both arguments scalar.
TRIM(STRING): STRING (scalar) with trailing blanks removed.

C.4   Functions Relating to Numeric Representation

These functions relate to the models used to represent integers and reals internally. The parameters of the models may vary from processor to processor.
An example of a model for the set of integers i represented is:

$$i = \pm \sum_{k=1}^{q} w_k \times 2^{k-1},$$

where w_k is 0 or 1.
An example of the representation of reals x is:

$$x = 0 \quad \text{or} \quad \pm 2^e \left[1/2 + \sum_{k=2}^{p} f_k \times 2^{-k} \right],$$

where $-126 \le e \le 127$, for example, and f_k is 0 or 1.
Values for p and q could be 24 and 31, for example. A base other than 2 might also be used.

Numeric inquiry functions   Arguments may be scalars or arrays. The value of the argument need not be defined.

DIGITS(X): number of significant digits in the model for real or integer X, i.e. p or q.

EPSILON(X): number that is almost negligible compared with 1 in the model that includes real X, i.e. 2^{1-p}.

HUGE(X): largest value in the model that includes real or integer X, i.e. $(1 - 2^{-p})2^{127}$ for reals.

MAXEXPONENT(X): maximum exponent (integer) in the model that includes real X, i.e. 127.

MINEXPONENT(X): minimum exponent (integer) in the model that includes real X, i.e. -126.

PRECISION(X): decimal precision (number of decimal places) for real or complex X.

RADIX(X): base (integer) in the model that includes real or integer X, i.e. 2.

RANGE(X): decimal exponent range in the model that includes integer, real or complex X.

TINY(X): smallest positive number in the model that includes real X, i.e. 2^{-127}.

Elemental functions to manipulate reals

EXPONENT(X): exponent (integer) part e of the model for X.

FRACTION(X): fractional part of the model for X, i.e. $X2^{-e}$.

NEAREST(X, S): nearest different machine number in direction given by sign of real S.

RRSPACING(X): reciprocal of relative spacing of model numbers near X, i.e. $|X2^{-e}|2^p$.

SCALE(X, I): $X2^I$ (real).

SET_EXPONENT(X, I): real whose sign and fractional part are those of X and whose exponent part is I, i.e. $X2^{I-e}$.

SPACING(X): absolute spacing of model numbers near X, i.e. 2^{e-p}.

C.5 Bit Manipulation Functions

These are based on an integer model like the one in Section C.4.

Inquiry function

BIT_SIZE(I): maximum number of bits that may be held in the model for I.

Elemental functions

BTEST(I, POS): TRUE if bit POS of integer I has value 1.
IAND(I, J): logical AND on all corresponding bits of I and J.
IBCLR(I, POS): value of I with bit POS cleared to zero.
IBITS(I, POS, LEN): value equal to LEN bits of I starting at bit POS.
IBSET(I, POS): value of I with bit POS set to 1.
IEOR(I, J): logical exclusive OR on all corresponding bits of I and J.
IOR(I, J): logical inclusive OR on all corresponding bits of I and J.
ISHFT(I, SHIFT): value of I with bits shifted SHIFT places to left (right if negative) and zeros shifted in from other end. Since shifting all the bits of an integer one position to the left (right) multiplies (divides) it by 2 this provides a much faster means of multiplying (dividing) by powers of 2. E.g. ISHFT(2, 4) returns 16, and ISHFT(2, -1) returns 1.
ISHFTC(I, SHIFT [,SIZE]): value of I with SIZE right-most bits shifted circularly SHIFT places to left (right if negative); if SIZE is absent all bits are shifted.
NOT(I): logical complement of all bits in I, i.e. all the bits of I are flipped.

Elemental subroutine

CALL MVBITS(FROM, FROMPOS, LEN, TO, TOPOS): copies the sequence of bits in FROM that start at position FROMPOS and has length LEN, to TO, starting at position TOPOS.

C.6 Vector and Matrix Multiplication Functions

DOT_PRODUCT(VECTOR_A, VECTOR_B): scalar (dot) product for real and integer arguments. Both arguments must be rank-one and the same size. If the arguments are logical, ANY(VECTOR_A .AND. VECTOR_B) is returned.
MATMUL(MATRIX_A, MATRIX_B): matrix product. For numeric arguments, there are three possible cases (arguments have been shortened to A and B):

- A is (n, m), B is (m, k), result is (n, k);
- A is (m), B is (m, k), result is (k);
- A is (n, m), B is (m), result is (n).

E.g. in the first case, element (I,J) of the result is

        SUM(MATRIX_A(I,:) * MATRIX_B(:,J))

If the arguments are logical, SUM and * are replaced by ANY and .AND..

C.7   Array Reduction Functions

The following seven functions all have array arguments. MASK is a logical array, e.g. an array expression.

ALL(MASK): TRUE if all elements of MASK are true, otherwise FALSE.
ANY(MASK): TRUE if any elements of MASK are true.
COUNT(MASK): number of true elements of MASK.
MAXVAL(ARRAY): element with maximum value in real or integer ARRAY. If ARRAY has zero size, largest negative value on system is returned.
MINVAL(ARRAY): element with minimum value in real or integer ARRAY. If ARRAY has size zero, largest positive value on system is returned.
PRODUCT(ARRAY): product of elements of integer, real or complex array, or 1 if ARRAY has size zero.
SUM(ARRAY): sum of elements of integer, real or complex array, or zero if ARRAY has size zero.

Optional argument DIM   All these functions take an optional second argument DIM. If it is present, the operation is performed on all rank-one sections spanning through dimension DIM, and returns an array of rank reduced by 1. E.g.

```
INTEGER :: A(2,3)  = RESHAPE( (/ 1,2,3,4,5,6 /), (/2,3/) )
PRINT*, SUM(A,2)
```

produces the output 9 12.

Optional argument MASK   MAXVAL, MINVAL, PRODUCT and SUM take MASK as a third optional argument. The operation is then applied to elements of ARRAY corresponding to true elements of MASK (which must obviously have the same shape).

C.8   Array Inquiry Functions

ALLOCATED(ARRAY): TRUE if ARRAY is currently allocated.
LBOUND(ARRAY [,DIM]): rank-one array holding lower bounds if DIM is absent; otherwise lower bound in dimension DIM.
SHAPE(SOURCE): rank-one array holding shape of SOURCE. If SOURCE is scalar, result has size zero.
SIZE(ARRAY [,DIM]): (scalar) size of ARRAY if DIM is absent; otherwise extent along dimension DIM.
UBOUND(ARRAY [,DIM]): similar to LBOUND except that it returns upper bounds.

C.9   Array Construction and Manipulation Functions

Note that array elements are manipulated in array element order.

CSHIFT(ARRAY, SHIFT [,DIM]): returns an array of the same shape and type as ARRAY with every rank-one section that extends across dimension DIM shifted circularly SHIFT times. If DIM is omitted it has the value 1. If SHIFT is an array it must have the shape of ARRAY with dimension DIM omitted, and supplies a separate value for each shift. Some experiments should make this clear!

EOSHIFT(ARRAY, SHIFT [,BOUNDARY] [,DIM]): identical to CSHIFT except that values are shifted off at the end (end-off shift) and boundary values inserted into the vacated positions. If ARRAY has an intrinsic type, BOUNDARY may be omitted; values of zero, FALSE, or blank are shifted in as the case may be. If BOUNDARY is present and scalar, it supplies all needed values; if it is an array, it must have the shape of ARRAY with dimension DIM omitted, and supplies a separate value for each shift.

MAXLOC(ARRAY [,MASK]): returns the subscripts of the largest element of ARRAY in a rank-one array of size equal to the rank of ARRAY. The operation is restricted to elements corresponding to true elements of MASK if it is present. If there is more than one maximum, the first in array element order is taken.

MERGE(TSOURCE, FSOURCE, MASK): (elemental function) returns TSOURCE if MASK is TRUE, FSOURCE otherwise. E.g. if the three arguments are conformable arrays, the first two are merged under the control of MASK.

MINLOC(ARRAY [,MASK]): similar to MAXLOC except that the subscripts of the smallest element are returned.

PACK(ARRAY, MASK [,VECTOR]): rank-one array of elements of ARRAY according to true elements of MASK, if VECTOR is absent. Otherwise result has size equal to size n of VECTOR, which must have size at least equal to the number of selected elements t; if $t < n$, elements i of the result for $i > t$ are the corresponding elements of VECTOR.

RESHAPE(SOURCE, SHAPE [,PAD] [,ORDER]): array with shape given by rank-one integer array SHAPE and type of SOURCE. The size of SHAPE must be constant. If PAD and ORDER are absent, the elements of the result are the elements of SOURCE (in array element order). If PAD is present, it must be an array of the same type as SOURCE; copies of PAD are inserted into the result after SOURCE. ORDER must be an integer array with the same shape as SHAPE. Its value must be a permutation of $(1, 2, \ldots, n)$. It appears to control the way in which SOURCE and PAD are combined.

SPREAD(SOURCE, DIM, NCOPIES): makes NCOPIES duplicates of SOURCE by increasing its rank by 1. DIM is the dimension of the result along which duplication takes place. See Chapter 15 for a program which generates examples.

TRANSPOSE(MATRIX): transpose of rank-two array MATRIX.

UNPACK(VECTOR, MASK, FIELD): array of type of VECTOR and shape of MASK. VECTOR must be rank-one array of size at least the number of true elements of MASK. The element of the result corresponding to the ith true element of MASK is the ith element of VECTOR; all others are equal to corresponding elements of FIELD if it is an array (with the same shape as MASK), or to FIELD if it is a scalar.

C.10 Inquiry Functions for Any Type

ASSOCIATED(POINTER [,TARGET]): If TARGET is absent, result is TRUE if POINTER is associated with a target, FALSE otherwise. The status of POINTER must not be undefined. If TARGET is present, result is TRUE if POINTER is associated with it.

If TARGET itself is a pointer, its target is compared with the target of POINTER, and FALSE is returned if either POINTER or TARGET is disassociated.

PRESENT(A): TRUE if the actual argument corresponding to the dummy argument A is present in the current call to a subprogram.

C.11   Elemental Logical Function

LOGICAL(L [,KIND]): converts between kinds of logical value. Returns the value of logical L (with a kind parameter value of KIND, if it is present). If KIND is present, it must be a scalar initialization expression.

C.12   Functions Relating to Kind

KIND(X): kind parameter value of X.

SELECTED_INT_KIND(R): kind parameter value for an integer data type able to represent all integer values n in the range $-10^R < n < 10^R$, where R is a scalar integer. -1 is returned if no such kind is available.

SELECTED_REAL_KIND([P] [,R]): kind parameter for a real data type with decimal precision at least P, and decimal exponent range at least R (as returned by PRECISION and RANGE). At least one of the scalar integers P and R must be present. -1 is returned if the precision is unavailable, -2 if the range is unavailable, and -3 if neither are available.

C.13   Transfer Function

TRANSFER(SOURCE, MOLD [,SIZE]): same physical representation as SOURCE, but type of MOLD. Scalar if MOLD is scalar, otherwise of rank one and size just sufficient to hold all of SOURCE. If SIZE is present, result is of rank one and size SIZE.

C.14   Non-elemental Intrinsic Subroutines

Random numbers   Pseudo-random numbers are generated from a seed held as a rank-one integer array.

RANDOM_NUMBER returns the random numbers, and RANDOM_SEED allows inquiries about the seed array, and the seed to be reset.

CALL RANDOM_NUMBER(HARVEST): random number x uniformly distributed in the range $0 \leq x < 1$, or an array of such numbers, in HARVEST, which has intent OUT and must be real.

CALL RANDOM_SEED([SIZE] [,PUT] [,GET]):
> SIZE (scalar integer) has intent OUT and is set by the system to the size N of the seed array;
> PUT (rank-one integer array size N) has intent IN and is used by the system to reset the seed;
> GET (rank-one integer array size N) has intent OUT and is set by the system to the current value of the seed.
>
> Not more than one argument may be specified; if none is specified, the seed is set to a system-dependent value. See Chapter 14 for examples.

Real-time clock

CALL DATE_AND_TIME([DATE] [,TIME] [,ZONE] [,VALUES]): returns (values are
> blank or −HUGE(0) if there is no clock)
> DATE (character) as *ccyymmdd* (century–day);
> TIME (character) as *hhmmss.sss* (hours–milliseconds);
> ZONE (character) as *Shhmm* (difference between local and Co-ordinated Universal Time—UTC—*S* is the sign);
> VALUES (rank-one integer array) holding the year, month, day, time difference in minutes with respect to UTC, hour, minutes, seconds, and milliseconds.

CALL SYSTEM_CLOCK([COUNT] [,COUNT_RATE] [,COUNT_MAX]): returns
> COUNT (integer) holding current value of system clock;
> COUNT_RATE (integer) holding number of clock counts per second;
> COUNT_MAX (integer) holding maximum value COUNT may take.

D

ASCII Character Codes

The ASCII (American Standard Code for Information Interchange) collating sequence is as follows:

Code	Char	Code	Char	Code	Char	Code	Char	Code	Char
0	(null)	26	→	52	4	78	N	104	h
1	☺	27	←	53	5	79	O	105	i
2	☻	28	∟	54	6	80	P	106	j
3	♥	29	↔	55	7	81	Q	107	k
4	♦	30	▲	56	8	82	R	108	l
5	♣	31	▼	57	9	83	S	109	m
6	♠	32	(blank)	58	:	84	T	110	n
7	•	33	!	59	;	85	U	111	o
8	◘	34	"	60	<	86	V	112	p
9	○	35	#	61	=	87	W	113	q
10	◙	36	$	62	>	88	X	114	r
11	♂	37	%	63	?	89	Y	115	s
12	♀	38	&	64	@	90	Z	116	t
13	♪	39	'	65	A	91	[	117	u
14	♫	40	(	66	B	92	\	118	v
15	☼	41	)	67	C	93	]	119	w
16	►	42	*	68	D	94	∧	120	x
17	◄	43	+	69	E	95	_	121	y
18	↕	44	,	70	F	96	'	122	z
19	‼	45	-	71	G	97	a	123	{
20	¶	46	.	72	H	98	b	124	¦
21	§	47	/	73	I	99	c	125	}
22	▬	48	0	74	J	100	d	126	~
23	↕	49	1	75	K	101	e	127	⌂
24	↑	50	2	76	L	102	f		
25	↓	51	3	77	M	103	g		

E
Solutions to Selected Exercises

Chapter 1

1.1
```
PROGRAM Arith
REAL A, B
PRINT*, "Enter A and B:"
READ*, A, B
PRINT*, "Sum:        ", A + B
PRINT*, "Difference:", A - B
PRINT*, "Product:    ", A * B
PRINT*, "Quotient:   ", A / B
END PROGRAM Arith
```

1.2
```
PROGRAM Energy
REAL C, E, V
READ*, C, V
E = C * V ** 2 / 2
PRINT*, "Stored energy:", E
END PROGRAM Energy
```

Chapter 2

2.2 (a) comma should be replaced by decimal point
    (e) asterisk should be omitted
    (f) exponent must be integer
    (h) comma should be replaced by decimal point

2.3 (b) decimal point not allowed
    (c) first character must be a letter
    (d) apostrophes not allowed
    (f) first character must be a letter
    (h) blanks not allowed

(i)   decimal points not allowed
(k)   asterisk not allowed
(l)   allowed but not recommended!

```
2.4       REAL, PARAMETER :: Pi = 3.1415927
     (a) PRINT*, 2 ** (0.5)
     (b) PRINT*, (5. + 3) / (5 * 3)      ! real division
     (c) PRINT*, (2.3 * 4.5) ** (1.0/3) ! real division in exponent
     (d) PRINT*, (2 * Pi) ** 2
     (e) PRINT*, 2 * Pi ** 2
     (f) PRINT*, 1000 * (1 + 0.15/12) ** 60

2.5 (a) P + W / U
    (b) P + W / (U + V)
    (c) (P + W / (U + V)) / (P + W / (U - V))
    (d) X ** (1 / 2.0)
    (e) Y ** (Y + Z)
    (f) X ** Y ** Z
    (g) (X ** Y) ** Z    ! ** goes from right to left by default
    (h) X - X ** 3 / (2.*3) + X ** 5 / (2.*3*4*5)

2.6    I = 2 ** 30 - 1 + 2 ** 30

2.7    REAL A, B, C, X
       READ*, A, B, C
       X = (-B + (B ** 2 - 4 * A * C) ** (0.5)) / (2.0 * A)
       PRINT*, X
       END

2.8    REAL G, P, L
       PRINT*, "Enter gallons and pints:"
       READ*, G, P
       P = 8 * G + P
       L = P / 1.76
       PRINT*, L, "litres"
       END

2.9    IMPLICIT NONE
       REAL Km, L, Km_L, L_100Km
       Km = 528
       L = 46.23
       Km_L = Km / L
       L_100Km = L / (Km / 100)
       PRINT*, " Distance", "  Litres used", " Km/L", " L/100Km"
       PRINT*
       PRINT*, Km, L, Km_l, L_100Km
       END

2.10   T = A
```

```
          A = B
          B = T

2.11      A = A - B
          B = B + A
          A = B - A

2.13      REAL L, P, R
          INTEGER N
          L = 50000
          PRINT*, "Enter N and R (as a decimal):"
          READ*, N, R
          P = R * L * (1 + R/12) ** (12*N)
          P = P / 12 / ((1 + R/12) ** (12*N) - 1)
          PRINT*, "Monthly payment:", P
          END

2.14      REAL L, N, R, P
          PRINT*, "Capital amount, monthly payment, interest rate"
          READ*, L, P, R
          N = LOG( P / (P - R*L/12) )
          N = N / 12 / LOG( 1 + R/12 )
          PRINT*, "Repayment period in years/months:", N, 12 * N
          END

2.15      REAL, PARAMETER :: Pi = 3.1415927
          REAL C, E, I, I1, L, R, Omega
          R = 5; C = 10; L = 4; E = 2; Omega = 2
          I1 = 2 * Pi * Omega * L - 1 / (2 * Pi * Omega * C)
          I = E / (R ** 2 + I1 ** 2) ** 0.5
          PRINT*, "Current:", I
          END
```

Chapter 3

```
3.1 (a) I = I + 1
    (b) I = I ** 3 + J

    (c) IF (E > F) THEN
           G = E
        ELSE
           G = F
        END IF

    (d) IF (D > 0) X = -B
    (e) X = (A + B) / (C * D)

3.2      REAL F
         INTEGER C
```

```
        DO C = 20, 30
            F = 9 * C / 5 + 32
        PRINT*, C, F
        END DO
```

3.3
```
        INTEGER I
        DO I = 10, 20
            PRINT*, I, SQRT(1. * I)
                    ! SQRT may not have an integer argument
        END DO
```

3.5
```
        INTEGER I, SUM
        SUM = 0
        DO I = 1, 100
          SUM = SUM + 2 * I
        END DO
```

3.7
```
        INTEGER I, N, NumPass
        REAL Avg, Mark
        NumPass = 0
        Avg = 0
        N = 10
        OPEN( 1, FILE = "Marks"  )
        DO I = 1, N
           READ (1, *) Mark
           Avg = Avg + Mark
           IF (Mark >= 5) NumPass = NumPass + 1
        END DO
        Avg = Avg / N
        PRINT*, "Average:", Avg
        PRINT*, NumPass, "passed"
```

3.9 $A = 4, X = 1 + 1/2 + 1/3 + 1/4.$

3.10
```
        X = 0
        DO K = 1, 4
           X = X + 1 / K
        END DO
```

3.11   The limit is π.

3.13
```
        REAL Bal, Dep, Intr, Rate
        INTEGER Mon
        Bal = 0
        Dep = 50
        Rate = 0.01
        PRINT*, "Month", "    Balance"
        DO Mon = 1, 12
           Bal = Bal + Dep
```

```
            Intr = Rate * Bal
            Bal = Bal + Intr
            PRINT*, Mon, "     ", Bal
         END DO
         END
```

3.16   ```
        REAL A, B, K, P
        INTEGER T
        K = 197273000
        A = 0.03134
        B = 1913.25
        PRINT "(A5, A20)", "Year", "USA Population"
        DO T = 1790, 2000, 10
          P = K / (1 + EXP(-A * (T - B)))
          PRINT "(I5, F20.0)", T, P
        END DO
        END
        ```

3.18    ```
        INTEGER Feet, Yards
        REAL Inches, Metres
        READ*, Metres
        Inches = 39.37 * Metres
        Yards = Inches / 36
        Inches = MOD( Inches, 36.0 )          ! inches left
        Feet = Inches / 12
        Inches = MOD( Inches, 12.0 )
        PRINT*, "Imperial:", Yards, Feet, Inches
        ```

3.19 (a) ```
         C = SQRT(A * A + B * B)   ! * is quicker than **
         ```
     (b) ```
         Theta = Theta * Pi / 180         ! convert to radians
         C = SQRT(A * A + B * B - 2 * A * B * Cos(Theta))
         ```

3.20 (a) ```Y = LOG(X + X * X + A * A)```
     (b) ```Y = (EXP(3 * T) + T * T * SIN(4 * T)) * COS(3 * T) ** 2```
     (c) ```Pi = 4 * ATAN(1.0)```
     (d) ```Y = 1 / COS(X) ** 2 + 1 / TAN(Y)```
     (e) ```Y = ATAN(ABS(A/X))```

Chapter 4

4.1 You should get a picture of tangents to a curve.

4.2 (a) 4 (b) 2
    (c) The algorithm (attributed to Euclid) finds the HCF (Highest Common
        Factor) of two numbers by using the fact that the HCF divides exactly into
        the difference between the two numbers, and that if the numbers are equal,
        they are equal to their HCF.

4.3   ```REAL C, F```

```
          READ*, F
          C = (F - 32) * 5.0 / 9
          PRINT*, "Celsius:", C

4.5       REAL A, B
          READ*, A, B
          IF (A > B) THEN
             PRINT*, A, "is greater"
          ELSE
             PRINT*, B, "is greater"
          END IF

4.6       REAL X, MaxX
          INTEGER I, MaxPos
          OPEN( 1, FILE = "MARKS" )
          MAxX = -HUGE(0)              ! smallest (most negative) number
          DO I = 1, 10
             READ (1, *) X
             IF (X > MaxX) THEN        ! X is biggest so far
               MaxX = X
               MaxPos = I              ! record position
             END IF
          END DO
          PRINT*, MaxX, "in position", MaxPos

4.7       REAL :: Sum = 0             ! initialization
          INTEGER N
          DO N = 1, 100
             Sum = Sum + 1.0 / N   ! remember integer division
             IF (MOD( N, 10 ) == 0) PRINT*, Sum
          END DO

4.8       INTEGER Secs, Mins, Hours
          READ*, Secs
          Hours = Secs / 3600
          Secs = MOD( Secs, 3600 )        ! number of seconds over
          Mins = Secs / 60
          Secs = MOD( Secs, 60 )
          PRINT*, Hours, ":", Mins, ":", Secs
```

Chapter 5

```
5.1       REAL A, B
          READ*, A, B
          IF (A > B) THEN
             PRINT*, A, "is larger"
          ELSE IF (B > A) THEN
             PRINT*, B, "is larger"
          ELSE
```

```
      PRINT*, "number are equal"
      END IF
```

5.2   1. Repeat 10 times:
              Read number
              If number < 0 then
                    increase negative counter
              otherwise if number $= 0$ then
                    increase zero counter
              otherwise
                    increase positive counter
    2. Print counters.

```
      INTEGER I, Num, NPos, NZer, NNeg
      NPos = 0; NZer = 0; NNeg = 0;
      DO I = 1, 10
        READ*, Num
        SELECT CASE (Num)
        CASE (:-1)
          NNeg = NNeg + 1
        CASE (0)
          NZer = NZer + 1
        CASE DEFAULT
          NPos = NPos + 1
        END SELECT
      END DO
      PRINT*, NNeg, NZer, NPos
```

5.5   1. Read a, b, c, d, e, f
    2. $u = ae - db$, $v = ec - bf$
    3. If $u = 0$ and $v = 0$ then
        Lines coincide
      Otherwise if $u = 0$ and $v \neq 0$ then
        Lines are parallel
      Otherwise
        $x = v/u$, $y = (af - dc)/u$
        Print x, y
    4. Stop.

```
      REAL A, B, C, D, E, F, U, V, X, Y
      READ*, A, B, C, D, E, F
      U = A * E - D * B
      V = E * C - B * F
      IF (U == 0 .AND. V == 0) THEN
        PRINT*, "Lines coincide"
      ELSE IF (U == 0 .AND. V /= 0) THEN
        PRINT*, "Lines parallel"
      ELSE
        X = V / U
```

```
              Y = (A * F - D * C) / U
              PRINT*, "x, y:", X, Y
           END IF
```

Chapter 6

```
  6.2    INTEGER X
         REAL Ang, Pi
         Pi = 4 * ATAN(1.0)
         DO X = 0, 90, 15
           Ang = X * Pi / 180              ! convert to radians
           PRINT "(I3, 2F7.4)", X, SIN(Ang), COS(Ang)
         END DO


  6.3    REAL Bal, Rate
         INTEGER Month, Year
         Bal = 1000
         Rate = 0.01
         DO Year = 1, 10
           DO Month = 1, 12
             Bal = (1 + Rate) * Bal
           END DO
           PRINT*, Year, Bal
         END DO


6.4 (a)  REAL Pi
         INTEGER K, N, Sign
         Pi = 1
         Sign = 1
         PRINT*, "Number of terms?"
         READ*, N
         DO K = 1, N
           Sign = -Sign
           Pi = Pi + Sign / (2 * K + 1.0)
                              ! avoids integer division
         END DO
         Pi = 4 * Pi


6.4 (b)  REAL :: Pi = 0
         INTEGER K, N
         PRINT*, "Number of terms?"
         READ*, N
         DO K = 1, N
           Pi = Pi + 1.0 / (4 * K - 3) / (4 * K - 1)
                              ! avoids integer division
         END DO
         Pi = 8 * Pi

  6.7    REAL(2) E, X            ! greatest precision
```

```
       X = 0.1
       DO I = 1, 20
         E = 1.0 / (1 - X) ** (1/X)
         PRINT*, X, E
         X = X / 10
       END DO
```

6.8
```
       REAL, PARAMETER :: Pi = 3.1415927
       REAL Fourier, T
       INTEGER K, N
       PRINT*, "N:"
       READ*, N
       T = 0
       DO WHILE (T <= 1 + SPACING(T))    ! make sure we hit 1.0
         Fourier = 0
         DO K = 0, N
           Fourier = Fourier + SIN( (2*K+1) * Pi * T ) / (2*K+1)
         END DO
         Fourier = 4 * Fourier / Pi
         PRINT*, T, Fourier
         T = T + 0.1
       END DO
```

6.10
```
       INTEGER Ans, I, NumTerms, Sum
       Sum = 0; I = 0;
       DO
        IF (Sum >= 100) EXIT
        Ans = Sum                 ! since Sum will go over 100
        NumTerms = I
        I = I + 1
        Sum = Sum + I
       END DO
       PRINT*, Ans, "after", NumTerms, "terms"
```

6.12
```
       INTEGER M, N
       READ*, M, N
       DO WHILE (M /= N)
         DO WHILE (M > N)
           M = M - N
         END DO
         DO WHILE (N > M)
           N = N - M
         END DO
       END DO
       PRINT*, "HCF is", M
```

6.14   The final payment is $157.75 in the 54th month (don't forget the interest in the last month).

Chapter 8

8.2
```
REAL X
READ*, X
PRINT*, X, Expo(X), EXP(X)

CONTAINS
  FUNCTION Expo( X )
    REAL Expo, Term
    REAL, INTENT(IN) :: X
    INTEGER K
    Expo = 1
    K = 1
    Term = 1
    DO WHILE (ABS(Term) >= 1e-6)
      Term = Term * X / K
      Expo = Expo + Term
      K = K + 1
    END DO
  END FUNCTION Expo
END
```

8.5
```
FUNCTION Normal( X )
REAL Normal, R, T
REAL, INTENT(IN) :: X
  REAL :: A = 0.4361836
  REAL :: B = -0.1201676
  REAL :: C = 0.937298
  REAL :: Pi = 3.1415927
  R = EXP( -X * X / 2 ) / SQRT(2 * PI)
  T = 1 / (1 + 0.3326 * X)
  Normal = 0.5 - R * (A * T + B * T * T + C * T ** 3)
END FUNCTION Normal
```

8.6
```
INTEGER N
DO N = 1, 20
  PRINT "(I4, F9.1)", N, Fibo(N)
END DO
CONTAINS
  RECURSIVE FUNCTION Fibo( N ) RESULT (F)
    REAL F
    INTEGER N
    IF (N == 0 .OR. N == 1) THEN
      F = 1
    ELSE
      F = Fibo(N-1) + Fibo(N-2)
    END IF
  END FUNCTION Fibo
END
```

Chapter 9

9.1
```
INTEGER, DIMENSION(100) :: Num
(a)    Num = (/ (I, I = 1, 100) /)
(b)    DO I = 1, 50
          Num(I) = 2 * I
       END DO
(c)    DO I = 1, 100    ! or Num = (/ (I, I = 100, 1, -1) /)
          Num(101-I) = I
       END DO
```

9.2
```
REAL F(100), F1, F2
READ*, F(1), F(2)
DO N = 3, 100
  F(N) = F(N-1) + F(N-2)
END DO
```

9.3
```
REAL :: S(7) = (/ 9, 10, 12, 15, 20, 35, 50 /)
INTEGER :: Emps(7) = (/ 3000, 2500, 1500, 1000, 400, &
                                         100, 25 /)
INTEGER :: NumScales = 7
INTEGER I, Above, Below
REAL AvLevel, AvSal
Above = 0; Below = 0
AvLevel = SUM( S ) / NumScales          ! intrinsic SUM
DO I = 1, NumScales
  IF (S(I) < AvLevel) THEN
    Below = Below + Emps(I)
  ELSE
    Above = Above + Emps(I)
  END IF
END DO
AvSal = 1000 * SUM( S ) / SUM( Emps )   ! intrinsic SUM
```

9.4
```
INTEGER X(10), Num, I
REAL Mean, Dist
READ*, X
Mean = SUM( X ) / 10                ! intrinsic SUM
Dist = ABS(X(1) - Mean)            ! it may be the first one
Num = X(1)
DO I = 2, 10
  IF (ABS(X(I) - Mean) > Dist) THEN
    Num = X(I)                         ! furthest number
    Dist = ABS(X(I) - Mean)           ! distance from mean
  END IF
END DO
```

9.5   1. Initialize: $N = 3$, $P_1 = 2$, $j = 1$ (prime counter)
    2. While $N < 1000$ repeat:
              $i = 1$
              $R = \text{MOD}(\ N,\ P_i\ )$ (remainder)
              While $R \neq 0$ and $P_i < \sqrt{N}$ repeat:
                      Increase i by 1
                      $R = \text{MOD}(\ N,\ P_i\ )$
              If $R \neq 0$ then
                      Increase j by 1 (that's another prime)
                      $P_j = N$
              Increase N by 2
    3. Print all the P_j's
    4. Stop.

Chapter 10

10.3
```
CHARACTER (1) :: ch = ""
INTEGER :: NonBlank = 0
INTEGER :: IOEnd  = 0
OPEN( 1, FILE = 'TEST' )
DO WHILE (IOEnd /= -1)                    ! for EOF under FTN90
   READ (1, "(A1)", IOSTAT = IOEnd, ADVANCE = "NO") ch
   IF (ch /= ' ') NonBlank = NonBlank + 1
END DO
PRINT*, NonBlank
CLOSE (1)
```

Chapter 11

11.1
```
CHARACTER(80) Line
INTEGER :: Blanks = 0
INTEGER I
READ*, Line      ! use quotes if text contains blanks
DO I = 1, LEN_TRIM( Line )
   IF (Line(I:I) == " ") Blanks = Blanks + 1
END DO
```

11.2
```
INTEGER I, PosStop
CHARACTER(80) Sentence
READ*, Sentence  ! enclose in quotes if blanks in text
PRINT*, Sentence
PosStop = INDEX( Sentence, "." )
PRINT*, PosStop
DO I = PosStop-1, 1, -1
   WRITE (*, "(A1)", ADVANCE = "NO") Sentence( I:I )
END DO
```

```
11.3    PROGRAM Zeller
        CHARACTER (9), DIMENSION(0:6) :: DayOfWeek = &
           (/ "Sunday   ", "Monday   ", "Tuesday  ", &
              "Wednesday", "Thursday ", "Friday   ", "Saturday " /)
        INTEGER Centy, Day, Month, Year, F
        PRINT*, "Enter day, month, year:"
        READ*, Day, Month, Year
        Month = Month - 2
        IF (Month <= 0) Month = Month + 12
        IF (Month >= 11) Year = Year - 1
        Centy = Year / 100
        Year = MOD( Year, 100 )        ! year in century now
        F = INT(2.6 * Month - 0.2) + Day + Year + Year / 4 &
                                      + Centy / 4 - 2 * Centy
        F = MOD( F, 7 )
        PRINT*, DayOfWeek(F)
        END


11.4    PROGRAM BinToDec
        CHARACTER(80) StrBin          ! maximum length is 80
        INTEGER, ALLOCATABLE :: Bin(:)
        INTEGER Dec, I, N
        READ*, StrBin
        N = LEN_TRIM( StrBin )        ! number of binary digits
        ALLOCATE( Bin(N) )
        READ (StrBin, "(80I1)") Bin ! reads first N digits
        Dec = 0
        DO I = 1, N
          Dec = Dec + Bin(I) * 2 ** (N-I)
        END DO
        PRINT*, Dec
        END


11.5    PROGRAM Upper
        CHARACTER (1) :: ch
        INTEGER :: IOEnd  = 0
        OPEN( 1, FILE = "TEXT" )
        DO WHILE (IOEnd /= -1)                 ! for EOF under FTN90
          READ (1, "(A1)", IOSTAT = IOEnd, ADVANCE = "NO") ch
          IF (ch >= "a" .AND. ch <= "z") THEN
            ch = ACHAR( IACHAR(ch) - 32 )   ! ASCII codes
          END IF
          WRITE (*, "(A1)", ADVANCE = "NO") ch
          IF (IOEnd == -2) PRINT*            ! for EOR under FTN90
        END DO
        CLOSE (1)
        END


11.12   FUNCTION TIS()
```

```
      REAL TIS
      INTEGER TIMES(8)
        CALL DATE_AND_TIME( VALUES = TIMES )
        PRINT*, TIMES
        TIS = TIMES(5) * 3600 + TIMES(6) * 60 + TIMES(7) &
            + TIMES(8) / 1000.0
      END FUNCTION TIS
```

Chapter 13

```
13.1   INTEGER, POINTER :: P1, P2, Temp
       INTEGER, TARGET :: I, J
       I = 1; J = 2
       P1 => I
       P2 => J
       PRINT*, P1, P2
       Temp => P1
       P1 => P2
       P2 => Temp
       PRINT*, P1, P2    ! check where they point now
```

Chapter 14

```
14.1   PROGRAM Bingo
       INTEGER Bing(99), I, Temp, Seed(1), Count, R
       REAL Rnd
       CALL SYSTEM_CLOCK( Count )
       Seed = Count
       CALL RANDOM_SEED( PUT = Seed )
       Bing = (/ (I, I = 1, 99) /)
       DO I = 1, 99
         CALL RANDOM_NUMBER(Rnd)
         R = INT( 99 * Rnd + 1 )
         Temp = Bing(R)
         Bing(R) = Bing(I)
         Bing(I) = Temp
       END DO
       PRINT "(10I3)", Bing
       END
```

```
14.2   PROGRAM Walk
       INTEGER, PARAMETER :: Xmax = 20
       INTEGER X, F(-Xmax:Xmax), I, N
       REAL R
       X = 0
       F = 0
       READ*, N
       DO I = 1, N
         CALL RANDOM_NUMBER(R)
```

```
        IF (R < 0.5) THEN
          X = X + 1
        ELSE
          X = X - 1
        END IF
        F(X) = F(X) + 1          ! that's another one at X
      END DO
      DO X = -Xmax, Xmax
        PRINT "(80A1)", ("*", I = 1, F(X))
      END DO
      END
```

14.3
```
      PROGRAM MonteCarlo
      REAL R, X, Y, Pi
      INTEGER I, N
      Pi = 0
      READ*, N
      DO I = 1, N
        CALL RANDOM_NUMBER(R)
        X = -1 + 2 * R                 ! -1 to 1
        Y = -1 + 2 * R                 ! ditto
        IF (X*X + Y*Y < 1) Pi = Pi + 1
      END DO
      Pi = 4 * Pi / N
      PRINT*, "Pi is very roughly", Pi
      END
```

14.5 Theoretically (from the binomial distribution), the probability of a DFII crashing is 1/4, while that of a DFIV crashing is 5/16; more can go wrong with it since it has more engines!

14.6 On average, *A* wins 12 of the possible 32 plays of the game, while *B* wins 20, as can be seen from drawing the game tree. Your simulation should come up with these proportions. (However, it can be shown from the tree that *B* can always force a win, if she plays intelligently.)

Chapter 15

15.1
```
      SUBROUTINE MyTrans( A )
        REAL, DIMENSION(:,:) :: A
        INTEGER J, K
        REAL Temp
        DO J = 1, SIZE(A,1)
          DO K = J, SIZE(A,1) ! start at J to avoid swopping back
            Temp = A(J,K)
            A(J,K) = A(K,J)
            A(K,J) = Temp
          END DO
        END DO
      END SUBROUTINE MyTrans
```

Chapter 16

16.1 (a) The real roots are 1.856 and −1.697, the complex roots are
          −0.0791 ± 1.780*i*.
      (b) 0.589, 3.096, 6.285, … (roots get closer to multiples of π).
      (c) 1, 2, 5.
      (d) 1.303
      (e) Real roots at 1.768 and 2.241.

16.2 Successive bisections are: 1.5, 1.25, 1.375, 1.4375 and 1.40625. The exact
      answer is 1.414214..., so the last bisection is within the required error.

16.3 22 (exact answer is 21.3333).

16.4 After 30 years the exact answer is 2117 ($1000e^{rt}$).

16.5 The differential equations to be solved are

$$dS/dt = -r_1 S,$$
$$dY/dt = r_1 S - r_2 Y.$$

The exact solution after 8 hours is $S = 6.450 \times 10^{25}$ and $Y = 2.312 \times 10^{26}$.

16.6
```
PROGRAM IMPALA
INTEGER I, N
REAL A, B, H, R, T, X
PRINT*, "Enter R, B, A, X(0), H:"
READ*, R, B, A, X, H
N = INT( 24/H + SPACING(H) ) + 1      ! trip count
T = 0
DO I = 1, N
  IF (MOD(I-1, INT(1/H + SPACING(H))) == 0) THEN ! output
            ! every month starting with initial value
    PRINT "(2F8.2)", T, X
  END IF
  T = T + H
  X = X + H * (R - B * X * SIN(A * T)) * X
END DO
END
```

16.7 With 10 intervals ($n = 5$), the luminous efficiency is 14.512725%. With 20
      intervals it is 14.512667%. These results justify the use of 10 intervals in
      any further computations involving this problem. This is a standard way of
      testing the accuracy of a numerical method: halve the step-length and see
      how much the solution changes.

Index

table 235
tabulation in I/O 152
TAN 39, 317
TANH 39, 317
TARGET attribute 204
  argument with 206
Taylor series
  exponential 122
  sine 82
terminal velocity 278
TINY 318
token 8
top down programming 48
traffic flow 229
TRANSFER 322
transfer function 69
transpose 249
TRANSPOSE 321
Trapezoidal Rule 273
triangular matrix, representation
    with pointers 208
tridiagonal matrix 290
TRIM 317
trip count 71
truncation error 293
type 9
  declaration 12
  derived 180
  implicit rule 12
  logical 58
  non-numeric 9
  numeric 9
  parameter 35
TYPE 186

UBOUND 320
unary operator 15

undefined variable 12
unformatted I/O 159
unit 155
unit number 19, 155
unknown amount of data, reading 82,
    129
UNPACK 321
unreferenced storage 207
USE
  ONLY 112
  rename 112

value argument 114
Van der Pol's equation 294
variable 6, 11
  defined 12
  generalized definition 186
  initialization 12
  scalar 12
  subscripted 125
  undefined 12
vector subscript 140
VERIFY 317
vertical motion under air resistance 278

WHERE construct 142
WHILE 78
word count 170
word extraction 170
WRITE
  formatted 155
  non-advancing 161
  output to screen or printer 155

Zeller's congruence 175
zero-trip loop 71